Internet Handbooks

1001 Web Sites for Writers on the Internet
Books and Publishing on the Internet
Building a Web Site on the Internet
Careers Guidance on the Internet
Chat & Chat Rooms on the Internet
Creating a Home Page on the Internet
Discussion Forums on the Internet
Exploring Yahoo! on the Internet
Finding a Job on the Internet
Getting Started on the Internet
Gardens & Gardening on the Internet
Graduate Job Hunting on the Internet
Homes & Property on the Internet
Human Resource Management on the Internet
Internet Explorer on the Internet
Internet for Schools
Internet for Students
Internet for Writers
Law & Lawyers on the Internet
Marketing Your Business on the Internet
Medicine & Health on the Internet
Music & Musicians on the Internet
Naming a Web Site on the Internet
News and Magazines on the Internet
Overseas Job Hunting on the Internet
Personal Finance on the Internet
Promoting a Web Site on the Internet
Protecting Children on the Internet
Shops & Shopping on the Internet
Studying English on the Internet
Studying Law on the Internet
Travel & Holidays on the Internet
Using Credit Cards on the Internet
Using Email on the Internet
Using Netscape on the Internet
Where to Find It on the Internet
Wildlife & Conservation on the Internet
Working from Home on the Internet

Many other titles in preparation

Books & Publishing on the internet

An essential guide for writers, readers, booksellers, librarians & publishing professionals

Roger Ferneyhough
MA(Oxon)

www.internet-handbooks.co.uk

First published in 2000 by Internet Handbooks, a Division of International Briefings Ltd, Plymbridge House, Estover Road, Plymouth PL6 7PY, United Kingdom.

Customer services tel:	(01752) 202301
Orders fax:	(01752) 202333
Customer services email:	cservs@plymbridge.com
Distributors web site:	http://www.plymbridge.com
Series web site:	http://www.internet-handbooks.co.uk

Note: The contents of this book are offered for the purposes of general guidance only and no liability can be accepted for any loss or expense incurred as a result of relying in particular circumstances on statements made in this book. Readers are advised to check the current position with the appropriate authorities before entering into personal arrangements.

Printed and bound by The Cromwell Press Ltd, Trowbridge, Wiltshire.

Contents

Contents

List of illustrations

Preface

Whether you are a reader of books, a published or unpublished writer, or working in the publishing or bookselling industry, this is the book for you. It is believed to be the first of its kind to be published in the UK, and part of the rapidly growing Internet Handbook series which began in 1999. It is designed to help you find out about the amazing new world of books and book publishing online. It is intended for members of the general public, booksellers, writers, editors, publishers, illustrators, designers, printers, agents, librarians, journalists, researchers, teachers and students – in fact everyone interested in exploring this exciting new world of publishing information online.

In these pages you will find search engines and directories, and many leading 'portal' (gateway) sites to book information and publishing services online. There are links to book publishing companies, writers groups, job opportunities, industry news, booksellers, book clubs, dictionaries and reference databases of all kinds – in fact a vast new world of digital information at your fingertips. The answers are all here, and 99 per cent of the information listed in the book is available free. All you need is access to a computer, a phone line, and an internet service provider.

The internet is set to completely transform the way we live, and the field of book publishing is no exception. Indeed, as an 'information industry' it is in the front line, and the world of books faces massive transformations. For example, the retail price of books is under massive attack by the new online suppliers such as Amazon – great news for book buyers, but a huge challenge to commercial publishers and high street booksellers. The evaluation of new book proposals can now be carried out online between publisher and author, as can their subsequent dealings. As an example, Macmillan Publishers are developing an online facility along these lines called AuthorNet. Beyond this, authors can even publish their work directly online, cutting out publisher, agent, printer and bookshop altogether, as pop musicians have begun to bypass traditional record manufacturers and distributors. Many authors now have their own web sites. Perhaps some of them will even become internet service providers for their fans, as David Bowie has in the music industry.

Indeed, the whole concept of a 'book' is likely to change, with more and more information providers turning to the internet. Now, they can offer content to a global readership at a fraction of the cost and time involved in traditional publishing. In addition, that content is increasingly interactive, and includes sound, video and film clips. Non-fiction, especially educational and reference publishing, is likely to see a revolution.

The Oxford University Press for example recently announced that it would no longer publish the complete Oxford Dictionary in volume form: it is now to be a web site, available on subscription, and with the material updated constantly instead of only once every few years. The Encyclopedia Britannica is another example of a publishing company which has decided to publish most of its content on the web, instead of in cumbersome and costly printed form. Other educational and professional publishers such as

Heinemann are setting up dedicated web sites to support individual books and series, for example offering online tutorial material and additional reference content. All the major legal, medical, financial, scientific and reference publishers are migrating to the internet. In the future, looking up something in a 'book' online may mean reading a piece of text while listening to a soundtrack, watching a video clip, and emailing the publisher or fellow users.

The internet transcends traditional national boundaries and takes little account of geographical factors. You can easily make contact with book publishers and editors, authors, literary agents, library resources, booksellers, official organisations and fellow book-lovers and collectors almost anywhere in the world. This is going to create many complexities and uncertainties in fields such as taxation, copyright, defamation and other topics rooted in local national law, and government officials everywhere will be keen to extend their reach into cyberspace.

Using the internet, it is now very easy for firms to set up offshore to escape ever-rising taxation and regulation. For example within the last year, William Hill and Ladbrokes moved their online betting offshore to Gibraltar, immediately saving the betting levy. Thousands more companies are likely to do the same, using the internet to migrate from their national high tax-and-regulation environments, and thereby winning a huge competitive advantage. It would easy for a professional author or publishing firm to do the same: the information business after all is essentially digital, requiring little more than web servers and telecommunication links which can be set up anywhere.

Governments of course will not easily surrender tax revenues or law enforcement powers which they use to justify their existence. Gordon Brown has already spoken of imposing a new 'offshore telephone tax' on people who make phone calls to countries such as Jersey, Monaco, Gibraltar, or the Cayman Islands. Is this supporting ecommerce? It is interesting, if depressing, to compare the reaction of the British government to the internet with that of other governments around the world.

In all sorts of ways, the internet is a new challenge to the way we live. Should all information, however controversial, be publishable across the internet? What are the limits of free speech? With varying degrees of public support, governments and agencies of control all over the world fear the power of the internet to distribute unwelcome material within their boundaries. There are many new moves towards censorship, surveillance and state invasion of personal privacy online. How far is this desirable?

In Singapore, all internet service provision is state-controlled, so the government can read people's emails and web logs at will. The government of Australia has just made it a criminal offence for its citizens to view 'pornography' on the internet (the definitions are vague). France criminalised the free use of strong encryption on the internet: be prepared give the authorities your private key (password) or go to jail. In Burma, there is now a 15-year jail sentence for owning a modem. In the UK, the New Labour government is seeking to force ISPs to install surveillance software, which will allow the police to routinely read a cross-section of emails and web logs without reference to the courts. Similar surveillance is being set up Japan and in several EU countries, with very little public awareness or debate. In the UK, with CCTV cameras, DNA testing and internet surveillance in both home and workplace, we will soon be living our lives under total surveillance. Is this really what we want?

Throughout history, publishing has been a target for censorship and state control, and the internet is rapidly developing into the most powerful publishing medium in history. It is up to every internet user in Britain as elsewhere to help define the future of the medium. As a publisher, author, bookseller or book lover, how far do you want *your* use of the internet subject to surveillance, regulation, censorship and taxation? Do you trust the politicians in these areas? This is your country and your future. Email your MP and MEP and let them know. Public apathy opens the door to ever greater state control.

This book assumes that you know the basics of using the internet, and that you already have access, perhaps through FreeServe, America On-line, CompuServe, BT, Virgin Net, Demon, GlobalNet or one of the many others in the UK and elsewhere. Many web site addresses (URLs) are given in this book. To go to one of them, simply type the address – exactly as shown – in the 'address' or 'location' box near the top of the window of your web browser (normally Internet Explorer or Netscape Navigator). Once you have typed it in, press the 'enter' key on your keyboard. Your screen will then display the web site you want.

The contents of this book are provided for general guidance only. Many of the links are to reputable organisations and the information they offer can be extremely valuable. However, not all resources on the internet are authoritative or current, and they can sometimes be controversial. While care has been taken to ensure the accuracy of the information contained in this book, no responsibility can be accepted for the consequences of any action taken based on the material contained within these pages.

Please also note that comments made about the web sites and other internet pages mentioned in this book are based on how they appeared at the time of writing. A web page may well appear differently at different times. Finally, if you would like to submit details of a web site you think should be included in a future edition of this book please feel free to email the details to the email address shown below. Happy surfing!

Roger Ferneyhough
ref@internet-handbooks.co.uk

1 Searching for information

In this chapter we will explore:

- *internet search engines*
- *portal sites for books and publishing*
- *book news online*
- *book trade information*
- *newsgroups and mailing list services*

Internet search engines

- *Search engines* – A search engine is a means of finding something on the internet. Popular search engines have now become big web sites in their own right, usually combining many useful features. As well as search boxes where you can type key words to summarise what you are looking for, you will probably also find handy directories of information, news, email and other services. There are hundreds if not thousands of search engines freely available, but the biggest and best known are probably AltaVista, Excite, Infoseek, Lycos and Yahoo!. The best idea is to try out several and see which one you like the best.

AltaVista
http://www.altavista.com
AltaVista is one of the most popular search sites among web users

Fig. 1. The well known AltaVista search engine and directory, used by millions of people every day. It can lead you to a vast amount of online publishing information.

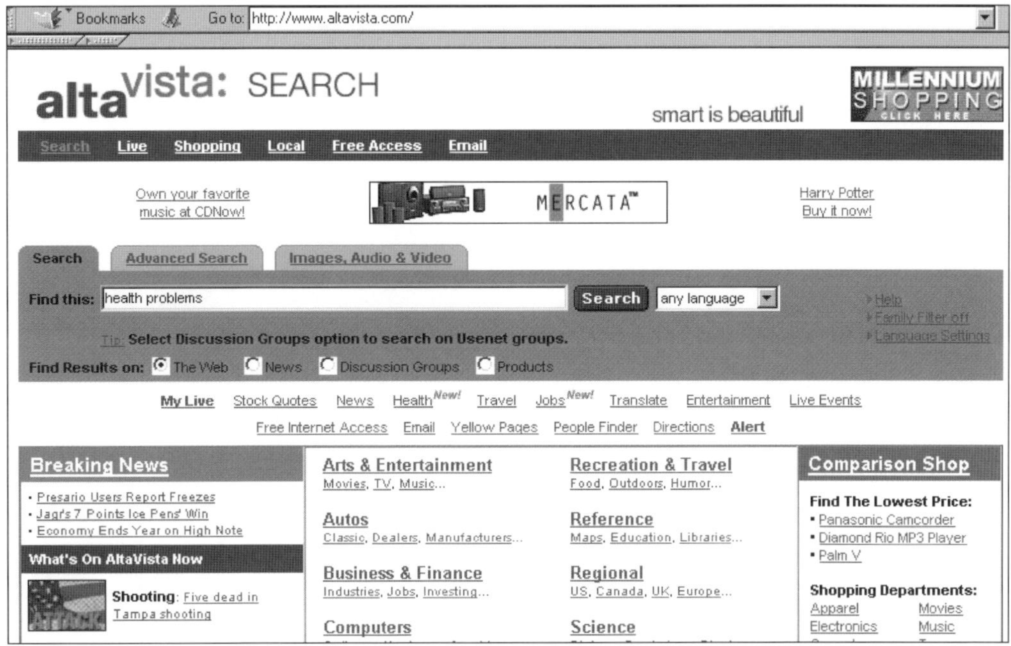

worldwide. It contains details of more than 30 million web pages on its massive and ever-growing database. You can either follow the trails of links from its home page, or (better) type in your own key words into its search box. You can even search in about 25 different languages.

Ask Jeeves
http://www.askjeeves.com/
Ask Jeeves offers a slightly different approach to searches. It invites you to ask questions on the internet just as you would of a friend or colleague. For example you could type in something like: 'Where can I find out about literary agents?' Jeeves retrieves the information, drawing from a knowledge base of about millions of standard answers.

Electronic Yellow Pages
http://www.eyp.co.uk
Before the internet, when looking for book information, what did you do? Most people simply opened up their Yellow Pages and started ringing round. In a more sophisticated way you can now do this online. These electronic yellow pages are organised on the same lines as the paper edition. Just type in the details of the information you need – anything from booksellers to publishers – and it quickly searches for appropriate services in your local area.

Excite
http://www.excite.com
Excite is another of the top ten search engines and directories on the internet. To refine your search, simply click the check boxes next to the words you want to add and then click the Search Again button. There are separate Excite home pages for several different countries and cultures including Australia, Chinese, France, German, Italy, Japan, Netherlands,

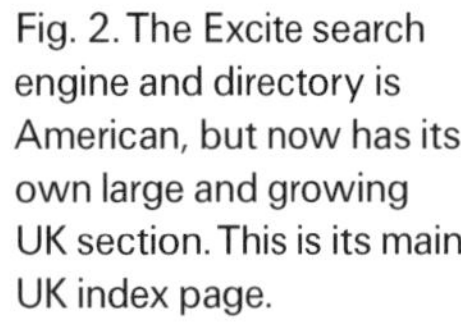
Fig. 2. The Excite search engine and directory is American, but now has its own large and growing UK section. This is its main UK index page.

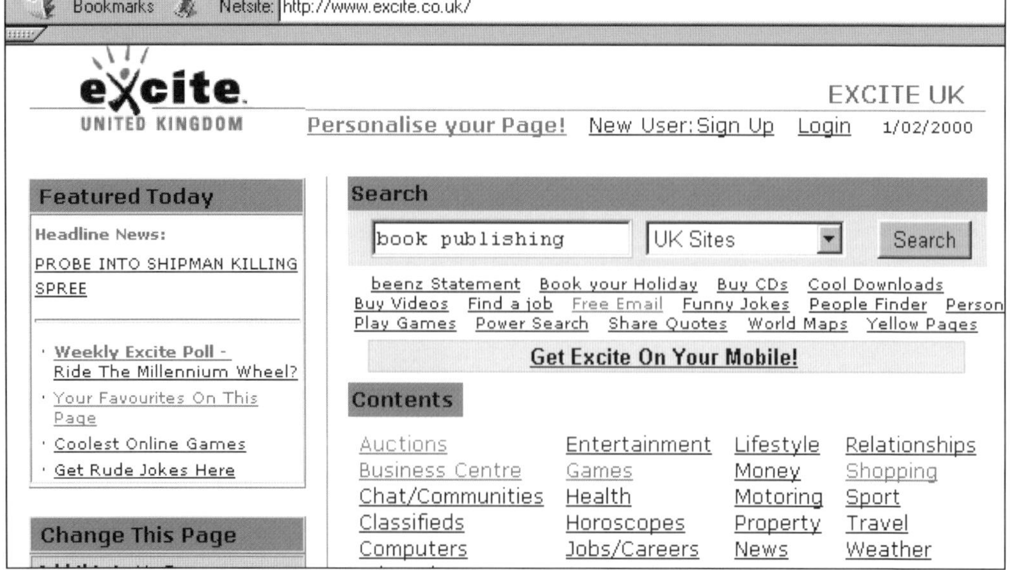

Spain, Sweden, and the USA. You will find its dedicated UK site at: http://www.excite.co.uk/

Global On-line Directory
http://www.god.co.uk/
Launched in 1996, GOD is fairly unusual among search engines in that it is UK-based, and aims to be a premier European search service. Features of the site include a 'global search' where you can search for web sites by country, state, province, county or even city by city, narrowing down the information and arriving at a more focused result. This is advantageous as the web grows, and as the information thrown up by general search engines becomes ever more overwhelming.

Google
http://www.google.com
A new and innovative search site is Google. It matches your query to the text in its index, to find relevant pages. For instance, when analysing a page for indexing, it looks at what the pages linking to that page have to say about it, so the rating partly depends on what what others say about it. Google was founded in 1998 by Larry Page and Sergey Brin, two Stanford PhD students.

HotBot
http://www.hotbot.com/
This is an impressive and well-classified search engine and directory, run by Wired Digital. Wired Digital's properties include HotBot, *Wired News* (www.wired.com), a premier service for news of the digital world, and HotWired (www.hotwired.com), the award-winning site about web technology and culture. It also owns Webmonkey, a leading web enthusiast's how-to site, and Suck (www.suck.com) which features unpopular opinions on pop culture from the web's longest running daily column.

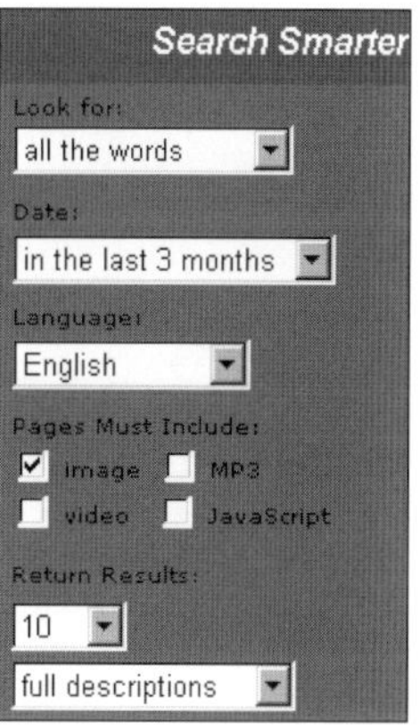

Infoseek (Go Network)
http://infoseek.go.com/
Infoseek is one of the leading search engines on the internet. In 1994, the American 'netpreneur' Steve Kirsch founded Infoseek with the mission of helping people unleash the power of the internet. Infoseek pioneered a suite of powerful, high-quality and easy-to-use search tools. These tools allowed everyone – even those with limited computer skills – to access information online. Infoseek has recently joined up with the Walt Disney Company, to launch the GO Network, a large consumer internet portal.

Internet Address Finder
http://www.iaf.net/
The IAF is used by millions of web users for searching and finding the names, email addresses, and now Intel Internet video phone contacts, of other users worldwide. With millions of addresses it claims to be the most comprehensive email directory on the internet. When you register for this free service, you'll be instantly connected to the Finder database – no waiting for processing, or passwords to be sent. You can search for family

Fig. 3. The Infoseek search engine and directory is another of the top search utilities on the internet. This page shows the results of a search for 'publishers'.

and friends, colleagues, for the famous, and the not-yet-famous. By registering, you will also enable others to find you.

Internet Public Library
http://www.ipl.org/ref/
The 'Ask-A-Question' service at the Internet Public Library is experimental. They say 'We're doing the best we can with what we've got. Right now, our biggest problem is volume: each day, we receive more questions than we can answer with our current staff resources.' The librarians who work at the IPL Reference Centre are mostly volunteers with other full-time librarian jobs. Your question is received at the IPL Reference Centre and the mail is reviewed once a day and questions are forwarded to a place where all the librarians can see them and answer them. Replies will be sent as soon as possible, advising whether your question has been accepted or rejected. If it has been accepted, you should receive an answer to in a day or two a week or so if it is a harder question.

Internet Sleuth
http://www.isleuth.com
Internet Sleuth is a metasearch tool with over 3,000 databases to choose from. If you want to find something that may be rare or unusual, this is a great place to start. It is an easy site to use and provides an excellent base-camp from which to explore the web. This kind of site can easily bury you under an avalanche of information, so be specific in your search keywords and phrases.

List of Search Engines
http://www.merrydew.demon.co.uk/search.htm
This enterprising British site offers a free list of search engines, over 250

on different topics. There are software search engines, multiple search engines, email/news search engines web search engines, commercial search engines, word reference science search, law search, TV, film and music search, press search, image search, technology manufacturers search, and localised search engines.

Lycos
http://www.lycos.com
Lycos is another of the top ten worldwide web search engines. It is named after a type of ground spider. It searches document titles, headings, links, and keywords, and returns the first 50 words of each page it indexes for your search. Founded in 1995, Lycos was one of the earliest search and navigation sites designed to help people find information more easily and quickly on the world wide web. The core technology was developed at Carnegie Mellon University. In 1997, with Bertelsmann, it has launched Lycos sites in 11 European countries. UK Lycos is at: http://www.lycos.co.uk/

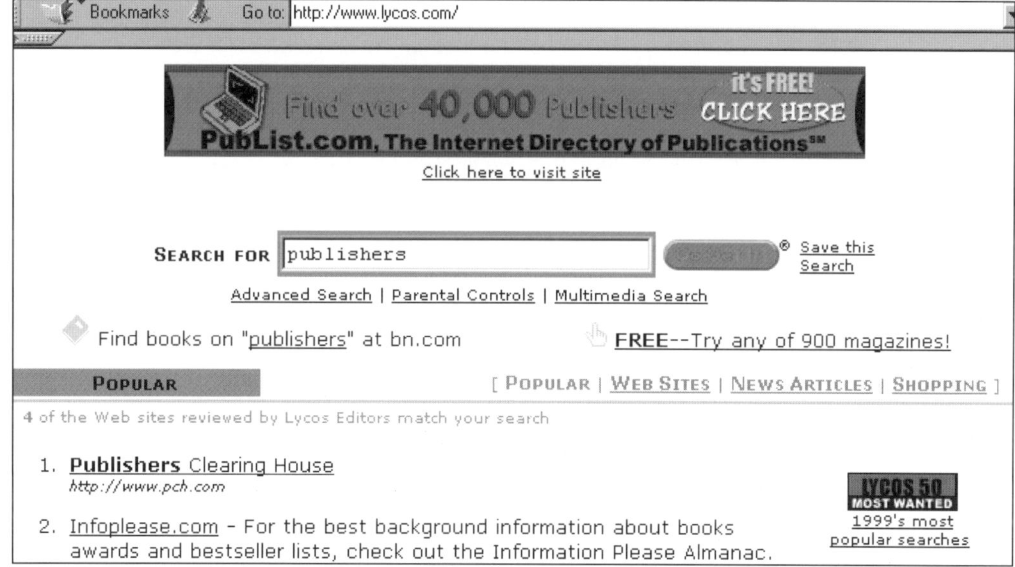

Fig. 4. The widely used Lycos search engine and directory is being used here to search for 'publishers'. The page includes a banner advertisement at the top, reflecting the subject matter of the search.

Metacrawler
http://www.metacrawler.com/
MetaCrawler was originally developed by Erik Selberg and Oren Etzioni at the University of Washington, and released to the internet in 1995. In response to each user query, it incorporates results from all the top search engines. It collates results, eliminates duplication, scores the results and provides the user with a list of relevant sites.

Metaplus
http://www.metaplus.com/uk.html
Metaplus is a meta-list of the best internet directories – and also offers direct links to some key general sites. This is its UK page, containing hundreds of classifications to explore, including UK regional links.

SavvySearch
http://www.savvysearch.com/
SavvySearch is one of the leading providers of metasearch services. Its search engine offers a single point of access to more than 200 search engines, guides, archives, libraries, and other resources. Users submit a keyword query which is then immediately and sent out to all appropriate internet search engines. The results are gathered and displayed clearly. SavvySearch has existed as a free internet search service since 1995.

Scoot Yahoo
http://scoot.yahoo.co.uk
Yahoo has combined with the British directory Scoot to offer an excellent search facility for those looking for a whole host of information. Once you have found the organisation you are looking for you can click straight into their web site if they have one.

Search.com
http://search.cnet.com/
This service is run by CNET, one of the world's leading new-media companies. From the home page you can click an A-Z list option which displays an archive of all its search engines. The list is long, but just about everything you need to master the web is there. You can search yellow pages, phone numbers, email addresses, message boards, software downloads, and easily do all kinds of speciality searches.

Search IQ
http://www.searchiq.com/
This site provides reviews of the most popular search engines and directories, including: Altavista, AskJeeves, Excite, Google, Hotbot, Inference, Infoseek, Lycos, and Yahoo. You can use the subject directory to locate what you are looking for quickly. Finding information on the web can be like looking for a needle in a haystack. Speciality search engines help you track down the precise information you want.

Starting Point MetaSearch
http://www.stpt.com/search.html
This is a powerful metasearcher that puts over 170 high-quality, popular, and comprehensive search tools – general and category specific – at your fingertips. These tools include AliWeb, AltaVista, Archie, Excite, DejaNews, InfoSeek, Inktomi, Lycos, Netfind, Open Text, SavvySearch, URLsearch,W3 Catalog, WebCrawler, WWWWorm, and Yahoo!.

UK Directory
http://www.ukdirectory.co.uk/
Based in Eastleigh, Southampton, this is a useful directory listing to UK-based web sites. You can browse it or search it. It has a well-classified subject listing. UK Directory is simple and intuitive to use. You don't need to know the name of the company, service or person to find the things you are interested in. Just look in the category that best suits your needs. It is as easy to use as a telephone directory.

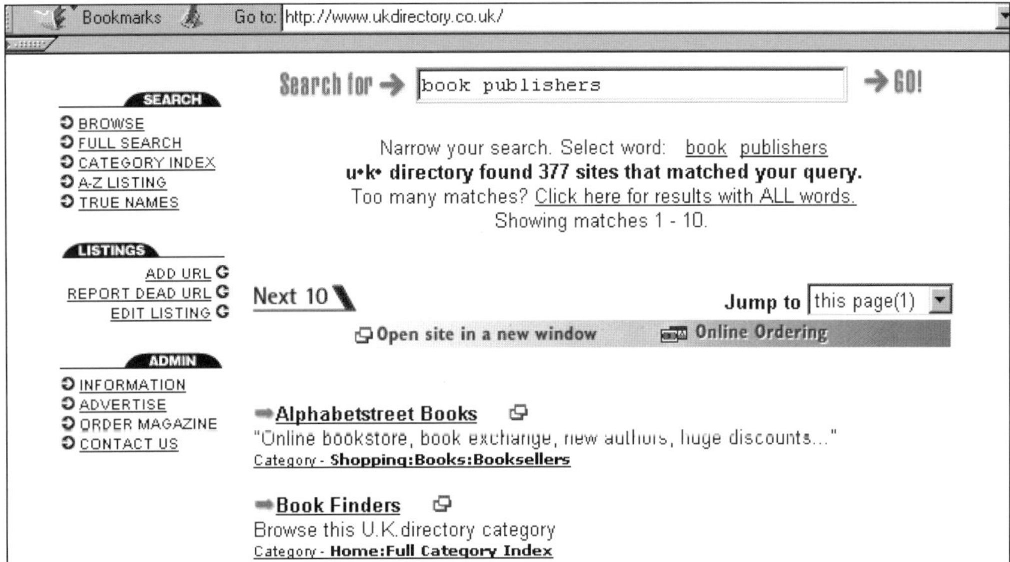

Fig. 5. UK Directory offers a local alternative to the many USA-based search engines. This search for 'book publishers' has yielded 377 matching results, the first two of which are visible at the bottom of the illustration.

UK Index
http://www.ukindex.co.uk/
This is another directory of sites in or about the UK. It assigns sites to broad categories to help you with searching. The depth of information seems variable.

UK Plus
http://www.ukplus.co.uk/
The parent company of this UK-oriented search engine and database is Daily Mail & General Trust – owners of the *Daily Mail,* the *Mail on Sunday, London Evening Standard* and a number of UK regional newspapers – so it draws on a rich tradition of quality publishing. It has built a vast store of web-site reviews supplied, not by an unselective computer robot, but by a team of experienced journalists. Although it concentrates on UK web sites of all kinds, you will also find many from all over the world which are included because it feels they are likely to be of interest to British-based readers.

UK Yellow Web Directory
http://www.yell.co.uk/
This site is operated by the yellow pages division of British Telecom. It is indexed 'by humans' and is searchable. A number of non-UK sites are included in the database. There is also an A to Z company listing, but note that companies whose names begin with 'The' are listed under T. A Business Compass lists 'the best' business internet resources, with links and brief descriptions.

Webcrawler
http://webcrawler.com/
Webcrawler is a fast worker and returns an impressive list of links. It analyses the full text of documents, allowing the searcher to locate key words which may have been buried deep within a document's text. Webcrawler is now part of Excite.

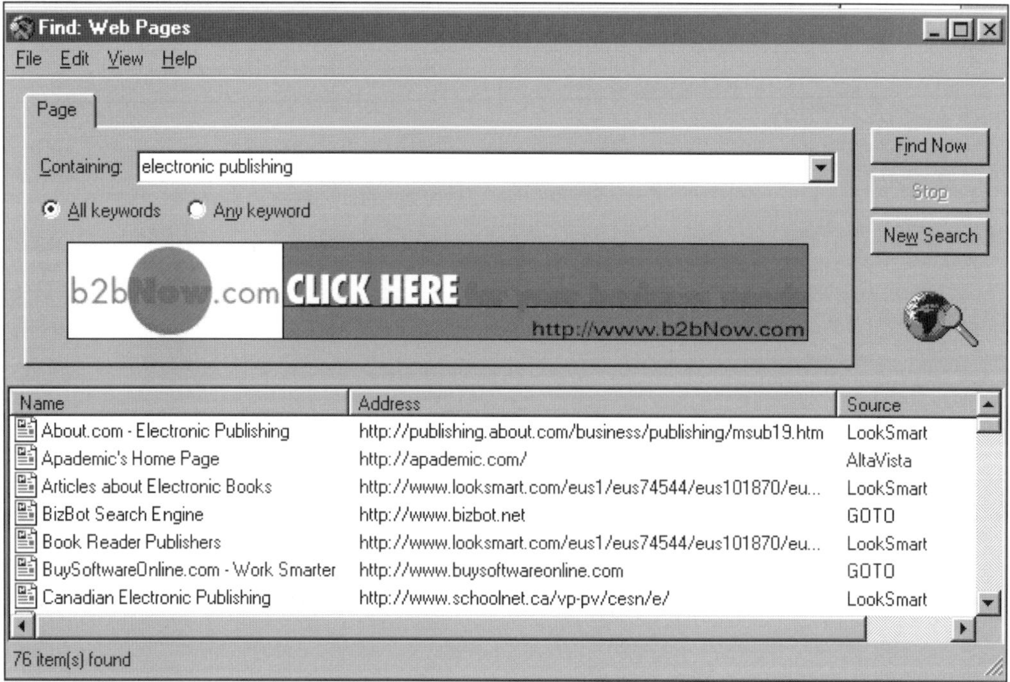

Fig. 6. Webferret is an excellent and popular piece of software that makes searching the web much easier and faster. It is produced by FerretSoft, and you can download a free version within a few minutes. Here it is being used to search for 'electronic publishing'.

WebFerret

http://www.ferretsoft.com

WebFerret is not a search engine as such, but a very handy search utility. You key in your query offline, and when you connect it searches the web until it has collected the number of references you have specified – up to 9,999 if you wish. WebFerret queries large web search engines to find sites matching the keywords you specify. It queries ten or more search engines simultaneously and discards duplicate results. The search engines it queries include AltaVista, Yahoo!, Infoseek, Excite, and others. You can immediately visit the URLs it finds, even while WebFerret is still running. The program is free and only takes a few minutes to download from FerretSoft. Highly recommended.

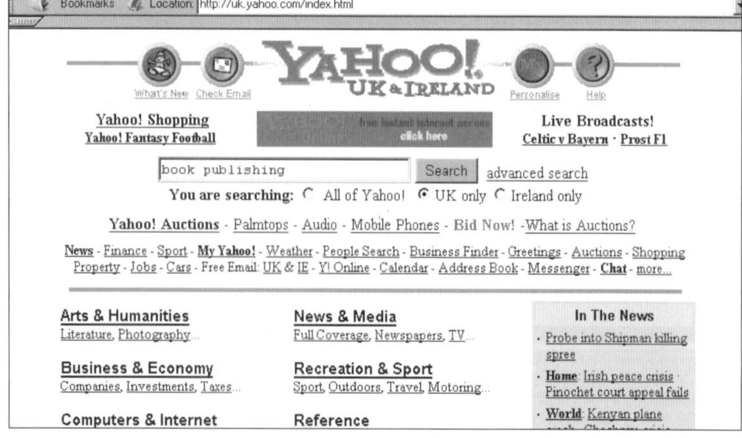

Fig. 7. As the world's biggest search engine and directory, the Yahoo! web site is an essential all-purpose bookmark. It offers home pages for many different countries, and this is its portal for the UK.

World Email Directory
http://www.worldemail.com/
This site is dedicated to email, email, more email, finding people and locating businesses and organisations. WED has access to an estimated 18 million email addresses and more than 140 million business and phone addresses worldwide. Here you'll find everything from email software, to email list servers, many worldwide email databases, business, telephone and fax directories and a powerful email search engine.

Yahoo! UK
http://www.yahoo.co.uk
Yahoo! was the first substantial search site on the internet, and is still one of the best for free general searching. It contains over a half a million links categorised by subjects. You can browse the categories or search through them using keywords. The site also contains links to specific information such as world news, sport and weather. Yahoo! is probably one of the search engines and directories you will use time after time, as do millions of people every day.

Portal sites for books and publishing

AcqWeb's Directory of Publishers and Vendors
http://www.library.vanderbilt.edu/law/acqs/pubr.html
This is an international directory of publishers and vendors used by libraries. It links to their web sites and email addresses. It is maintained for the benefit of the library community, and in particular acquisitions, collection development and serials librarians. AcqWeb is a sister publication of AcqNet and a gathering place for librarians and other professionals interested in acquisitions and collection development.

ABA Foundation for Free Expression
http://www.Ambook.org/
The American Booksellers Association campaigns against book censorship: this is its banned books page.

The Bookish Home Page
http://www.bic.org.uk/
The Bookish Home Page offers a gateway for book industry users of the internet. There are links to book industry communication, ecommerce, bibliographic and product information, standards, bar coding for books, electronic rights trading, publications, the Editeur home page, and other useful 'bookish' information. Information and links are updated and suggestions for inclusion are welcomed. The site is sponsored by the Publishers Association, Booksellers Association, Library Association and the British Library.

BookWeb
http://www.bookweb.co.uk/
BookWeb offers a useful miscellany of book trade information with hypertext links and email forms for book publishers and others. Any

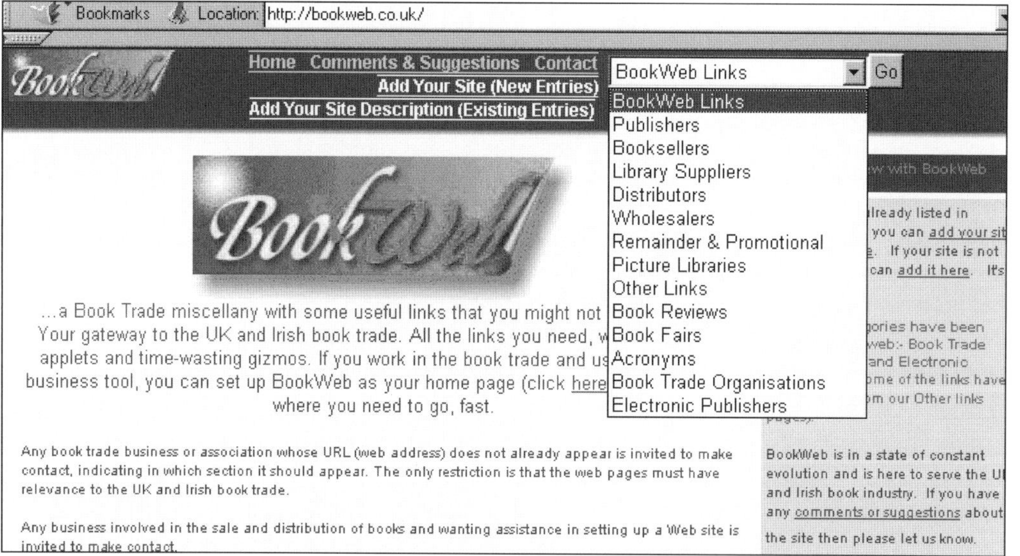

Fig. 8. BookWeb's guide to UK publishing. The drop-down menu offers quick links to everything from publishers and booksellers to acronyms and electronic publishers.

book trade business or association whose URL (web address) does not already appear is invited to make contact indicating in which section it should appear. The only restriction is that the web pages must be relevant to the UK book trade. The site includes a section on 'how to get published', containing useful advice about finding a publisher. BookWeb is sponsored by Sweetens Computer Services.

BookWire
http://ilmp.bookwire.com/
US-based BookWire can fairly claim to be the international book industry's most comprehensive online information source. It includes the latest book industry news, features, reviews, original fiction, guides to literary events, author interviews, and thousands of annotated links to book-related sites. Together with its sister magazine, *Publishers Weekly*, it brings you full coverage of book industry news, events, and personalities. *Library Journal Digital* offers inside information on the latest library news, multimedia, information technology, and views. BookWire also hosts groups such as the Book Industry Study Group, National Book Critics Circle, Mystery Writers of America, Poetry Society of America and the Association of Authors' Representatives. The site offers subscription to the leading reference directories, *Literary Market Place (USA)* and *International Literary Market Place* (global). The site is a service of the reference publishers Bowker, a division of Cahners Business Information.

Independent Book Publishers UK Web Ring.
http://www.gatewaybooks.com/i-book-uk.html
The idea of this web ring is to bring together web sites that promote books published by independent UK companies. Joining the ring is free. Your site will be checked for its suitability to join, and you will receive by email all the code needed to add to your HTML. All you have to do then is add it to your home page. The site is run by a small independent publisher called Gateway Books in Avon.

Infojump
http://www.infojump.com/corp/
InfoJump is a well-presented search engine that indexes electronic periodicals and online versions of print publications. It provides fast and relevant results by focusing on indexing selected periodicals. Its database consists of 5 million articles, said to be increasing at the rate of10,000 per day.

Knops Book Information Web site
http://www.xs4all.nl/-knops/index3.htm
This is a web site developed by a Dutch book restoration service, Knops Boekrestauratie, devoted to all aspects of books, book history, printing, bookbinding, auctions, manuscripts, antiquarian books, and dealers. The web site contains hundreds of useful book-related links.

Literary Market Place, Internet Edition
http://www.literarymarketplace.com/
LMP is an established and substantial print directory of the USA and international book publishing industry. This link takes you immediately to BookWire (see above).

Literary Resources on the Net
http://www.english.upenn.edu/-jlynch/Lit/
Jack Lynch's well-known resource is grouped into 16 main categories: classical & biblical, medieval, Renaissance, eighteenth-century, Romantic, Victorian British, twentieth-century British and Irish, American, theatre and drama, theory, women's literature and feminism, ethnic

Fig. 9. BookWire is an essential online guide to USA publishing. It combines news and features with links to all the main players on the American publishing scene.

nationalities, other national literatures, bibliography and history of the book, hypertext, and miscellaneous. It would benefit from more description of indexed sites.

NISS Information Gateway: Bookshops and Publishers
http://www.niss.ac.uk/reference/bookshops.html
This UK page provides links to bookshops and publishers offering on-line catalogue and how-to-order information for printed material. Other sections offer links to sources of electronic versions of texts, to sources dealing specifically with audio books, and to miscellaneous related resources (such as 'Books Out Of Print' and suppliers of videos).

Publishers on the Internet
http://www.lights.com/publisher/
With an easy-to-use menu, this site offers a very handy and easy way to visit the web sites of publishers large and small in almost every country of the world. The UK section for example gives hyperlinks to 340 publishers arranged A to Z. If you are shopping for books online, the site also enables you to compare prices from 25 internet bookstores.

University of Sheffield Library: Books and Publishing
http://www.shef.ac.uk/uni/services/lib/useful/books.html
This page provides links to sources for locating information about publications and publishers. It does not aim to provide links to the full text of publications. Full text services are available for some electronic journals and for some electronic books and texts.

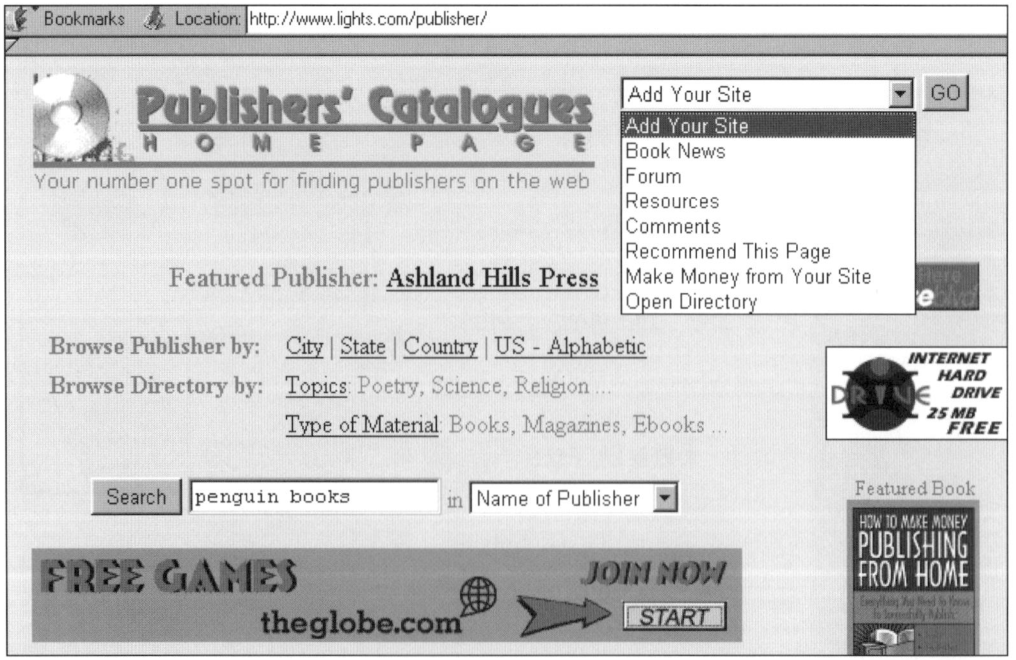

Fig. 10. The enterprising Northern Lights web site contains a substantial index of publishers on the internet. You can search by name of publisher (as in this case, Penguin Books), or browse its directory by topics or type of material such as books and magazines.

Book news

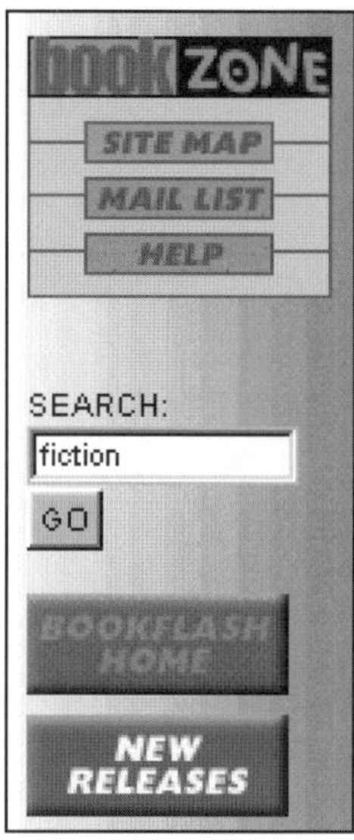

Book Flash
http://bookflash.com/
BookFlash posts publishing news releases online. The magazine-style site explains how you can post your own organisation's publishing news release, and what BookFlash will do to make sure people know about it.

Bookseller Magazine
http://www.thebookseller.com/
See page 42.

BookSpot
http://www.bookspot.com/
BookSpot is a general interest American book site which you can use to search for online texts, book reviews, reading lists, author and publisher information, book stores, book news, and events.

New York Books
http://www.nybooks.com/
'The web site for the intellectually curious': *The New York Review of Books*, from the *Reader's Catalog* and *Granta*.

Publishers Weekly - see *BookWire* above.

Book trade information

Book Data
http://www.bookdata.co.uk/
Book Data was founded in 1987 to provide information services to publishers, booksellers and libraries wherever English language books are sold. The company now employs some 90 full-time and part-time staff based in offices outside London. Book Data creates and maintains a database of title records of books and non-serial publications in other media. The largest part of the database consists of titles from subscribing publishers, who pay for the creation of descriptive records of their books and to secure inclusion in all Book Data services including online.

Books in Print
http://www.booksinprint.com
This is a paid subscription service which gives access to 1.6 million bibliographic records, over 300,000 full-text reviews, and full publisher information.

Newsgroups and mailing list services

- *Newsgroups* are public discussion groups freely available on the internet. Each newsgroup is a collection of messages, usually unedited and not checked by anyone ('unmoderated'). Messages can be posted in the newsgroup by anyone including you. The ever-growing newsgroups have been around for much longer than the world wide web and web pages, and are an endless source of information, news, scandal, entertainment, resources and ideas. The 80,000-plus newsgroups are collectively referred to as Usenet. To access newsgroups, you will need a news reader, a type of software that enables you to search, read, post and manage messages in a newsgroup. It will normally be supplied as part of your internet service when you first sign up, e.g. Internet Explorer/Outlook, or Netscape/Messenger.

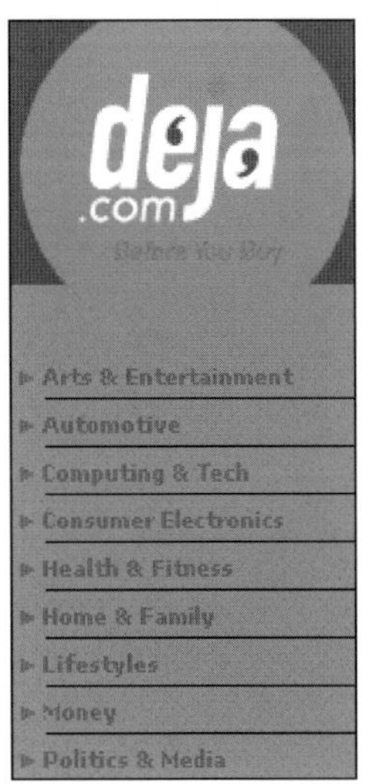

Deja.com
http://www.deja.com/
Deja.com (originally Deja News) was founded in 1995 as the first web site dedicated exclusively to online discussion, and capable of searching and archiving Usenet newsgroups. With more than six million page views per day, it offers access to tens of thousands of newsgroups. Deja is one of the web's most visited sites. More than a million people have registered (free) to take advantage of its expanding range of information and community services.

- *Mailing lists* In internet parlance, a mailing list is a forum where members can distribute messages by email to the members of the forum, and where all the members ('subscribers') can read the messages posted. There are two types of lists, discussion and announcement. Discussion lists allow exchange between list members. Announcement lists are one-way only and used to distribute information such as news or humour. A good place to look for specific mailing lists is Liszt (see below).

Liszt
http://www.liszt.com
Liszt offers the largest index of mailing lists available on the internet, covering every conceivable area of interest – more than 90,000 lists in all. It also offers a Usenet newsgroups directory and an IRC chat directory. You can obtain a great deal of information here.

MailBase
http://www.mailbase.ac.uk/
Run from the University of Sheffield, MailBase is the best known and largest source of special interest mailing lists in the UK, over 2,000 in all. You can search its database of lists to find the one(s) that interest you, and then subscribe (free) to read and post messages on that particular topic environmental health, clinical topics, health management, or what you will.

news:alt.books.reviews
news:uk.adverts.books
These are just two just examples of Usenet newsgroups, where people read and post messages about new and forthcoming books. To access any such group, just type the address exactly as shown above into your browser's address box: the name of the newsgroup, prefixed by 'news:'.

The messages in the newsgroup should open up for you automatically. Click on any of the headers (single line descriptions) in the upper panel, and you can then read the message in the lower panel.

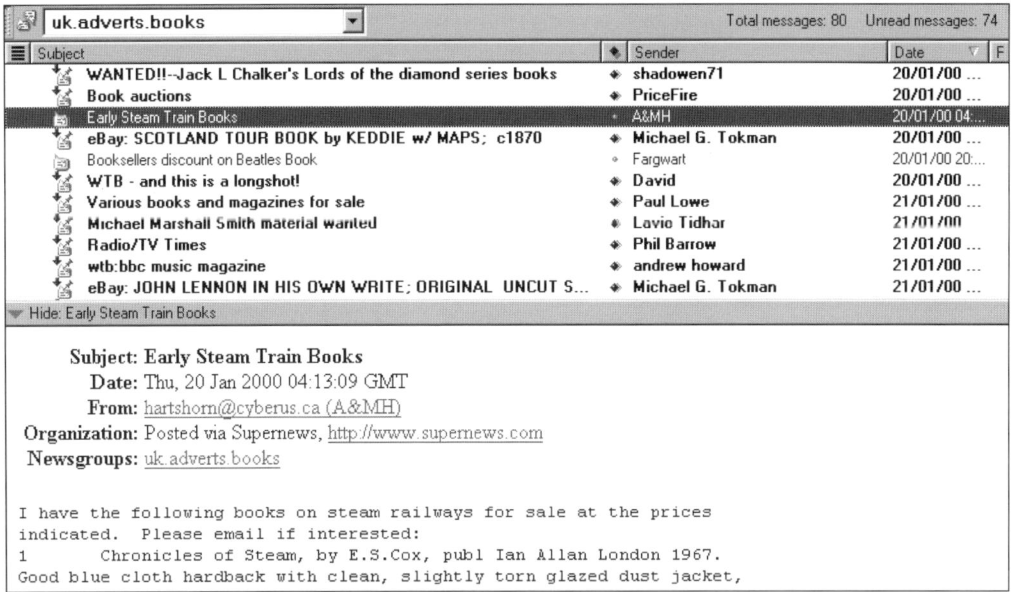

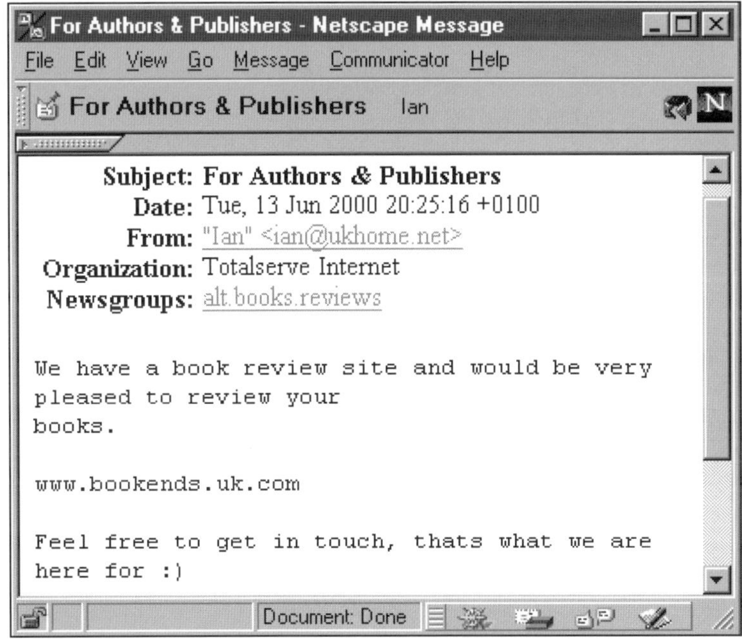

Fig. 11 (a). This is an example of a book-related newsgroup, 'uk.adverts.books'. The upper part of the screen shows some of the message headers. By clicking on a header, you can read a particular message, in this case one about early steam train books.

Fig. 11 (b). A message posted in the newsgroup called alt.books.reviews.

2 Books and booksellers

In this chapter we will explore:

- *booksellers' associations*
- *online bookshops*
- *book price comparison web sites*
- *general booksellers*
- *rare and secondhand online booksellers*
- *book clubs*
- *library suppliers and book wholesalers*

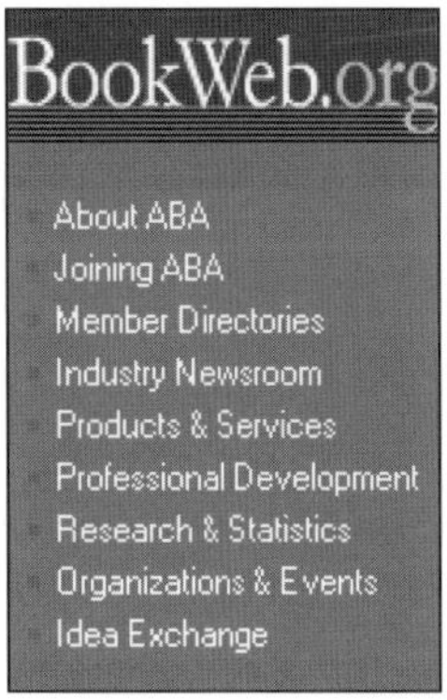

Booksellers' associations

American Booksellers Association
http://www.bookweb.org/aba/
Founded in 1900, the American Booksellers Association is a not-for-profit trade organization devoted to meeting the needs of its core members–independently owned bookstores with store front locations. It hosts the annual ABA Convention in conjunction with BookExpo America each spring. The site contains a searchable directory of members. You can browse these by location, and visit online bookstores by category.

American Wholesale Booksellers Association
http://www.awba.com/hist.html
The AWBA was formed in 1984. It represents a diverse group of book wholesalers of all sizes, and types, and from all areas of the US.

Antiquarian Booksellers' Association of America
http://www.abaa-booknet.com/
Established in 1949, the ABAA represents the antiquarian book trade. The site includes a Collectors' Corner with a compendium of articles and other resources on book collecting, essays by ABAA members, FAQs, and links to other useful sites. There is information about upcoming book fairs as well as links to the web sites of past and future ABAA fairs. The association has about 470 members.

Booksellers Association of Great Britain and Ireland
http://www.booksellers.org.uk/
The BA represents over 95 per cent of booksellers in these countries. The web site includes a bookshop and publishers search facility and numerous industry links, plus guides to competitiveness, marketing your bookshop, providing a forum, professional development, essential publications and advice, products for the bookshop, professional services, representing your interests in the trade and beyond, and contact list.

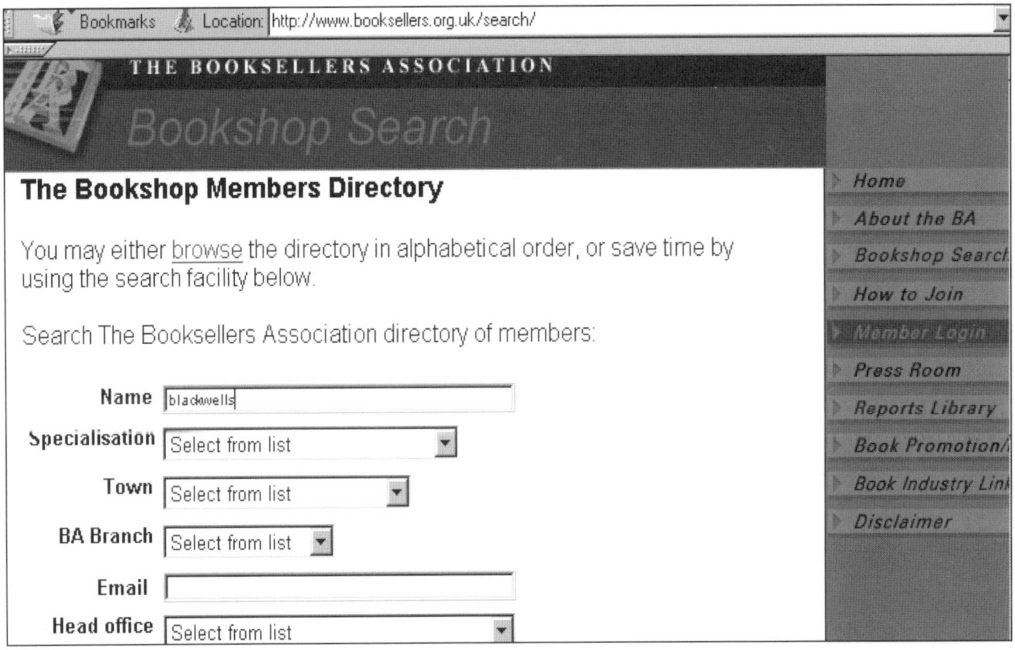

Fig. 12. The web site of the Booksellers Association (UK). This part of the site enables you to search its directory of members. The panel on the right contains links to other parts of this useful site.

British Internet Bookdealers Association
http://www.clique.co.uk/bibfind.htm
The site contains details of more than 1,300 British book dealers and their specialist subject-areas. There is a search engine where you can seek information by keying in a subject area, otherwise you will need to know the name of particular dealer you are looking for.

Canadian Booksellers Association
http://www.cbabook.org/
Based inToronto, the CBA works closely with booksellers and suppliers to promote the profitability of the industry, favourable trading terms, and operational practices. It also represents booksellers' interests to the government and wider public. The site features Bookline, an interactive discussion area for all CBA members. You can swap information on books, enquire about bookselling issues, and post questions on any matter relating to the book trade.

European Booksellers Federation
http://www.ebf-eu.org/
Each member state of the European Union is represented by delegates from its principal bookselling trade association, so that in effect nearly every bookshop in Europe is represented by this Brussels-based organisation, some 25,000 bookshops in all.

Hay-on-Wye Bookshops (UK)
http://www.hay-on-wye.com/
The picturesque town of Hay-on-Wye in Herefordshire is world-famous as a centre of secondhand bookselling. The site lists all the booksellers in the area, and gives details of the annual literature festival.

Provincial Booksellers Fairs Association
http://antiquarian.com/pbfa/
The PBFA is the largest trade association in the world for dealers in antiquarian and secondhand books, organising around 150 book fairs a year in the UK, and providing services and safeguards for booksellers and the public, worldwide. The site includes a directory of members, notice board, and details of fairs all over the UK, the highlight of which is the series of fairs held in May/June each at the Russell Hotel in London's Bloomsbury.

Online bookshops (new books)

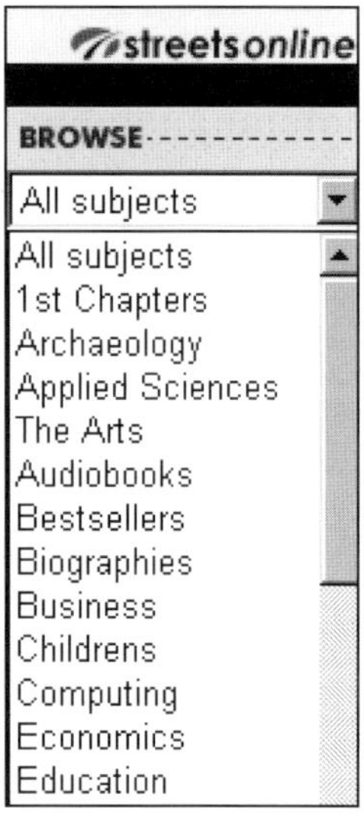

Alphabetstreet Books
http://www.alphabetstreet.com
This is one of the leading UK online bookstores, started in 1996 and now backed by FreeServe. If you wish, free 'informers' - sent to you by email every two weeks or so will keep you up to date on hundreds of subjects. You can search and browse for any book, and order using their secure internet credit and debit card payment system. The service is part of Streets Online. Its other online retailing sites sell CDs, DVDs and games. Most of its products include VAT and free delivery in the UK.

Amazon
http://www.amazon.com
Amazon.com opened its virtual doors in 1995 with a mission to transform book-buying into the fastest, easiest, and most enjoyable shopping experience possible. It has since achieved immortality (and a vast stockmarket value) in becoming the world's most popular online bookshop, with heavily discounted prices throughout. 12 million people in more than 160 countries have used it not just for books but for electronic greeting cards, online auctions, CDs, videos, DVDs, toys and games, and electronics. The site incorporates an Authors' Guide and Publishers' Guide explaining how you can sell your own titles using Amazon, and how you can build a store on your web site to sell books, music, videos, and other products. Whatever your interest in books and publishing, this site is unmissable.

Amazon UK
http://www.amazon.co.uk
This is the UK version of Amazon, which is now developing localised versions for other countries. Payment for book purchases is by credit card. You become an account-holder, following which you can view your order history, review any of your past or pending orders, and track the progress of your order online. Amazon works with UK wholesalers, and so your book will normally arrive within a couple of days. You can easily change your email address or password at any time. Amazon.co.uk contains more than 1.5 million locally published titles (not all are in print!).

Fig. 13. This is the home page of Amazon.com, the world's best known online bookshop. It uses local national book distributors to help deliver the books to its customers.

Barnes and Noble
http://www.barnesandnoble.com
Barnes and Noble is one of the top US retail bookstore chains, and this in-depth site reflects the company's position in the marketplace. You can search for what you want and browse in all sorts of ways for example by subject – biography, business, computers, entertainment, fiction, literature, kids' books, history, mind, body, and spirit and many more subjects. It can help you with out of print titles and specialist areas can help you find the professional or electronic titles you require. Since launching in 1997, this has become the world's fifth largest e-commerce site and among the 25 largest sites overall on the web, according to Media Metrix. It is also the exclusive bookseller on America Online.

Blackwells
http://bookshop.blackwell.co.uk/
The 'world's leading academic bookseller' would like you to be not just a customer but a member. Registration is free, and brings the following benefits: an alerting service for new books listings by email, a one-time entry of up to four delivery addresses, a personalised notebook with access to your own events diary, order history and profile, and a personalised homepage. But it's not essential for using the site. Blackwell's Online Bookshop offers free postage for any orders delivered to addresses within the UK.

BOL
http://www.bol.com
BOL is a heavyweight contender in the online bookselling market, offering dedicated services for the UK, USA, Germany, France, the Netherlands, Spain and Switzerland. You can choose to create your own profile, tailoring the service to suit your individual requirements.

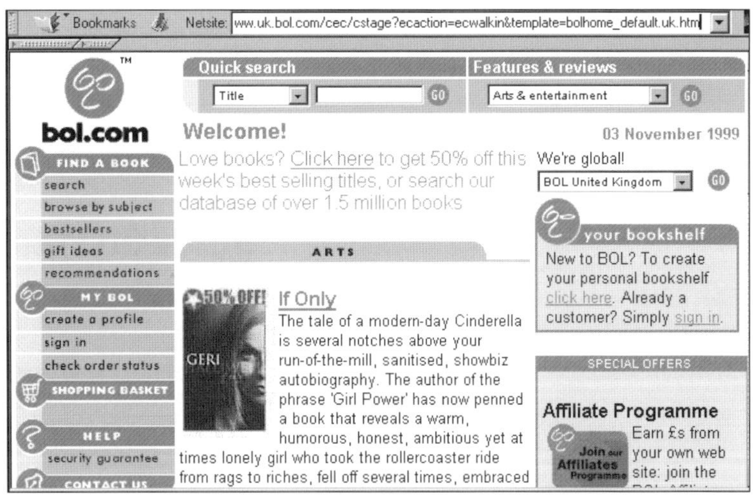

Fig. 14. BOL.Com is a major contender among the online bookshops. It allows you to personalise your usage of the site in various ways, for example by creating a 'personal bookshelf'.

You will then receive personalised book recommendations, details of new titles by your favourite authors and in your favourite subjects You can also receive a personalised email newsletter with all the latest news about the books and authors you like best. You can easily check the status of your order. BOL is a division of the media giant Bertlesmann.

Book Pl@ce
http://www.thebookplace.com
Bookpl@ce is another UK challenger in the fiercely competitive market for online bookselling. The site includes nearly one billion terms indexed for searching, including of course titles and author names. Book blurbs and jackets are shown where possible. It also offers *Book Ends,* a free online magazine and Fifth Dimension, its own sci-fi and fantasy bookshop. The service is owned and operated by Book Data (see above). Any non-stock item has to be ordered from the publishers, so delivery could take 14 days.

Booksearchengine
http://www.booksearchengine.com
If it is in print you can find the cheapest and nearest copy here. You do not need to type in the author's full name or the complete title in most cases. For example, if searching for *The Power and the Glory* by Graham Greene you need only type in Greene in the author field and Glory in the title field.

BookZone
http://www.bookzone.co.uk
You can search through BookZone by title, author or ISBN, check the state of your order or look for new releases by your favourite author, view its ordering policies and information on how to use the site, and 'take the escalator to our other stores for music, software and videos'. BookZone is a service of CDZone Ltd, based in Yorkshire.

Borders
http://www.borders.com
Now a publicly owned, independent corporation, Borders Group Inc. is

the world's second largest retailer of books, music, video and other informational, educational, and entertainment products. It has over 200 superstores in the USA, UK and Singapore. With a searchable and browseable catalogue of ten million books, CDs and videos – if it's a new or in-print product you want – you should be sure to find it on this buzzing site.

City Lights
http://www.citylights.com/
Founded in San Francisco in 1953 by poet Lawrence Ferlinghetti and Peter D. Martin, City Lights is one of the great independent bookstores in the United States. It is a place where book lovers from across the country and around the world come to browse, and soak in the ambiance of this literary landmark. If you want to explore beat literature, or surrealism, this is the place to come. Anti-authoritarian politics and insurgent thinking continue to be a strong influence in the store.

Computer Manuals Online Bookstore
http://www.compman.co.uk/home.htm
This attractively presented UK site should be able to supply almost any kind of computer manual or reference book you could want.

Countrybookstore
http://www.countrybookstore.co.uk
The Country Book Store is situated in the heart of the Peak District countryside and has become one of the most popular out-of-town bookstores in the UK. With its news and features, its secure shopping basket, international currency comparisons, and order tracking, this impressive web site is a testament to what can be achieved by a specialist book retailer.

Dillons
http://www.dillons.co.uk
This link now redirects visitors to the main Waterstones site.

Dog Lovers Bookshop
http://www.dogbooks.com
This is an typical example of an efficient niche online bookstore. Updated weekly, its listings are accessible via a table of contents organised by species, domestic breed, and topic. The firm is a member of the American Booksellers Association.

English Book Centre
http://www.ebcoxford.co.uk
The EGC in Oxford supplies all types of ELT materials, including books, videos, multimedia packages and computer software. Its customers come from all over the world and range from language schools and universities to businesses and government departments.

Grant & Cutler
http://www.grant-c.demon.co.uk
Founded in 1936, this London firm is the UK's largest foreign language bookseller, offering titles in French, German, Italian, Portuguese, Spanish, Russian, Dutch and the Nordic languages, plus software, CDs, and audiocassettes on a huge range of subjects. It has one of the world's biggest selections of dictionaries, language-learning books and audiocassettes for these and about 200 other languages.

Fred Hanna's Bookstore
http://www.adnet.ie/hannas/
Hanna is one of the top bookselling names in Ireland. In addition to comprehensive online searching and ordering facilities, the site also contains links to other Irish sites of interest.

Heffers
http://www.heffers.co.uk
Cambridge-based Heffers offers secure online shopping on this functional site, with use of a login name and password. Its database lists approximately 1.9 million titles. If the title you want is out of print or secondhand you can go to its antiquarian and out-of-print books search and make your request there. As a 'member', you can sign on to receive information on new books in any of over 3,400 subject categories. Heffers was recently acquired by Blackwell.

Helter Skelter
http://www.skelter.demon.co.uk
Based in London's West End, Helter Skelter claims to be the only rock 'n' roll bookshop in the world, and able to get any music book available anywhere in the world to anywhere in the world. You can download its current catalogue in MS Word format.

Hodges Figgis
http://www.hodgesfiggis.com
Hodges Figgis is one of the best-known bookshops in Ireland. To find a title on its online store you are invited to browse or search its catalogue of over 100,000 titles. You choose the subject category you want, and then further options are presented to you. Alternatively, you can key in a title, author or ISBN. If you cannot find the book you are looking for on the site, you can an email them and they will try to assist you.

Internet Bookshop
http://www.bookshop.co.uk/
Originally an independent internet start up business, the Internet Bookshop has been acquired by W. H. Smith, the high street retailer, and rebranded as WHSmith Online. This attractive site offers well over a million titles in all subject areas, many of them discounted, and is very well presented in a magazine style format, with news, reviews and features. The sjte also sells CDs, videos and games. It uses a secure credit card ordering system. Highly recommended.

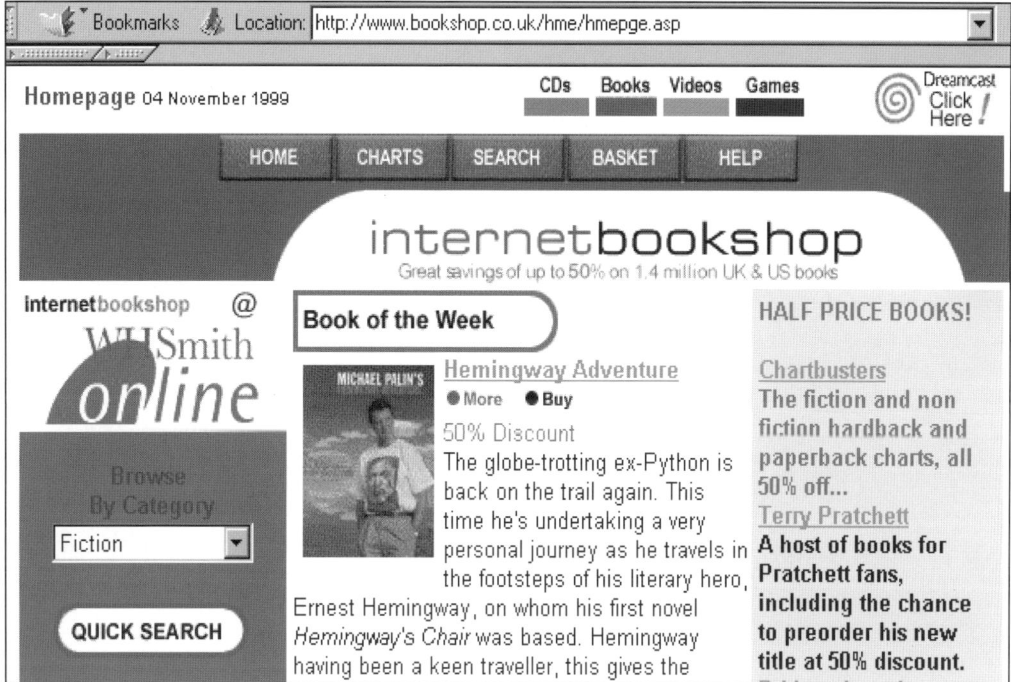

Fig. 15. The web site of the Internet Bookshop. Originally an independent venture based in Oxford, it was acquired by WH Smith as a platform for its entry into online retailing.

Internet Talking Bookshop
http://www.orma.co.uk/intabs.htm
The Internet Talking Bookshop invites you to enjoy shopping with its secure mail order service, using the shopping basket. You can browse through its catalogue which offers some 2,400 audio books, including all those produced by the BBC.

Modern Book Co
http://www.sonnet.co.uk/modern
Based in London, the Modern Book Co offers a broad range of titles in business, computers and computing, electronics & communications, medicine, and science and engineering. This is quite a functional looking site, but offers a 10% discount on all orders via this web site

Natural History Book Service
http://www.nhbs.co.uk/
The NHBS site offers catalogues of books on botany, zoology, biology, ecology, conservation, biodiversity, natural history, travel, palaeontology, evolution, earth and environmental sciences, physical sciences, and sustainable development.

Ottakars
http://www.ottakars.com/
Ottakars was set up in 1987, and now has about 70 bookshops across the UK. Its attractively produced online bookstore offers a 30-day satisfaction guarantee. You can search by author, title, ISBN or keywords, or browse by various subject categories. Each branch offers its own highly individual web site.

Peters Bookselling Group
http://www.peters-books.co.uk/index.html
Founded in 1935, Peters is a family-owned general bookselling business based in Birmingham.

Politico's Political Bookstore
http://www.politicos.co.uk
Politico's describes itself as Britain's only political bookstore and coffee house, located at the heart of political life in Westminster. It offers a wide selection of political books, magazines and publications, plus political giftware, postcards, and political art.

Post Mortem Books
http://www.postmortembooks.co.uk
Sussex-based Post Mortem offers crime and mystery fiction, UK and US books by mail order, new and used books, scarce and rare editions, signed copies, Sherlock Holmes, Drakulya and similar items. It also publishes selected reprints in the genre.

Postscript
http://www.sandpiper.co.uk/postscript
Postscript offers publishers' overstocks, reprints and remaindered editions from major publishing houses and independent and university presses. Its list covers everything from art and design to travel and transport.

Read Ireland
http://www.readireland.ie
Read Ireland is an internet bookstore dedicated exclusively to Irish interest books. It offers a free weekly email newsletter.

Scotweb
http://www.scotweb.co.uk/library/
Scotweb features a selection of Scottish books and magazines, Robert Burns and other literature, and multimedia CDs about Scotland.

Shetland Times Bookshop
http://www.shetland-times.co.uk/shop
The site offers books about Shetland, Scottish, maritime, Scandinavian and other specific interests. There is also a book-of-the-week slot and news of forthcoming local publications.

John Smith & Son
http://www.johnsmith.co.uk
Founded in Glasgow in 1751, John Smith is Scotland's oldest independent book retailer, and believes it may be the oldest continuously trading bookseller in the world. The company is owned by its shareholders, most of whom are staff. It has twelve shops in Scotland, of which eight are situated on university campuses. They say that every hundredth order received from this web site is supplied free of charge.

W H Smith
See the Internet Bookshop (above).

W H Smith Paris
http://www.paris-anglo.com/clients/whsmith
W H Smith has the largest English bookshop in Paris (and France) with more than 70,000 titles to choose from, including English & American fiction, management, computer and reference books, children's books, English language teaching material and magazines.

James Thin
http://www.jthin.co.uk/
Established in 1848, Thin's are famous Scottish and international booksellers. Their site offers a quick search facility through a database of around one million titles. It also features details of forthcoming events, signings and readings, and *Capital Letters*, an online magazine featuring news and reviews from the Scottish literary world.

Waterstones
http://www.waterstones.co.uk/
With its attractive presentation, quick search, links to branches, personal library, music, and numerous other features, Waterstones have developed an impressive and functional site. You can take a site tour, explore current title and author promotions, books of the month, signed first editions, out of print titles, and check out discounts on best-selling titles. You can check the status of your online order using a case-sensitive username and password. Recommended.

Fig. 16. Waterstones is a dominating force in the high street, but on the internet it faces stiff competition from Amazon and other newcomers, who offer across-the-board discounts and many innovative online services.

Book price comparison web sites

DealPilot
http://www.dealpilot.com/
You can use DealPilot to find almost any book, CD, video or DVD on the internet and then let it compare prices from all major online shops to track down the best offer. You are also invited to enhance your web site, increase your traffic and earn money by joining the DealPilot partner program. DealPilot.com AG was founded in July 1997 by Christopher Muenchhoff and Christoph Janz, to be an innovative German internet-based company setting its main focus on internet software robots and comparison shopping systems. Highly recommended.

Fig. 17. DealPilot is a leading web site for making online price comparisons, not only for books but also for CDs and videos.

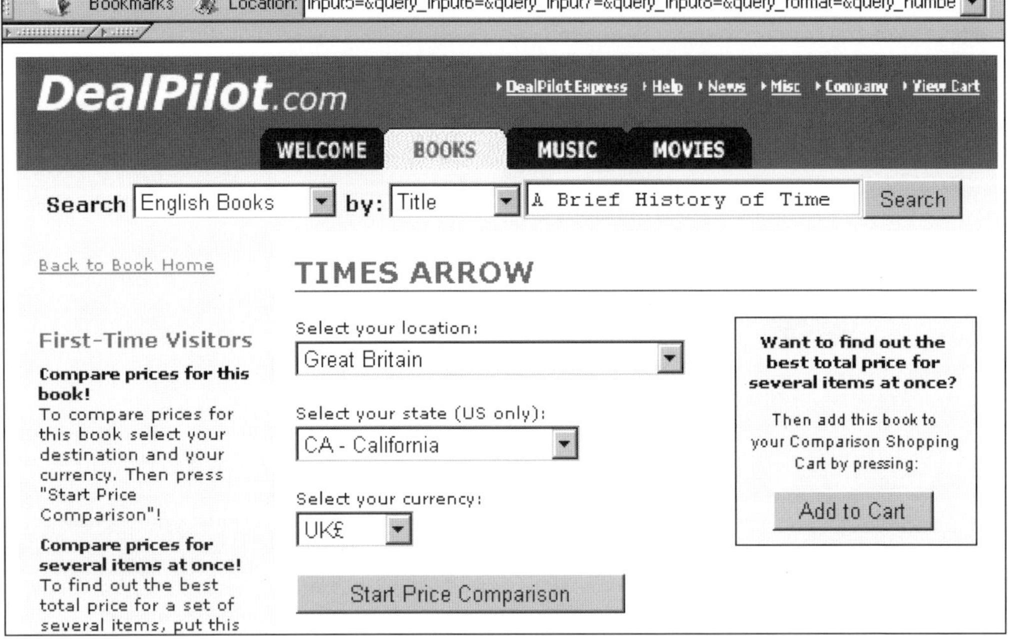

AddALL
http://www.addall.com/
AddALL is a free and independent web site and search engine built by book buyers for book buyers. 'Our search result is totally objective without favouring one bookstore over another.' You can search for any book you want, and compare the prices, from around 40 online bookstores worldwide. You can have the prices displayed in the currency you prefer, along with the delivery charge and any sales tax applicable to your region. You can also compare delivery times.

A1-BookMall
http://www.a1bookmall.com/
A1-BookMall is another very effective book-price search engine. You can compare the prices of 25 internet bookstores, and the shipping costs are included in the comparison.

Best Book Buys
http://www.bestbookbuys.com/
Finds the lowest price from several online bookstores including Amazon.com, Barnes & Noble, Big Words, Book Pool, BooksaMillion, Buy.Com, Christian Book, Fat Brain, Page One, Powell's Books, Textbooks, Varsity Books and many more. There is an associated web site called Best Music Buys.

Rare and secondhand online booksellers

Advanced Book Exchange
http://www.abebooks.com
The Canadian company ABE says it is the world's largest source of out of print books, representing the stocks of over 5,300 booksellers and with a massive 15 million titles listed. ABE works by networking together thousands of bookstores, almost all of them small family businesses, and giving them a range of services usually only available to large corporations. Want a copy of that elusive first edition, or the long-ago published memoirs of your great-grandfather? ABE is the place to come. Highly recommended.

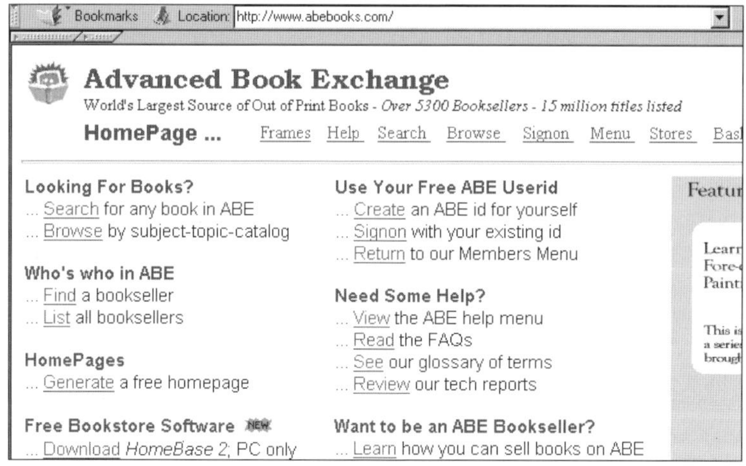

Fig. 18. If you collect rare and secondhand books, the Advanced Book Exchange is a must, offering 15 million titles from more than 5,000 booksellers. If you are interested in turning a hobby into a business, you can easily set up as an online bookseller yourself.

Alibris
http://www.alibris.com/
Visitors to Alibris gain immediate access to a database of millions of books, manuscripts, maps, photos, prints, and autographs. With sophisticated search capabilities, its attractively designed web store should help you find the books you want in just a few keystrokes. If you are not quite sure what you want, you can browse through about 30 subject categories. The company is based in San Francisco.

Antiquarian Bookstore
http://www.antiqbooks.com/
This New Hampshire firm specialises in rare and out-of-print books and magazines, with a stock of about 200,000 books.

Books and booksellers

Bibliocity
http://www.bibliocity.com/
Bibliocity can help you track down rare and collectible books from leading international antiquarian booksellers. The site features searching, online ordering, and automatic handling of wants, and you can also find out about forthcoming auctions. Bibliocity has recently joined forces with Alibris.

Bibliofind
http://bibliofind.com/
With more than ten million used and rare books, first editions, periodicals and ephemera offered for sale by thousands of booksellers around the world, Bibliofind is one of the most interesting book-selling sites on the web, and a must for collectors and dealers worldwide. The functionally laid out site gives you answers to your questions in seconds. Bibliofind has recently become part of the mighty Amazon group of online retailing services. Highly recommended.

Bookfinder.com
http://www.bookfinder.com
'Over 15 million new, used, rare, and out of print books at your fingertips...' BookFinder connects readers to over 15,000 booksellers from around the world with a real open marketplace for all their online book shopping needs. You can use this handy site to search ABE, Amazon Bibliofind, Bibliocity, BookAvenue, Antiqbook and Powell's of Oregon.

Booksearch.Com
http://www.booksearch.com/
BookSearch Inc was started in 1984 by Timothy Donahue. It is affiliated with over 1,700 retail bookstores in all fifty American states as well as in Canada, the United Kingdom and Japan. To initiate a search you are invited to phone, send an email, or use its online search request form, and they will notify you of the results. The site does not include a searchable database as such. Initiating a search includes no obligation to purchase. Visa, Mastercard, American Express and Discover cards are accepted.

Charing Cross Road Bookshop
http://www.anyamountofbooks.com/
These two London shops – Charing Cross Road Bookshop and Any Amount of Books – can supply rare books, first editions, modern literature, art, poetry, scholarly/academic books, antiquarian, leather bound sets, and general stock. The site contains their catalogue, plus some useful links to the secondhand book trade.

Rare Oriental Book Company
http://www.rareorientbooks.com/
Since 1967, Rare Oriental has been supplying libraries, museums, research institutes and private collectors. It maintain a 'copious and eclectic' collection of over 25,000 rare, scarce and choice titles on all

aspects of Japan, China, Korea, Tibet and south-east Asian countries and their cultures. It issues subject catalogues on everything from art reference, jade, furniture, and gardens, to carpets, ceramics and porcelains, woodblock print reference and netsuke.

Book clubs

Book-of-the-Month Club
http://www.bomc.com/
This is the main international home page of BOMC. Outside the USA you are referred to: http://www.englishbooks.com/

Club Internacional del Libro
http://www.cilsp.com/
CIL is the largest Spanish language mail order publisher, offering books, courses, educational books, multimedia and music.

Library suppliers and book wholesalers

Arts Bibliographic
http://www.artsbib.com
This London-based firm is a specialist art book supplier.

Baker & Taylor
http://www.btol.com/
Established over 170 years ago, Baker & Taylor is a gigantic American book wholesaler and library supplier of books, videos and music products. It has approximately 385,000 titles in its inventory and ships over a million unique ISBNs to 8,000 trade and institutional customers each year. It also provides its customers with value-added proprietary data products and customised management services. Its price/availability feature allows booksellers and librarians to receive up-to-the-minute information regarding the availability of its book products and an individual quotation.

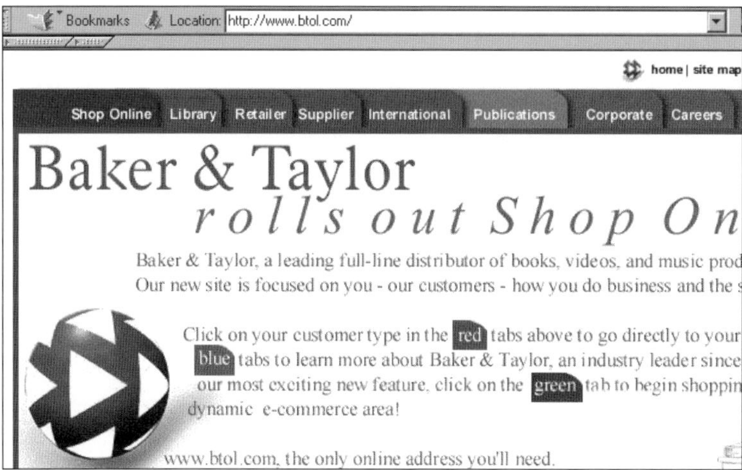

Fig. 19. This is the home page of Baker & Taylor, the leading US and international wholesale book distribution company.

Books and booksellers

Bertrams
http://www.bertrams.com
With a catalogue of more than 200,000 titles from 1,300 publishers, Bertrams is one of the leading UK book wholesalers. It only supplies bookshops, and does not sell direct to the general public. It also supplies software services to the book trade.

Blackwells
http://bookshop.blackwell.co.uk
Blackwells are library suppliers as well as general retailers.

Cypher Group
http://www.cyphergroup.co.uk/
The Cypher Group was formed in 1997 from three library supply companies, Morley Book Company, Library Services UK and Greenhead Books. It has since been joined by Bertrams, the wholesaler and is now the largest UK-based specialist library supplier with a turnover of £35 million, and a combined group turnover in book-related material of more than £100 million. It supplies public libraries, academic, specialist and medical institutions.

Dawsons
http://www.dawson.co.uk
Founded in 1809, Dawson Holdings is one of the world's largest information services organisations and is a publicly traded UK company. Its book division combines book procurement with technology to offer a comprehensive service to librarians all over the world. Its divisions include Surridge Dawson.

Everetts
http://www.everett.co.uk
Founded way back in 1793, Everetts is an international bookseller and subscription agent. Its services include consolidation, standing orders and back issue periodical and series runs.

Gardners
http://www.gardners.com
Gardners are one of the biggest UK book wholesalers. They say that this is a trade site, developed for prospective and existing account customers, and so it does not supply books direct to the public. Trade customers can enquire or place orders real time, view forthcoming titles, check back orders, view invoices and credits, view bestseller lists, and see the latest promotions and offers.

Greenhead Books – see Cypher Group.

Morley Books – see Cypher Group.

Starkmann Ltd
http://www.starkmann.com
Starkmann provides libraries with a supply service for books and CD-

roms published in Europe and North America. The site has links to special offers, reference title database, full title database, place an order, track your orders, news, and staff profiles.

Woodfield & Stanley
http://www.woodfield-stanley.co.uk
The Huddersfield firm of Woodfield & Stanley is an independent family-owned company established in 1946. It supplies libraries and schools all over the world with children's books, and claims to have been the first UK supplier to provide a fully functional book browsing and ordering system over the internet for its customers in 1995.

3 Readers and reading

In this chapter we will explore:

- *magazines and periodicals*
- *literature online*
- *children's books*
- *crime and mysteries*
- *drama*
- *horror*
- *literary fiction*
- *romance*
- *science fiction and fantasy*

Magazines and periodicals

Bookseller Magazine
http://www.thebookseller.com/
The Bookseller, popularly known as 'The Organ', is the leading weekly illustrated book trade magazine in the UK, published by Whitakers in London. The main links on the site lead you to information about the magazine, an archive of news, articles and features, bestsellers, digital dialogues, book trade careers, directories, members, professional publishing, Europe, and a buyer's guide. There is a searchable database of 'who owns whom' in British publishing, and book publishing in Britain. Anyone is free to explore the web site, though some of the facilities require a membership fee.

Fig. 20. The *Bookseller* magazine is published once a week, but is available on the internet 24 hours a day, complete with information from back issues.

Book Ends Magazine
http://www.bookends.co.uk
Book Ends is a searchable online magazine containing publishing news, reviews, short stories, features, trade news and 'top tens' from the world of books. Over sixty new titles are reviewed each month. The site offers subject home pages, a seven-page children's section, in-depth features, news of best sellers, book events, trade news, mystery book, bookmark awards and an ever-growing archive of publishing information. The magazine is a project of Book Data Ltd.

Free Pint
http://www.freepint.co.uk/
Functional in appearance, Free Pint is a well-established and popular internet newsletter which includes web site reviews and articles contributed by a group of UK information science professionals. It includes a 'Bookshelf' section. The newsletter is sent to more than 26,000 subscribers around the world every two weeks.

London Review of Books
http://www.lrb.co.uk
The *London Review of Books* was founded in 1979, during the year-long lock-out at the *Times*. It first appeared as an insert in the *New York Review of Books*, but in 1980 became a fully independent literary paper, published twice a month ever since. It aims to carry on the tradition of the English essay, giving contributors the space and freedom to develop their ideas. Its contributors include Frank Kermode, John Bayley, Alan Bennett, Marina Warner, Jenny Diski, Christopher Hitchens, Adam Phillips, Hilary Mantel, Stephen Sedley, Edward Said, Jonathan Coe and Tom Paulin. Its web site includes extracts from the current edition, as well as a searchable archive.

Magazine & Bookseller
http://www.napco.com/mb/mb1.html
Magazine & Bookseller is a guide to North American magazines and paperbacks, a comprehensive resource that lists virtually every magazine and book title currently available for sale on the continent. Each issue lists thousands of titles, accompanied with up-to date information such as price, frequency, publication dates, author, and ISBN number, as well as company names, phone numbers, and key contacts.

Media UK Internet Directory
http://www.mediauk.com/directory/
This site offers a substantial guide to the UK's radio, television, magazines and newspapers. Its searchable newspaper directory includes 247 newspapers - all national and online local papers, news services and resources. Its searchable magazine directory enables you to find listings of over 250 online consumer magazines. You can be notified by email of new additions. The site also includes a live jobs database, with over 14,000 vacancies listed.

Publishers Weekly (USA)
http://www.publishersweekly.com/
With its substantial offering of news, features, reviews and industry resources, *Publishers Weekly* is the number one American print and online magazine for the bookselling and publishing industries. You can check out the latest, exclusive information on book, movie, TV and other licensing deals in *PW Rights Alert*, a new email newsletter. Other features include classified advertising, bestseller ratings, forecasts, author news, and international publishing updates.

Publishing News
http://www.publishingnews.co.uk
Each week, *Publishing News* online brings all the hot news of the UK book trade direct to your screen: the major news stories, the gossip, the bestsellers and previews of new books. You can also register to receive news summaries by email. The site also includes a useful and fairly comprehensive set of hyperlinks to the web pages of UK publishers, booksellers and trade contacts of various kinds.

Fig. 21. The web site of *Publishing News* online, a lively competitor to *The Bookseller.* It includes hundreds of useful UK book trade links.

Pure Fiction
http://www.purefiction.co.uk
This is a web site intended for anyone who loves to read - or aspires to write - bestselling fiction. It contains book reviews and previews, a wealth of writing advice, an online bookshop, and a writers' showcase. Other features include links to about 100 sites devoted to published writers, a large list of links for anyone writing a novel, and the home pages of Pure Fiction visitors past and present. The site also runs its own writers' newsgroup, 'alt.books.purefiction'.

Richmond Review
http://www.richmondreview.co.uk
The *Richmond Review* was established in October 1995 as the UK's first literary magazine to be published exclusively on the world wide web. Updated at least monthly, it has a team of around 25 regular contributors and editors, many of whom work in London book publishing. Reviewers are not allowed to review books published by the companies they work for.

Scottish Book Collector
http://www.scotbooksmag.demon.co.uk
This web site is the baby of the *Scottish Book Collector* magazine, a quarterly periodical that specialises in in-depth features about collectable, old and rare books alongside profiles of contemporary Scottish writers and publishers – usually with a collector's spin. It is a gateway to everything you might want to know about the world of books in Scotland. It links you to secondhand booksellers, publishers, authors, bookshops and arts organisations, as well as providing up-to-the-minute listings and news.

Spike
http://www.hedweb.com/spike/
First arriving online in June 1996, *Spike* offers updates on a frequent but irregular basis of publishing interviews, features, reviews and new writing, both by established and unpublished authors. *Spike* is based in the UK and edited by Chris Mitchell, 'under whose benevolent dictatorship the magazine has existed since its inception in a squalid Brighton back street over three years ago.' *Spike* invites outlines for suggested book reviews of not more than 700 words and interviews and features no longer than 2,000 words.

Times Literary Supplement
http://www.the-tls.co.uk
Each week the *TLS* offers weekly authoritative reviews of fiction, poetry, history, politics, philosophy, the arts and just about every other subject under the sun. Each year the print version reviews some 2,500 books, plays, films and exhibitions. The web site offers subscribers a free back issues search facility giving instant access to all back issues from October 1994 onwards. Each issue is added to the archives but not until six months after publication.

Literature online

Books On-line
http://www.cs.cmu.edu/books.html
Books On-line indexes more than English-language 2,500 works which are available electronically. In addition, this main page lists of the most big repositories of online texts, both in English and in other languages.

British Literature
http://www.britishliterature.com
This is a popular online literary magazine with a large number of general interest items, covering both the UK and commonwealth countries. Contributions are invited.

Complete Works of William Shakespeare
http://the-tech.mit.edu/Shakespeare/works.html
This site makes available the text of all Shakespeare's plays and poems. It offers a discussion area, a list of Shakespearean resources on the net, a glossary, chronological and alphabetical listings of the plays, and Bartlett's familiar quotations from Shakespeare. There are also links to other Shakespeare resources on the internet.

Cyber Classics
http://www.cyberclassics.com
This site offers reprints of classic literature in print and electronic formats. More than 200 titles are available.

Drew's Scripts-o-Rama
http://www.script-o-rama.com
Drew's describes itself as 'the most comprehensive index of movie and television scripts available on the internet'. You will find links to TV and film scripts which can be downloaded from the net. Some of these are simply transcripts of films and TV programmes, but others are the actual scripts used, including shooting scripts and early drafts.

Fictionsearch
http://www.fictionsearch.com
Fictionsearch is a community search engine specialising in the art of literature. You can use the search field or choose to browse through one of the directories covering authors, resources and genres. The resources section offers links to such topics as courses, self-publishing, reviews, publishing law, literary agents, chat lines, college texts, web rings and more. The site is maintained by the Caelin Day Group in Australia.

A B C D E F G H

Browse by Dewey

000 General
100 Philosop
200 Religion
300 Social S
400 Languag
500 Natural
600 Technolo
700 The Arts
800 Literatur
900 Geograp

Internet Classics Archive
http://webatomics.com/Classics/index.html
This is a searchable archive of around 375 classical Greek and Roman texts in English translation.

The Internet Public Library
http://www.ipl.org/reading/books/
The public online texts collection at the reading room of the Internet Public Library contains over 3,700 titles that can be browsed by author, by title, or by Dewey subject classification as well as by keyword.

Online Books Page
http://www.cs.cmu.edu/books.html
Begun in 1993, this is a valuable free directory of books that can be

freely read on the internet. It includes an index of more than 10,000 online books, pointers to significant directories, archives of online texts, special exhibits and similar resources. The page is now hosted by the University of Pennsylvania Library.

Online Book Store
http://www.obs-us.com/
OBS is a publisher of full-text, distributive online books. Its subject areas include business titles, computers, e-commerce, cookery books, travel and fiction.

Project Gutenberg
http://www.promo.net/pg/
Project Gutenberg aims to make information, books and other materials freely available to the general public in forms that the vast majority of the computers, programs and people can easily read, use, quote, and search. This well-established site includes the text of hundreds of books now in the public domain, which you can read online or download for later study and analysis. There are three main areas of the Project Gutenberg Library. These include light literature containing such titles as *Alice in Wonderland, Through the Looking-Glass, Peter Pan* and *Aesop's Fables*; 'heavy literature' such as the Bible or other religious documents, Shakespeare, *Moby Dick*, and Milton's *Paradise Lost*; and reference works such as *Roget's Thesaurus*, almanacs, and assorted encyclopedias and dictionaries. Highly recommended.

Fig. 22. Project Gutenberg was one of the first internet ventures to offer online texts, and has now established itself as a leader in this field. You can search for online texts by browsing through its A to Z index of authors.

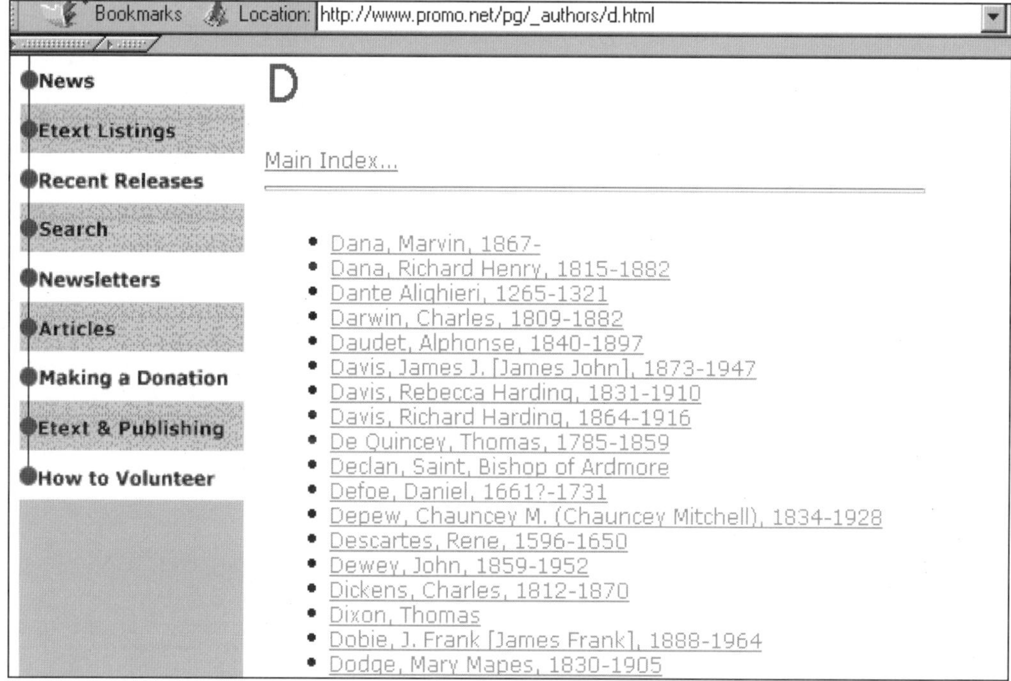

Project Bartleby
http://www.columbia.edu/acis/bartleby
Developed at Columbia University, the main focus of Project Bartleby is poetry. The collection includes electronic copies of the work of many major English poets.

The University of Virginia Electronic Text Center
http://etext.lib.virginia.edu
This organisation offers an ongoing and exhaustive programme of digitalisation of public-domain electronic texts. Many of these are available for viewing by visitors, though some are restricted to students, faculty, and staff at the university. If you're looking to see if you can pull down an electronic version of a public-domain text, this is a good starting point.

Children's books

Children's Literature Ring
http://www.geocities.com/Athens/3777/ring.html
The Children's Literature Ring is a ring of sites devoted to books for young people.

Enid Blyton
http://www.blyton.com/
This is the online shop window of The Enid Blyton Company, which owns the rights to the work of the famous children's writer.

The Federation of Children's Book Groups
http://www.fcbg.mcmail.com/index.htm
The Federation is a national, voluntary organisation concerned with children and their books. It aims to promote enjoyment and interest in children's books and reading, and to encourage the availability of a range of literature for all ages, from pre-school to teenage. The Federation liaises with schools, playgroups, publishers, libraries and other official bodies. It provides a meeting point for parents, professionals and everyone who shares its aims.

The Harry Potter Fan Site
http://www.angelfire.com/wi/harrypotter/mainharry.html
This site is dedicated to the outstandingly popular Harry Potter series. It includes photos, articles, and lots of other Potter-related information.

The Roald Dahl Club
http://www.roalddahlclub.com
Lots of online fun and games for Willie Wonka and Farmer Bean enthusiasts.

Yahooligans
http://www.yahooligans.com/
One of the best online entertainment areas for children, run by Yahoo! and guaranteed safe for surfing.

Crime thrillers and mysteries

Agatha Christie
http://www.stmarymead.com/
This useful resource is organised by author and by detective (Hercule Poirot and Miss Jane Marple), and includes book titles and publication dates. The site includes numerous links and a bulletin board.

Bibliomysteries
http://www.bibliomysteries.com/
The site features mysteries with settings, plots or main characters related to the world of books, archives, and libraries.

Crime Fiction Database
http://www.crimefiction.com
This is a fairly substantial and well-organised UK database of crime fiction which you can explore by name of author and by name of detective.

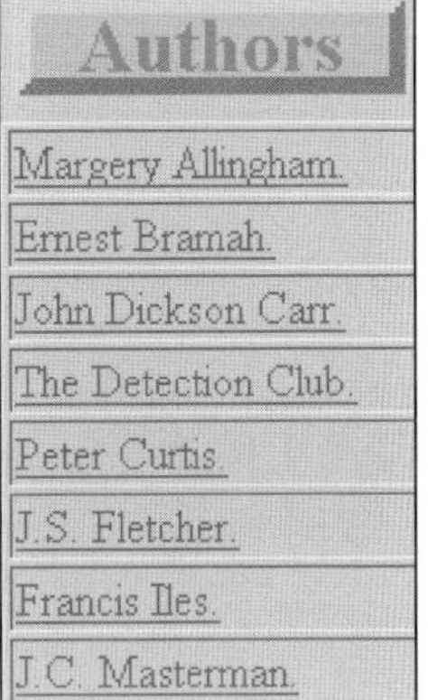

Stop! You're Killing Me!
http://www.stopyourekillingme.com/
Stop! features the work of hundreds of authors with complete chronological lists of their books in this sub-genre.

Drama

Dramatic Literature: The Bookshelf
http://www.geocities.com/Athens/Forum/7186/drama.html
Contains reviews and recommendations of plays and playwrights.

Harold Pinter Society
http://www.odc.edu/academic/pinter/

Playwrights on the Web
http://www.stageplays.com/writers.htm
Playwrights on the Web is an international database of playwrights and their web sites, offering directors, producers and publishers a unique way to discover new plays and fresh talent. If the play you want is already in print, visit The Internet Theatre Bookshop and access virtually every play currently published in the English language. If it's out-of-print, you can try searching the Rare Plays catalogue.

Shakespeare Birthplace Trust
http://www.shakespeare.org.uk
This is the official Shakespeare site. Includes information on the historic houses, educational courses, and library, museum and archive collections.

Erotica

Erotica Readers Association
http://www.erotica-readers.com/
Full of book reviews, links, and stories.

Horror

DemonMinds Universe of Horror
http://www.demonminds.com/horror.html
The site showcases examples of new horror writing, art, and poetry.

Stephen King
http://stephen-king.net/
A web site dedicated to the life and work of the American horror writer. Everything you want to know about *The Dark Tower* and more.

HorrorNet
http://www.horrornet.com/
This is a resource for horror, suspense and dark fantasy fiction, including indexes of magazines, publishers, bookstores, reviews, author email addresses and author sites.

News:alt.fan.authors.stephen-king
A newsgroup for fans of Stephen King. There are hundreds of such author-related newsgroups. Use your newsreader (e.g. Outlook, or Netscape Messenger) to search for the ones you want.

Skin and Bones
http://www.skinandbones.net/
The site aptly describes itself as a literary showcase of the grotesque, the gothic and the erotic.

Literary fiction

Jane Austen
http://www.austen.com/
The site offers information about the author, and a collection of fan fiction inspired by her works. There are also links to many sites with information on Jane Austen, her life, and to Jane Austen societies around the world.

Iain Banks
http://www.phlebas.com/
The name of the web page is Culture Shock, and it provides resources and a study in depth of the life and work of this Scottish fiction and science fiction writer.

The Brontë Sisters
http://www2.sbbs.se/hp/cfalk/bronte1e.htm
The site contains a large number of links to Charlotte, Emily and Anne Brontë web sites around the world wide web.

A.S. Byatt
http://www.asbyatt.com/
The site includes a book list, essays by the author, and other information.

Lewis Carroll
http://www.lewiscarroll.org/carroll.html
This is an excellent comprehensive resource for the life and writings of Charles Dodgson, author of *Alice in Wonderland, Alice Through the Looking-Glass, The Jabberwocky* and other memorable works. The site incorporates a large number of international links.

Charles Dickens
http://www.geocities.com/Athens/Styx/8490/
'The Dickens, you say!' is the title of this web page which includes a mass of information and illustrations about the great man, plus links to other Dickens and Victorian England web sites.

Ian Fleming
http://www.mcs.net/-klast/www/fleming.html
Old Etonian writer Ian Fleming (1909-1964) created the unforgettable character of British secret agent 007James Bond, who first appeared in the 1952 novel *Casino Royale.*

Graham Greene
http://members.tripod.com/-greeneland/
Entitled 'Greeneland – the World of Graham Greene', the site features a biography, bibliography, photographs, and a bulletin board for discussion of the author whose works included *Brighton Rock, The Power & the Glory, The Comedians*, and *Our Man in Havana*.

Frederick Forsyth
http://www.whirlnet.demon.co.uk/forsyth/
This is an unofficial page that includes news, bibliography and other

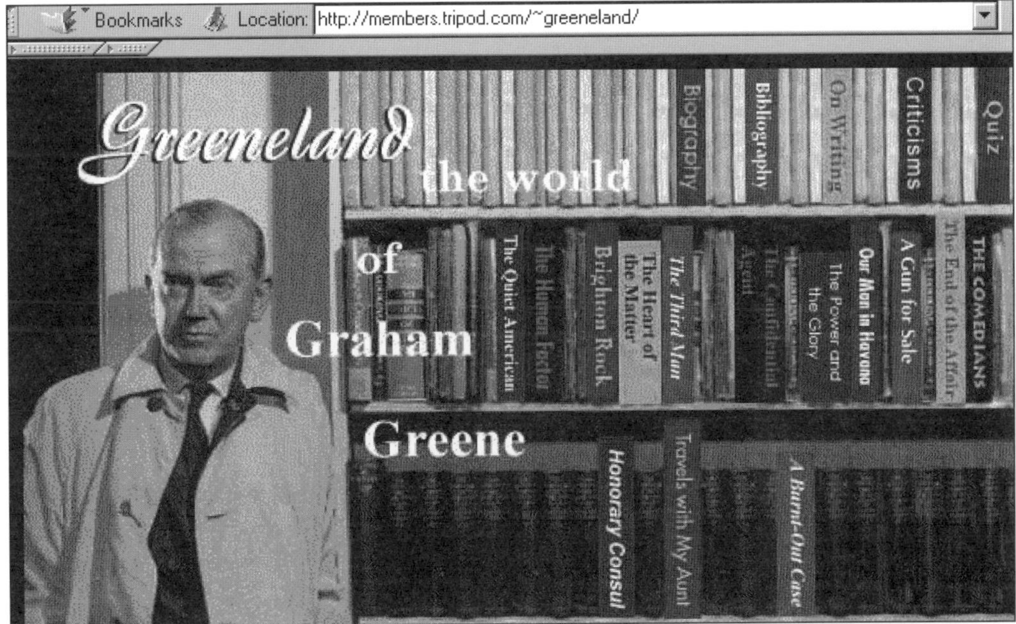

Fig. 23. A Graham Greene web site. There is a growing number of sites like this, created by fans or collectors to celebrate the life and works of their favourite authors.

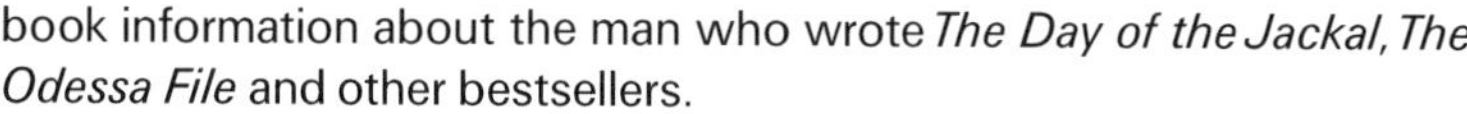
book information about the man who wrote *The Day of the Jackal*, *The Odessa File* and other bestsellers.

Edward Lear
http://www2.pair.com/mgraz/Lear/index.html
This is a good place to explore the poems and art, early nonsense comic strips, bibliographies of books by and about Lear and Nonsense literature in general.

Iris Murdoch
http://www.mcs.net/-jorn/html/jorn/iris.html
This useful web page includes a timeline of the Oxford author's life and summaries of her works, such as *Flight from the Enchanter, A Severed Head, The Bell, The Nice and the Good, The Black Prince,* and *The Sea The Sea.*

George Orwell
http://www.k-1.com/Orwell/
Here you will find a short biography and essays, plus summaries and synopses of his books, such as *The Road to Wigan Pier, Down and Out in Paris and London, Nineteen Eighty Four* and *Animal Farm.* George Orwell was the pen name of Eric Blair.

Evelyn Waugh
http://e2.empirenet.com/-jahvah/waugh/
This site is dedicated primarily to Waugh as writer, and provides a basic introduction to his life and times, and to promote knowledge about and enjoyment of Waugh and his work (*Decline and Fall, Vile Bodies, A Handful of Dust, Brideshead Revisited* etc.). There is a chronology, a mailing list service, summaries of his works, and numerous links to sites of related interest.

Virginia Woolf Web
http://orlando.jp.org/
This is a project of the Virginia Woolf Society of Great Britain.

Romance

Barbara Cartland
http://www.sound.net/-tomasonr/cartland.htm
You can find a large number of links here to the life and works of the undisputed queen of popular British romantic writing.

New Writers' Scheme
Join Now
What's New
Author Links
Aims
Beginnings

Romantic Novelists Association
http://freespace.virgin.net/marina.oliver/rna.htm
The RNA aims to promote the various types of romantic and historical fiction, to encourage good writing in all its many varieties, to learn more about the craft, and help readers enjoy it. This is its official home page, where you can find out about activities, events, awards, conferences, its new writers scheme, officers, memberships and more.

Science fiction and fantasy

About.com's Fantasy and Science Fiction Books
http://fantasy.about.com/
This is a substantial online guide to various science fiction and fantasy resources.

Douglas Adams
http://www.douglasadams.com
This the official web site of the author of *The Hitchhiker's Guide to the Galaxy,* which combines information, links and other resources with a discussion forum

Terry Pratchett's Discworld
http://www.geocities.com/Area51/1777/
This is the place to look up Discworld information, pictures and links. The site is maintained by theTerry Pratchett Fan Club.

SFF-NET
http://www.sff.net/sff/index.htp
The web site of the Science Fiction & Fantasy Network.

J. R. R. Tolkien
http://www.tolkien-archives.com
These 'Tolkien Archives' are packed with information on the author, *The Lord of the Rings,* his writings, and related phenomena.

▶ *Search engines* – Don't forget to use your favourite search engine to extend your search.

Fig. 24. TheTerry Pratchett Discworld web site, created by fans for use by fans.

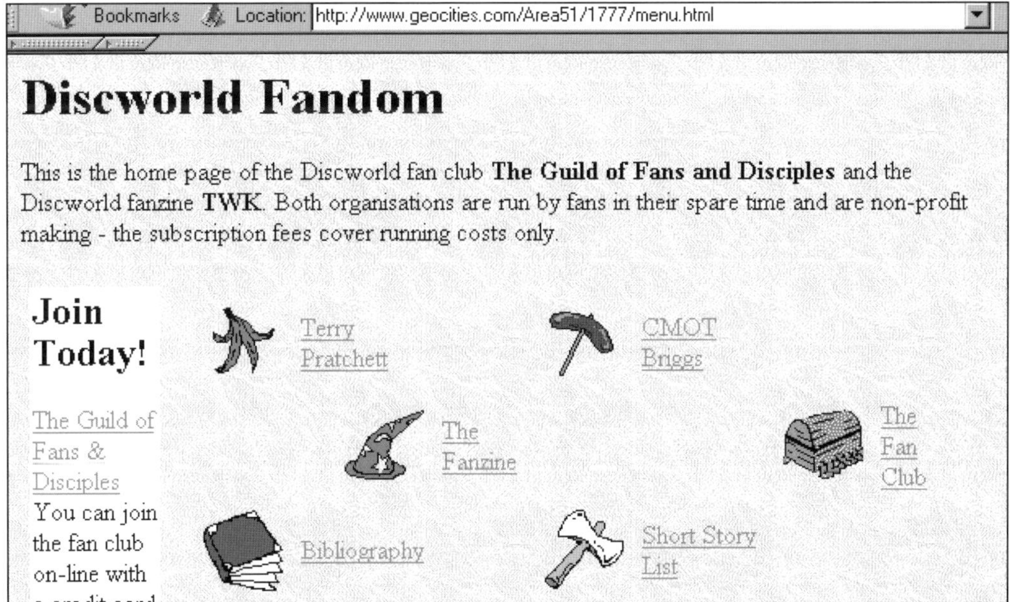

4 Writers and writing

In this chapter we will explore:

- *writers' associations*
- *writers' periodicals*
- *literary agents*
- *publishing your work online*
- *copyright*
- *miscellaneous services*
- *newsgroups for writers*

Writers' associations

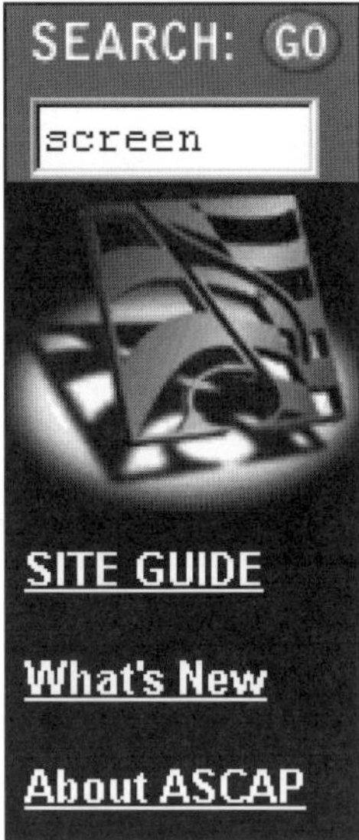

American Society of Composers, Authors & Publishers
http://ascap.com/ascap.html
ASCAP is a membership association of over 80,000 composers, songwriters, lyricists and music publishers. Its function is to protect the rights of its members by licensing and paying royalties for the public performances of their copyrighted works.

Australian Book WebRing
http://www.bookshop.com.au/webring/
This web ring consists of Australian sites whose content is primarily concerned with books, whether as authors, book lovers, booksellers or publishers. It includes a comprehensive listing of Australian booksellers and publishers online, with pointers to much Australian book-trade information.

Australian Society of Authors
http://www.asauthors.org/
ASA promotes and protects the professional interests of Australian literary creators. It represents members in negotiations and disputes, and provides advice on industry standards and practices. The site includes practical guidance on getting published and getting paid.

Authors Guild
http://www.authorsguild.org/
From 1919, the New York-based Guild has lobbied for free speech, copyrights and other issues of concern to authors. Its web site includes contract advice, guidance on electronic rights and other legal information, an index to its *Bulletin,* and a 'publishers' row' containing book trade news.

Authors' Licensing & Collecting Society
http://www.alcs.co.uk
The ALCS exists to help UK writers reap the full rewards of their work. It

administers a special scheme for collecting revenues from photocopying, electronic rights and recording, which it then distributes according to certain rules. You can explore the work of the Society and discover how to register your own work with them.

Canadian Authors Association
http://www.CanAuthors.org/national.html
Founded in Montreal in 1921, the CAA has had some 25,000 members over the years. You can follow the links at the top and bottom of each page to explore the scope and history of the Association and its impact on Canadian writing. There is an extensive collection of links to other internet writing resources. The site includes a public message area that enables you to ask questions directly in a public forum where a wider audience may be able to help you.

Canadian Science Writers' Association
http://www.interlog.com/-cswa/index.html
The CSWA web site provides information about the association, its constitution and mandate, its members, membership categories, news and coming events, articles from a quarterly newsletter, *Science Link*, and links to other science-related sites.

Chartered Institute of Journalists
http://www.users.dircon.co.uk/-cioj/
The Institute is the world's oldest organisation for journalists. Its site gives details of membership, some historical background, a section on ethics and some links to similar organisations around the world.

HTML Writers Guild
http://www.hwg.org/
This is a group of html/web writers and creators committed to excellence in html design, a master-apprentice approach to learning html, and to promoting its members in the jobs market.

The Inner Circle Writers Club
http://www.geocities.com/circlefaq.htm
The Inner Circle is a free club for fiction writers from around the world, with around 1,500 members. To join, you must complete a questionnaire, details of which are posted on the membership profile pages. This resource can help you track down find writers with particular interests and backgrounds. You can then contact them to ask if they will appraise your work (and they may do the same).

Institute of Scientific and Technical Communicators
http://www.istc.org.uk
ISTC is the largest UK body representing professional communicators and has been established for more than 50 years. It aims to set and improve standards for communication of the scientific and technical information that support products, services or business. The site includes details of courses, conferences, publications and local groups.

International Women's Writing Guild
http://www.iwwg.com/
Founded in 1976, the IWWG is a network for the personal and professional empowerment of women through writing. Its web pages give details of its aims, membership, member profiles, conference tapes, letters and links to other sites. Membership costs $35 inside the USA and $45 outside.

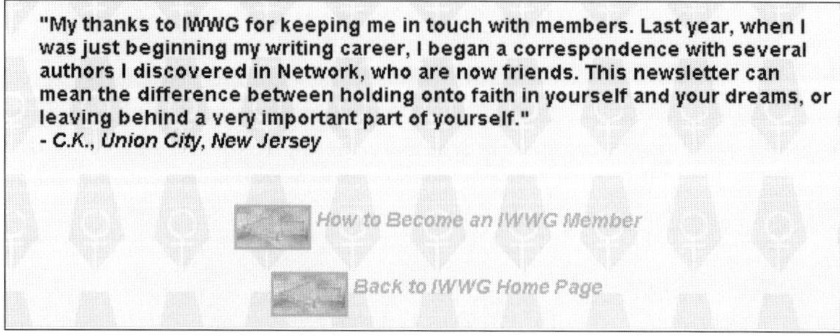

Journalism Education Association
http://www.jea.org
The JEA is made up of journalists, teachers and other media professionals. It aims to 'make a permanent contribution to the dignity of the journalistic profession'. The web site contains various learning resources and a catalogue of publications for sale. Details of forthcoming conferences and other events are also shown.

National Association of Writers in Education
http://www.nawe.co.uk
Formed in 1987, NAWE aims to promote and support the development of creative writing of all genres in all educational settings. Its Directory of Writers is a detailed and fully searchable database of writers who work in schools, colleges and the community. It is funded by six of the Regional Arts Boards of England. The database, featuring over 1,100 writers, is updated each week. There is a wealth of supporting information.

National Union of Journalists
http://www.gn.apc.org/media/nuj.html
The NUJ is the world's biggest union of journalists, with some 25,000 members in England, Wales, Scotland, and Ireland. The site contains useful information on digital technology, copyright, moral rights, contracts and how to negotiate them. You will also find resources covering journalistic training and qualifications, and an online newsletter called *Freelance*.

Poetry Book Society
http://www.poetrybooks.co.uk/
T S Eliot founded the Poetry Book Society in 1953 in order to promote a love and understanding of contemporary poetry. The PBS is a membership organisation which exists to keep people all over the world up to date with the best new English language poetry being published in the UK and Ireland today. It is also a specialist book club and a non-profit

registered charity funded by the Arts Council of England. The site is itself a very useful resource.

Poetry Society
http://www.poetrysoc.com
The Poetry Society provides advice and information for poets, as well as publishing the *Poetry Review.* There are links to membership, *Poetry Review*, poetry places, competition, National Poetry Day, links, education, poetry workshop, poetry café, poetry news, interview archives, and email. The Society is supported by the Arts Council, the National Lottery and BT.

Fig. 25. The Poetry Society web site includes information about National Poetry Day, competitions, education and membership.

Quill Society
http://www.quill.net/
The Quill Society is a 'communication centre for adept writers wishing to refine their writing skills, and novice writers to step into the realm of their imagination.' The site contains an online library, resources, activities, membership details, and community area. The Society is administered from Brookline, Massachusetts.

Science Fiction & Fantasy Writers of America
http://www.sfwa.org/
These web pages contain quite detailed information and advice about the practical aspects of being a writer, as well as news and information about this ever popular genre. The Society was founded in 1965.

Scottish Writers on the Internet
http://www.users.globalnet.co.uk/-crumey/scot.html
This resource is maintained by edited by novelist and critic Andrew

Crumey. It contains an author index from Robert Burns and Iain Banks to Sir Walter Scott and W. S. Graham, a history of Scottish literature and artistic movements, Scottish history, frequently asked questions, contacting an author, tracing ancestry, and pricing old books. There are useful resources including handy links and an extensive bibliography for the serious student, plus book reviews, and a quick guide to the 'classics'.

Society of Authors
http://www.writers.org.uk/society/
Founded in 1884, the Society of Authors is the UK's leading association for writers of fiction and non-fiction. Its 6,500 members also include artists, illustrators, playwrights, and scriptwriters (for both radio and television). These pages give details of the Society, as well as many topics related to writing, publishing, copyright, electronic rights, and multimedia. There is a book list dealing with various aspects of the art of writing, and hyperlinks to useful reference material and sources of information.

Society of Indexers
http://www.socind.demon.co.uk
The Sheffield-based Society exists to promote indexing, the quality of indexes and the profession of indexing. The site includes details of services for publishers and authors, and services for indexers. You can find out which indexers are available online. The Society also runs an email discussion list called Sideline.

Society for Technical Communication
http://www.stc-va.org
The STC is meant for technical writers, editors, designers and illustrators all those whose work involves communicating technical information to those who need to apply it. The site contains details of publications, competitions, and employment opportunities.

Society of Professional Journalists
http://spj.org/spjhome.htm
This American site offers links to all kinds of resources for journalists, plus extracts from *Quill*, its monthly magazine.

Writers Guild of America
http://www.wga.org/
The Writers Guild is an established labour union that represents over 8,000 professional writers for the movies, television programs and interactive games.

Writers' Guild of Great Britain
http://www.writers.org.uk/guild/
The Writers' Guild of Great Britain was established in 1958 with the aim of representing the interests of writers of all media. Its books section campaigned for the creation of the public lending right (PLR) and also helped establish the first minimum terms agreements (MTAs) for book writers, for example with BBC Publications, Bloomsbury, André

Fig. 26. The web site of the Writers Guild of America. It contains masses of practical help on the craft and business of fiction and nonfiction writing.

Deutsch, Faber & Faber, HarperCollins, Hodder Headline, Penguin, and Transworld. It web site offers detailed accounts of its activities, supported with a range of links.

Writers Net
http://www.writers.net/
Writers Net is a privately developed US-based initiative intended to foster relationships between writers, publishers, editors, and literary agents. It currently offers two sections: *the Internet Directory of Published Writers*, and the *Internet Directory of Literary Agents*. The former is a searchable directory of hundreds of published writers on the Net arranged by categories such as biography, feminism and popular science. Each entry contains a listing of published works, biographical statement, and contact information. The *Internet Directory of Literary Agents* is a searchable directory of literary agents on the Net. Each entry contains areas of specialisation, a description of the agency, and contact information. Both writers and agents can add/edit their entries online. Also, an *Internet Database of Writing Assignments* is promised soon.

Writers' periodicals

Ept Magazine
http://www.inept.com
Ept describes itself as 'a gormful publication for the immaculate readership. We present the best and shiniest cut-throat modern thinking on aspects of culture, lifestyle, sport and travel.' Ept is based in Dublin, Ireland. 'If you have an idea for an article and are not sure whether or not it fits our brief, email us with a brisk synopsis and we can advise you.'

Inklings Web Page
http://www.inkspot.com/inklings
Inklings is a free email newsletter for writers, published by Inkspot, a popular online resource for writers.

Fig. 27. Inkspot is a popular internet resource for writers. The web site now runs to more than 2,000 pages of information, and includes news, archives, features, and free membership.

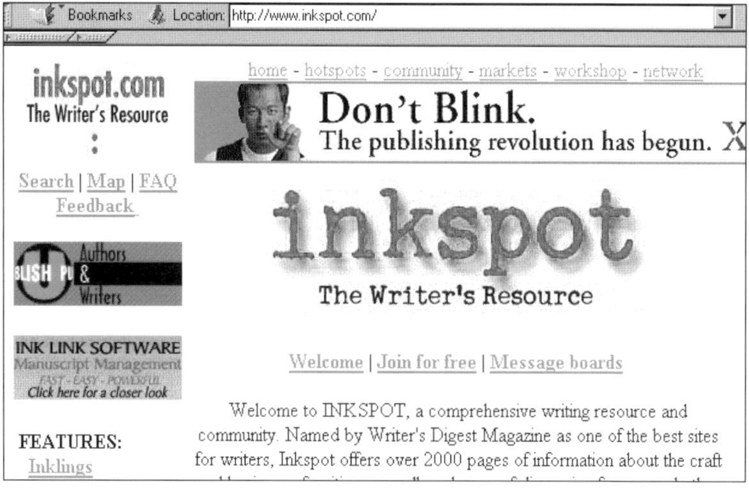

Internet Free Press
http://www.free-press.com/
Sponsored by MCB University Press, the Internet Free Press describes itself as 'the complete solution for academic publishing online.' It offers to serve as your meeting place, your library, your place of publication, your guide through the intricacies of publishing for profit or not-for-profit, your technical helper, and your market place for exchange and trade. Members wishing to publish a journal on Internet Free-Press start by completing an online new journal proposal form.

Fig. 28. The Internet Free Press offers a useful facility for academic journal publishing online.

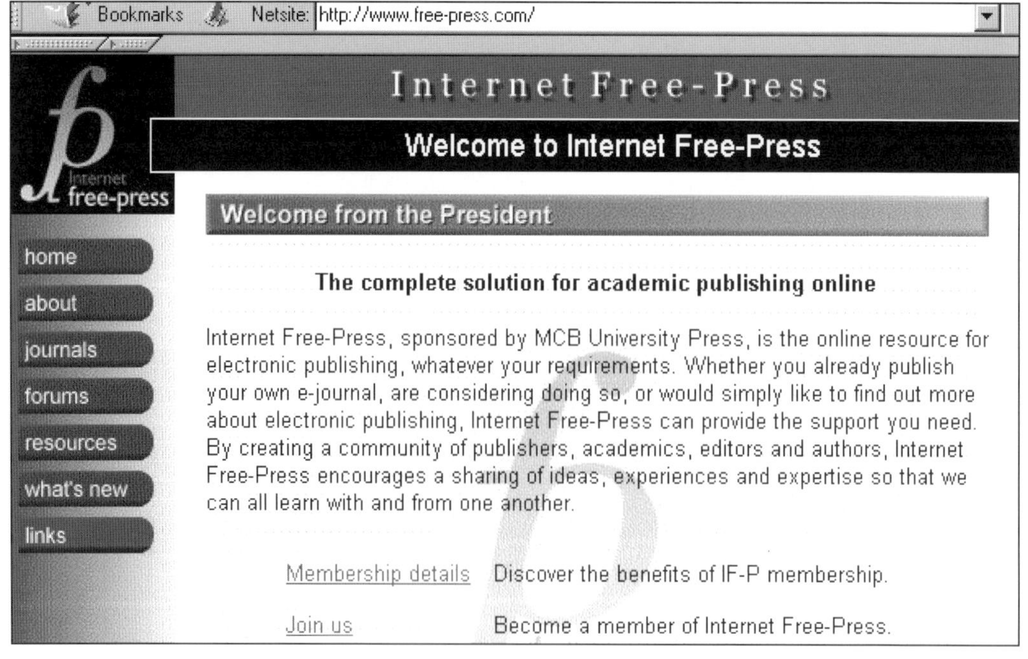

Literary Review
http://www.litreview.com/
The content of the site is limited, but there are a few sample articles and poetry, and subscription information.

North Words Magazine
http://www.highlanderweb.co.uk/nortword.htm
North Words feature poetry, short stories, guest writers and more from the Highlands of Scotland. Although produced in the Scottish Highlands, Northwords has also featured the work of writers from Ireland, Wales, Norway, Finland, the USA, Poland and Japan.

Novel Advice Newsletter
http://www.noveladvice.com
'A cyber-journal for writers devoted totally to the craft of writing', this regular newsletter focuses on fiction-writing, but actually covers more than fiction alone. You can explore courses, resources, audio tapes, chat room, bookstore, a message board and more. There is a useful archive of previous issues.

Writers' Digest
http://www.writersdigest.com/index.htm
'Your online guide to getting published.' Its index of writer's guidelines lets you browse more than 1,100 guidelines, prepared by book and magazine editors themselves. Turn to Writer's Market for a complete rundown of a market's needs, then search for more of the editor's viewpoint. Writer's Market presents more than 4,200 markets for your work, and every month Writer's Digest magazine reports on dozens of markets for writers. There are also links to 100 of the best web sites for writers.

Fig. 29. Writers Digest is another top web site for writers, containing a variety of useful market information.

AUTHORLINK NEWS
Successes, Statistics
What People Say
Authorlink Awards
About Authorlink

EDITOR/AGENT RESOURCES
Manuscripts and screenplays for sale
Author Showcase
Emerging Writers
Author Index
Film/TV Scripts
Who's Hot
Add Agency Listing
Add A Publisher

Publishing your work online

Authorlink
http://www.authorlink.com
Authorlink is a highly professional American site claiming more than 125,000 readers a year. It is packed with news of the US publishing industry, and includes plenty of market information. You can also submit your unpublished book or manuscript for possible showcasing on the site.

Hafod Publishing
http://www.hafod.demon.co.uk
The Welsh home-run business of Hafod Publishing invites the submission of unpublished novels which they can market on their web site.

Online Originals
http://www.onlineoriginals.com
Online Originals offers an electronic publishing service. It distributes book-length works in digital form, with email orders and delivery. It pays authors royalties of 50%. The company publishes both non-fiction and fiction. Readers can view extracts of each work online and pay a fee if the want to obtain receive the complete publication.

The Poetry Exchange
http://www.w3px.com
Based in Hertfordshire, UK, the Poetry Exchange enables poets to publish their poems free of charge.

Copyright

The Berne Convention
http://www.law.cornell.edu/treaties/berne/overview.html
The site contains the 1971 Paris Text of the Berne Convention for the Protection of Literary and Artistic Works.

Canadian Copyright Licensing Agency (CanCopy)
http://www.cancopy.com/
A reproduction rights organisation, CanCopy provides legal access to copyright-protected works for millions of Canadian copyright users. It also provides administrative services for Canadian copyright owners. In fact, more than 3,500 Canadian creators (writers, editors, artists) and publishers are members, and some 30 member organisations (Canadian creator and publisher associations) support its work. Copyright users from more than 800 organisations depend on their CanCopy licence as a means of legal access to copyright-protected works. The agency not only represents domestic works, but also published works by foreign creators and publishers through bilateral agreements with sister organisations in other countries.

Copyright Agency Limited (Australia)
http://www.copyright.com.au/
CAL provides efficient copyright management for authors and publish-

ers, by collecting and distributing licensing fees charged for copying published works. The site includes information on news & publications, CAL and copyright, licensing options, membership and payment. There is a directory of members and links to related organisations and web sites.

Copyright and Fair Use
http://fairuse.stanford.edu/
This Stanford University Libraries site contains a general description of the applicability of US copyright law and the so-called 'fair use' exemptions to its general prohibition on copying. It also describes 'safe harbor' guidelines applicable to classroom copying

Copyright Basics
http://palimpsest.stanford.edu/bytopic/intprop/circ1.html
This Circular from the US Copyright Office contains an excellent and authoritative summary of American copyright its legal nature, extent, duration, applications and exemptions in a variety of media.

Copyright Clearance Center (USA)
http://www.copyright.com/
Formed in 1978, the CCC is the largest licenser of photocopy reproduction rights in the world. It provides licensing systems for the reproduction and distribution of copyrighted materials in print and electronic formats throughout the USA and worldwide. It currently manages rights relating to over 1.75 million works and represents more than 9,600 publishers and hundreds of thousands of authors and other creators, directly or through their representatives. CCC-licensed customers in the US number over 9,000 corporations and subsidiaries plus thousands of government agencies, law firms, document suppliers, libraries, academic institutions, copy shops and bookstores.

Copyright Licensing Limited (New Zealand)
http://www.copyright.co.nz
The site includes a 'copyright hotline' you can call with your questions.

Copyright Licensing Agency Ltd (UK)
http://www.cla.co.uk/
Formed in 1982, the CLA is the UK's reproduction rights organisation and a member of IFRRO, the International Federation of Reproduction Rights Organisations. It looks after the interests of rights owners in copying from books, journals and periodicals. It encourages respect for copyright, licenses users for copying extracts from books, journals and periodicals, collects fees from licensed users for such copying, and pays authors and publishers (via ALCS and PLS) their shares of the copying fees collected. The CLA is a non-profit making company limited by guarantee and owned by its members, the Authors' Licensing and Collecting Society (ALCS) and the Publishers Licensing Society (PLS).

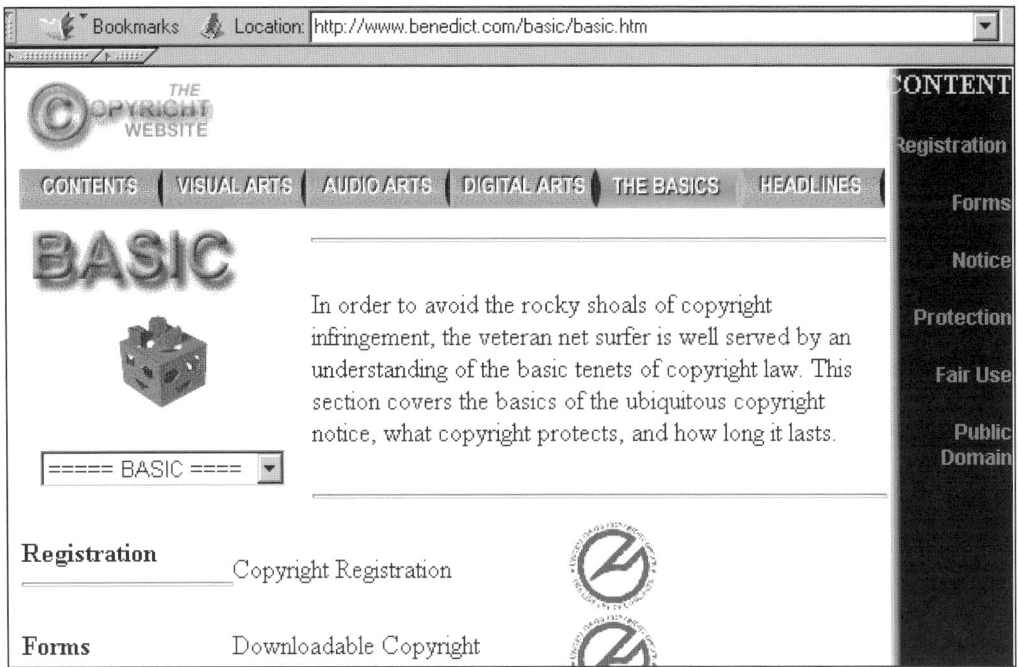

Fig. 30. The internet has created all sorts of new problems and questions about copyright. This Copyright Web Site aims to guide you through the maze.

Copyright Website
http://www.benedict.com
Launched in 1995, this enterprising site aims to provide 'real world, practical and relevant copyright information of interest to infonauts, netsurfers, webspinners, content providers, musicians, appropriationists, activists, infringers, outlaws, and law abiding citizens'. In particular, it seeks to encourage discourse and invite solutions to the myriad of copyright tangles that now permeate the web.

Creators' Copyright Coalition
http://www.gn.apc.org/media/cccindex.html
The CCC was formed in 1995 in response to the 'assault' by several UK publishers on freelancers' rights in their work. It recommends that all contracts for use of creators' work should always specify exactly what rights are being obtained, for what price and for what period. The web site includes a summary of the coalition's aims, updates on its campaigning, and links to related organisations.

International Federation of Reproduction Rights Organisations
http://www.ifrro.org/
IFRRO began in 1980 as a working group of the Copyright Committee of the International Publishers Association and the International Group of Scientific, Technical & Medical Publishers. Its site contains all kinds of useful and up-to-date information about existing copyright laws, conventions, and working papers.

Public Lending Right Office
http://www.earl.org.uk/partners/plr/index.html
Under the UK's PLR scheme, authors receive payments from govern-

ment funds for the free borrowing of their books from public libraries in the UK. To qualify for payment, authors must apply to register their books with the PLR Office. Payments are made annually on the basis of loans data collected from a sample of public libraries in the UK. The site explains how you can apply for PLR, how loans data is collected from libraries, how payment is calculated and distributed to registered authors and copyright owners, the most borrowed authors and books, and recent and forthcoming developments.

US Copyright Office
http://lcweb.loc.gov/copyright/
The Copyright Office provides expert assistance to Congress on intellectual property matters. It is also an office of record, a place where claims to copyright are registered and where documents relating to copyright may be recorded when the requirements of the copyright law are met. The site provides information about the provisions of the copyright law and the procedures for registration, and explains its operations and practices. The Office also administers various compulsory licensing provisions of the law, which include collecting royalties. The site gives details of publications, registrations, fees, the work of the Library of Congress, announcements and records, a historical overview, and contacts.

When Works Pass into the Public Domain
http://www.unc.edu/-unclng/public-d.htm
This US site contains a handy up-to-date chart summarising the legal position on copyright expiration.

World Intellectual Property Organisation
http://www.wipo.org/
WIPO is an intergovernmental organisation of the UN based in Geneva, Switzerland. It promotes the protection of intellectual property throughout the world, and administers multilateral treaties dealing with intellectual property. 'Intellectual property' comprises industrial property (inventions, trademarks, an industrial designs) and copyright (literary, musical, artistic, photographic and audiovisual works). Much of WIPO's work is devoted to assisting developing countries in this field. The site contains a catalogue of publications and documents, and you can explore such issues as internet domain names and ecommerce as well as the more traditional aspects of intellectual property.

Miscellaneous services

Authorlink
http://www.authorlink.com/
Authorlink is a US commercial resource designed to link authors, manuscripts, agents and publishers. The site contains previews of about 600 ready-to-publish evaluated manuscripts and screenplays seeking sales to editors, agents or producers. It claims 240,000 readers and two million page views per year.

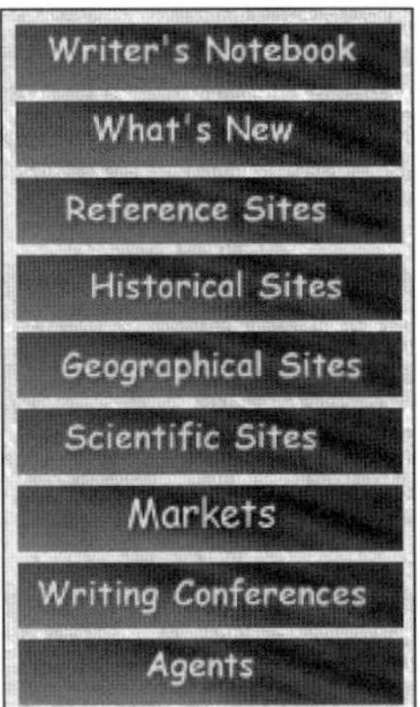

Thebookshelf.org
http://thebookshelf.org
This site is dedicated to increasing the accessibility of quality books, manuscripts and screenplays to the general public. It does not sell or publish books, and does not make any money on book sales. It takes submissions directly from the authors, and provides direct access back to the authors. On a cyclical basis, it features books on the opening page, under the title 'Off the Shelf'. It covers fiction, travel, humour, poetry, children's books, hobbies, non-fiction, screenplays and educational titles.

Children's Writing Resource Center
http://www.write4kids.com/
On this site you can access a free library of how-to information for both new and experienced children's writers, with articles, tips and more. You can use it to scour the internet for instant access to the world's research databases. There is also a message board dedicated to children's writing.

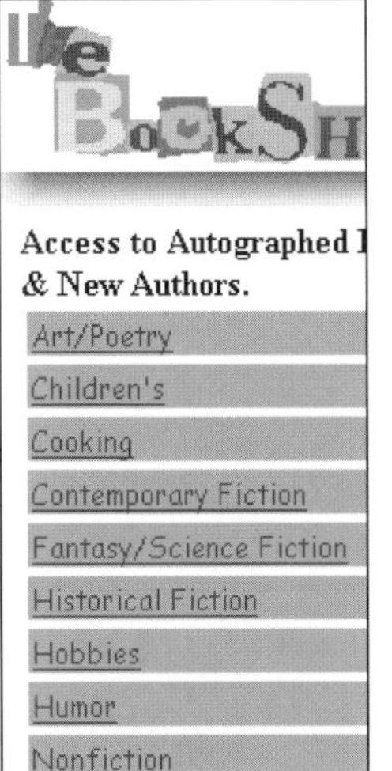

For Writers
http://www.forwriters.com
For Writers contains links to hundreds of authors' web sites, writers' groups, markets, awards and conferences. It also provides historical, geographical, scientific and reference sites for information.

Inkspot
http://www.inkspot.com
Inkspot is one of the leading sites on the internet for writers. It offers over 2,000 pages of information about the craft and business of writing, as well as dozens of discussion forums and other online networking opportunities. This popular site contains news and market information, interviews with published writers, articles about the writer's craft, writers' forums, classified advertisements, and lots more. It also publishes an email newsletter called Inklings and maintains an archive of back issues. Highly recommended.

International Writer
http://www.ndirect.co.uk/-int.writer
International Writer lists services available to writers, explain various aspects of how to write and get your work published and maintains a directory of writers' groups, including those who wish to twin with other groups. There are FAQs, and guides to markets and services for writers, and writers' circles.

WordUp
http://www.wordup.co.uk
WordUp is a new London-based online writers' resource. The site contains reviews, information about writing workshops, newsletters, events, prizes, women's writing and more. If you belong to a group or organisation for writers then you are invited to complete an online form and they will add it to their database. If you have your own writer's web site, or you are an author with a site, then you can send them your details.

Writers Write
http://writerswrite.com
The site is well-geared to the needs of authors seeking commercial outlets for their work in the United States. Its detailed annotated section on 'paying markets' is well worth a visit. There are also classified ads, online forums for writers, a jobs section, a writer's bookstore and many other useful features.

- The Write News™
- The Write Jobs™
- Author Interviews
- Author Directory
- Classified Ads
- Writer's Bookstore
- Oprah's Book Club
- The A-Lists
- Marketplace

Literary agents

Agent Research & Evaluation Inc
http://www.agentresearch.com/
The site aims to empower authors by providing them with extensive information about virtually every active literary and dramatic rights agent in the US, Canada and the UK. It will tell you which literary agents sell what to whom and for how much. The site includes an agents' database, online newsletters and other services for writers.

Association of Authors' Representatives
http://www.bookwire.com/AAR/
The AAR offers a canon of ethics, FAQs, a member list, and other information for writers seeking representation in the USA and wider afield.

Directory of Literary Agencies
http://www.writers.net/agents.html
Use the search or browse button to see the listing at WritersNet.

OzLit Literary Agents
http://home.vicnet.net.au/-ozlit/agents.html
The site offers a short agency list for writers seeking to sell their work in Australian markets.

Peters, Fraser & Dunlop
http://www.pfd.co.uk
Representing virtually every form of creative talent - authors, producers, directors, actors, composers, and technical skills in film, television and on stage – PFD can justly claim to be a market leader in Europe in its field.

Richard Curtis Associates
http://www.curtisagency.com/
New York-based Richard Curtis Associates represents over 100 top authors in every category of popular fiction and nonfiction. The web site includes detailed submission guidelines.

Samuel French
http://www.samuelfrench.com/
Samuel French Inc is an old-established firm of play publishers and author's representatives with offices in New York, Hollywood, Toronto, and London. The firm seeks out the world's best plays and makes them available to the widest range of producing groups. Sources of its plays

range from Broadway and the London West End to publication of unsolicited scripts submitted by unpublished authors.

Writing.org
http://www.writing.org/html/a.agents4.htm
This page includes some very useful contacts and tips for authors seeking professional representation.

Finding out more

- ▶ For a more detailed guide to resources for writers on the internet, see Nick Daws' excellent and detailed paperback reference guide, *The Internet for Writers*, published in the Internet Handbooks series, and recommended in *The Author* magazine.

5 Libraries

In this chapter we will explore:

- *library associations*
- *online libraries*
- *library services*

Library associations

American Association of School Librarians
http://www.ala.org/aasl/
AASL is interested in the general improvement and extension of library media services for children and young people. This substantial web site contains news and announcements, information about events and conferences, library advocacy and support, library education and employment, ALA interests and activities, ALA marketplace, membership information and services, ALA's library, ALA divisions, units, governance and more.

American Library Association
http://www.ala.org/
The ALA provides leadership for the development, promotion, and improvement of library and information services and the profession of librarianship in order to enhance learning and ensure access to informa-

Fig. 31. The American Association of School Librarians is a good example of a well-produced professional web site. There are hundreds of links to help you find what you want.

tion for all. This site offers a substantial resource for all information professionals, such as library news and announcements, events and conferences, library advocacy and support, library links, education, and employment.

Association of Research Libraries
http://arl.cni.org/
This is a North American organisation based in Washington.

Association of UK Media Librarians
http://www.aukml.org.uk
AUKML is an organisation for print media and broadcast librarians and information professionals. Formed in 1986, its members come from newspaper and magazine publishing, broadcasting organisations and academic institutions.

Australian Library and Information Association (ALIA)
http://www.alia.org.au/
This is the substantial web site of ALIA, the professional organisation for the Australian library and information services sector. It contains extensive resources on such issues as training, membership, government, appointments, publishing, management, copyright, privacy and censorship. Over 3,000 people are now subscribed to its online newsletter.

International Federation of Library Associations
http://www.ifla.org/
IFLANET is the online presence of this international umbrella organisation.

Internet Library Association
http://www-org.usm.edu/~ila/
The ILA is a free-membership, non-profit organisation for both librarians and non-librarians. It says: 'This organisation is designed to teach and inform people about the internet. It is truly an exciting time to be a librarian. The information age and technology revolution are just beginning, and we can be the leaders of this revolution.' The site reviews hot topics about the internet which directly affect librarians and libraries, and contains some library links.

Library Association (UK)
http://www.la-hq.org.uk/
Founded in 1877, the LA is the leading British professional body for librarians and information managers from all sectors. Its 25,000 members in the UK and overseas receive a monthly journal, *LA Record,* and a fortnightly vacancies supplement. The site contains details of careers and qualifications, professional and international issues, training and development, publications, and more.

Library Link
http://www.mcb.co.uk/liblink/
Based in Bradford, UK, Library Link offers an online information and discussion forum for librarians, researchers, lecturers, and students - anyone with an interest in the field of information management. Its membership stands at about 8,000. The two main areas of this well-signposted site are Library Services and Managing Information. There are useful comments about the linked sites.

Library LINK
Home
About
Join
News
Discussion
Workshops

UK Serials Group
http://www.uksg.org/
The UK Serials Group exists to encourage the exchange and promotion of ideas on printed and electronic serials and the process of scholarly communication.

Online libraries

Bibliothèque Nationale
http://www.bnf.fr/
The Bibliothèque Nationale is the national library of France. The Paris library contains not only books and periodicals, but also manuscripts, prints, drawings, photographs, music scores, records, cassettes, maps and plans, coins, medals, costume and stage designs, thus covering all fields of knowledge and all media. The web site offers an English language virtual tour and catalogue and more comprehensive English version of the web site is under development.

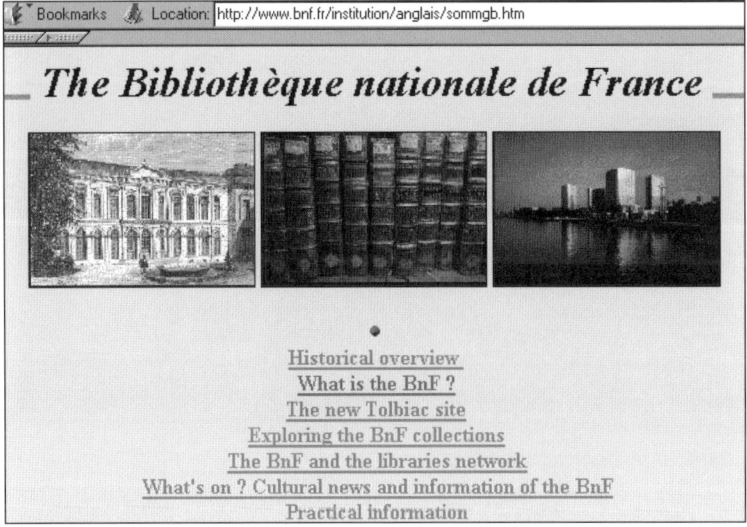

Fig. 32. The web site of the Bibliothèque Nationale, Paris, the French equivalent of the British Library. The site can be read in English as well as French.

Bodleian Library
http://www.bodley.ox.ac.uk/
The Bodleian Library in the University of Oxford is one of the oldest libraries in Europe, and in England is second in size only to the British Library. Since 1610 it has been a library of legal deposit and over almost four centuries has accumulated great collections of books, manuscripts,

and other sources of information which place it among the world's major research libraries. The site contains information about digital library projects under development, catalogue access, a shopping arcade, exhibitions, the Oxford Libraries Internet Gateway, and much more.

British Library
http://www.bl.uk/
http://portico.bl.uk/
From its futuristic new London headquarters at St Pancras, the British Library provides a state of the art reading room, a range of bibliographic, document supply and information services, as well as exhibitions, publications and events. This substantial web site gives details of library resources and services available free and on subscription, and of British Library Net, its free dial-up internet service. You can explore online some of its great treasures such as Magna Carta, Beowulf and the Lindisfarne Gospels. You can also find full details of BLAISE, the British Library National Bibliographic Service, an online subscription information retrieval service giving access to 21 databases containing over 19 million bibliographic records. Highly recommended.

Fig. 33. The British Library, London. The web site is a well-produced and substantial resource, giving access to millions of documents. Subscription is required for much of the site.

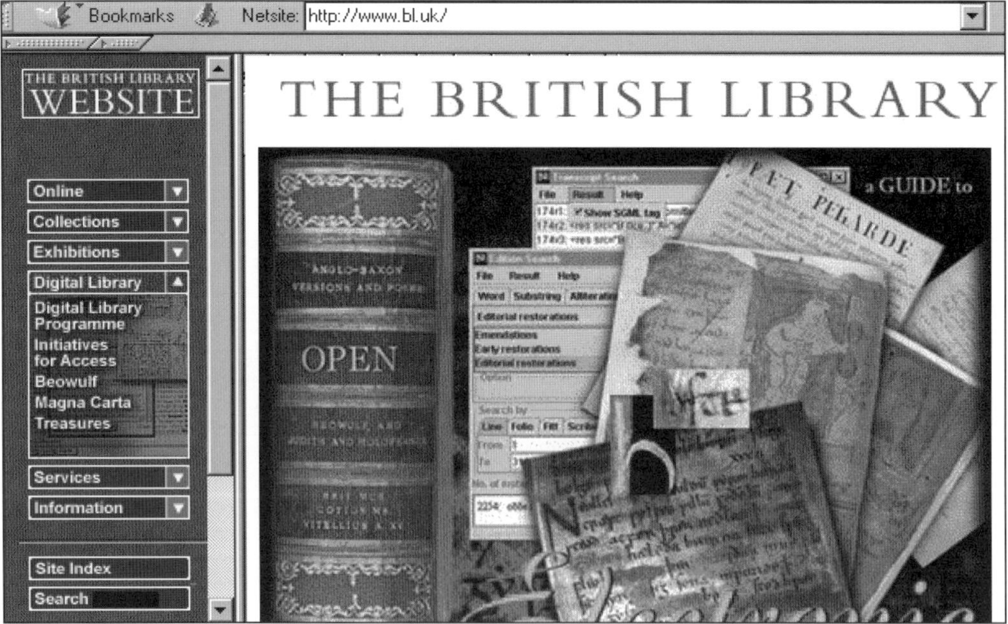

Cambridge University Library
http://www.lib.cam.ac.uk/
The site contains details of the Library's range of services. It is also piloting a web-based version of its catalogue, but this was still under development when the site was reviewed.

EARL
http://www.earl.org.uk
EARL stands for Electronic Access to Resources in Libraries. This con-

sortium of UK public libraries promotes the role of public libraries in providing library and information services across the network. It supports library authority policy makers, and demonstrates prototype networked services. The UK Electronic Library is being developed following a feasibility study in 1997. UKEL is to act as the national gateway to the New Public Library, providing electronic content and services relevant to the needs of public library users. It aims to make innovative use of networking tools, and exploit and widen access to the unique resources of public libraries.

Internet Public Library - see page 14.

Librarianship & Information Science Subject Gateway (PICK)
http://www.aber.ac.uk/~tplwww/e
PICK is a gateway to quality librarianship and information science resources on the internet. It is compiled by the Thomas Parry Library, the University of Wales, Aberystwyth. Its basic aim is to provide easy access to quality internet resources in the field of librarianship and information science. There is a vast amount of LIS material on the internet, but problems with locating and using such information. PICK aims to solve some of these problems by collecting, organising and reporting on selected librarianship and information science resources.

Library of Congress
http://lcweb.loc.gov/catalog/
The US Library of Congress in Washington is the largest library in the world, with more than 115 million items on 530 miles of shelves. The collections include 17 million books, 2 million recordings, 12 million photographs, 4 million maps, and 50 million manuscripts. The Library's mission is to make its resources available and useful to the Congress and the American people and to sustain and preserve a universal collection of knowledge and creativity for future generations. Its online catalogue is a database of some 12 million records covering books, serials, computer files, manuscripts, cartographic materials, plus music,

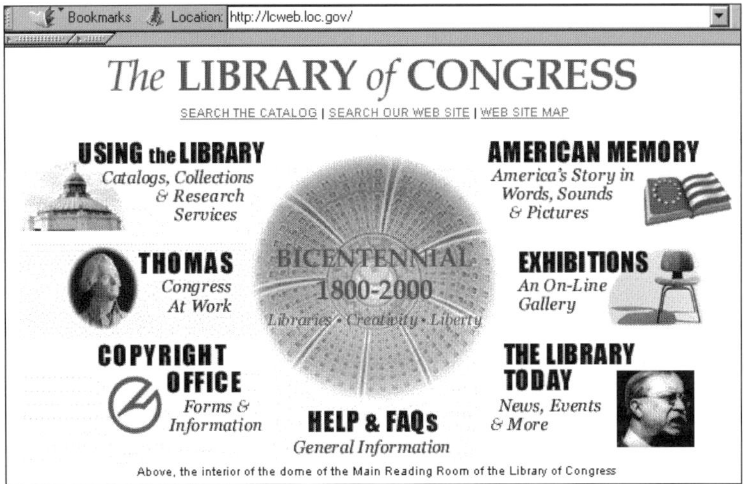

Fig. 34. The web site of the Library of Congress in Washington, USA. This is an essential resource for everyone wanting access to the historical documents and records of America.

sound recordings, and visual materials in the library's collections. Its online catalogue also provides references, notes, circulation status, and information about materials still in the acquisitions stage.

Library Job Postings on the Internet
http://topcat.bridgew.edu/-snesbeitt/libraryjobs.htm
This is a project developed by Sarah Nesbeitt, a former student at the University of Michigan School of Information. The site offers an extensive list of internet-based job listings for the United States, Canada, and also for the UK, Australia and New Zealand.

LibWeb
http://sunsite.berkeley.edu/Libweb/
LibWeb has the ambitious aim of providing links to all libraries whose catalogues or other resources are available on the web. Part of the Berkeley Digital Library, the site is updated daily, and lists about 2,500 sites from all over the world. You can search through them following a geographical listing, or by keyword. You may need a password or other information to access a particular library's site.

London Library
http://webpac.londonlibrary.co.uk/
The London Library, founded in 1841, is a subscription library serving the needs of scholars by lending books for use at home. Located in St James's Square in central London, the library contains about a million books in all European languages and a subject range across the humanities, with particular emphasis on literature, history and related subjects. Its web site contains details of its membership and facilities, and a searchable catalogue of its acquisitions since 1984 (slowly being extended back in time).

National Library of Scotland
http://www.nls.uk
This site brings you information on all the library's services, including how to use the reading rooms, and gives you instant access to its online catalogue. You can also explore the library's fascinating collections of manuscripts, maps and rare books as well as its tailor-made information service for business and industry, SCOTBIS.

National Library of Wales
http://www.llgc.org.uk/
The National Library of Wales was established by Royal Charter in 1907 and opened on its present site in Aberystwyth in 1916. The site gives brief details of services and job vacancies, but otherwise the online service appears to be rather limited.

Research Libraries Group of America
http://www.thames.rlg.org/toc.html
RLG is a not-for-profit membership corporation of institutions devoted to improving access to information that supports research and learning. Its

web site links into many national and international library networks and online services.

Higher Education

- Aberdeen Unive
- University of Ab
- Anglia Polytechn
- Aston University

- University of Bat
- University of Bir
- Bolton Institute I
- Bournemouth Ur
- University of Bra
- University of Brig
- University of Bris
- Brunel University

UK Higher Education and Research Libraries
http://www.ex.ac.uk/library/uklibs.html
This useful site contains links to more than 150 libraries and information services listed, including those of universities, university colleges, and institutes and colleges of higher education.

UK Libraries Plus
http://www.lisa.sbu.ac.uk/uklibrariesplus/
UKLP is a co-operative venture between higher education libraries. It enables part-time, distance, and placement students to borrow material from other libraries in close proximity to where you live or work. In addition, there is a provision for full-time students and for staff to use other libraries on a reference only basis. Membership is open to any higher education institution in the UK.

UK Office for Library & Information Networking
http://www.ukoln.ac.uk
This would be a useful bookmark for any information managers. The site offers information about current research, for example on the UK eLib project, electronic journals, key documents, and developments in information networking. You can also explore various subject gateways.

UK Public Libraries Page
http://www.dspace.dial.pipex.com/town/square/ac940/ukpublib.html
Developed by Sheila and Robert Harden since 1995, these pages aim to present the most complete and up-to-date picture of public library internet activity in the United Kingdom. This is a long web site address, but it does offer comprehensive information on library education, conferences, projects in progress, and library sites across the UK, Europe and wider afield.

Library services

Acqweb
http://www.library.vanderbilt.edu/law/acqs/acqs.html
Acqweb is a resource for librarians looking for help in making purchases. It also maintains a very extensive and full list of publishers around the world, including commercial, academic, and specialty imprints.

6 Publishers: UK and Ireland

In this chapter we will explore:

- *publishers' associations*
- *book fairs*
- *book distributors*
- *publishers A-Z*

Publishers' associations

Association of Learned and Professional Society Publishers
http://www.alpsp.org.uk/
Based in Worthing, West Sussex, ALPSP offers a meeting point for all those involved in the publication of academic and professional journals and books. It provides information and expertise in learned publishing, a wealth of contacts, training and support. The site offers links to the pages of most of its member organisations and to other sites relevant to the book and journal industry. The Association publishes its own journal, *Learned Publishing*.

Book Trust
http://www.booktrust.org.uk/
Based in Wandsworth, London, the Trust is an independent educational charity formed to promote books and reading and to encourage readers of all ages and cultures to discover and enjoy books. It offers information on children's books, books in the news, literary prizes, and its own pub-

Fig. 35. The Book Trust, London, is active in promoting the use of books, especially among children.

lications. The Trust offers a useful telephone book information service (premium number).

Directory & Database Publishers Association
http://www.directory-publisher.co.uk/
The DDPA aims to represent the interests of directory and database publishers, and to maintain and apply a code of professional practice. The site tells you all about the DPA, its membership, events and contacts. There is an online search facility and you can browse through its membership database.

Periodical Publishers Association
http://www.ppa.co.uk/
This is the web site of the trade association of UK magazine publishers. Its 200 members are responsible for the vast majority of magazines published in the UK.

Publishers Association
http://www.publishers.org.uk/
The PA is the representative body for book and journal publishers in the UK. It has campaigned for the continued zero-rating of books and journals for VAT, the protection of copyright, and for increased provision of books throughout the educational sector. The PA's specialist divisions include the General Book Council, and the Education Division comprising the Educational Publishers Council and the Council of Academic and Professional Publishers. Its weekly Headlines fax service gives members the news they need in the fastest way possible.

Scottish Publishers' Association
http://www.scottishbooks.org/
The association represents about 80 Scottish publishers.

Society of Freelance Editors and Proofreaders
http://www.sfep.demon.co.uk/
SFEP aims to promote high editorial standards and achieve recognition of the professional status of it 1,400 members. The site includes a descriptive online directory of its members and the services they provide.

Society of Young Publishers
http://www.thesyp.demon.co.uk/
Established in 1949, the SYP is open to anyone in publishing or a related trade or who is hoping to be soon. Originally intended for the 18 to 35 age group, over 35s can join as Associate Members. The site gives details of training, and forthcoming events and meetings.

Women in Publishing
http://www.cyberiacafe.net/wip/
The UK-based group WIP has been offering networking, training and mutual support to women in publishing since 1979. The site includes details of monthly meetings, training opportunities, an online publishing

tutorial, international contacts, membership details and an application form. The group is organised by committees of volunteers.

Book fairs

The Antiquarian Book Fair
http://www.aba.org.uk/olympia99.htm
The Antiquarian Book Fair is the finest international events of its kind. Over 150 of the world's top dealers attend the fair at Olympia each year.

Hay-on-Wye Bookshops (UK)
http://www.hay-on-wye.com/bookshop.htm
Sponsored by the *Sunday Times*, the Hay Festival of Literature takes place in May and June each year, along with the Hay Children's Festival of the Arts.

London International Book Fair (LIBF)
http://www.libf.co.uk
The LIBF is a major event in the calendar of the British and international book trade, staged for a few days each in March/April at the Olympia Exhibition Centre in west London. The web site was still under development when reviewed. There were email contacts to the organisers.

British Council
http://www.britcoun.org/publishing/index.htm
The British Council's Publishing Promotion Unit publicises British books and multimedia around the world through participation in international book fairs. Information about which writers are currently touring for the British Council and about literature festivals in the UK appear on its Literature Department web pages.

Book distributors

Eurospan
http://www.eurospan.co.uk
EurospanOnline offers comprehensive, easy-to-locate information on new, recent and bestselling titles from a core group of US academic, scholarly and professional publishers. Thousands of titles are featured in subjects ranging from art to zoology and comprising reference and multi-volume works, undergraduate and post-graduate textbooks, monographs, professional manuals, journals and multimedia.

International Book Distributors
http://www.ibdltd.com/
IBD specialises in the distribution of foreign language dictionaries and translation tools.

Littlehampton Book Services
orders@lbsltd.co.uk
LBS is a wholly owned subsidiary of the Orion Publishing group and

forms the distribution arm of the group. It also acts as third-party distributor for about 20 independent publishers who between them cover all areas of publishing. LBS services all sectors of the market including bookshops, book clubs, supermarkets and mail order.

Macmillan Distribution
http://www.macmillan-mdl.co.uk
The site contains a list of publishers and imprints distributed by Macmillan Distribution Ltd. Registration is required, and subsequent use of an ID and password. The site provides the opportunity to subscribe to Whitaker Book Bank, teleordering and product and service information.

Marston Book Services
http://www.marston.co.uk
Marston Book Services Ltd was incorporated as a wholly owned subsidiary of Blackwell Publishers in 1978. Total publishers' sales through MBS are around £45 million. The web site offers an online ordering and enquiry service free for booksellers.

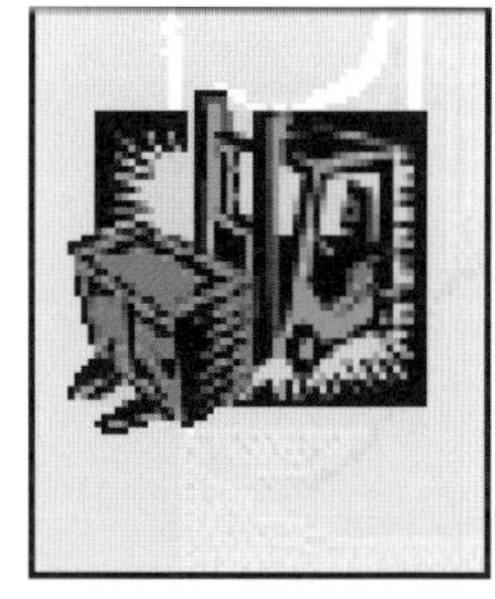

Penguin Books
http://www.penguin.co.uk
Penguin provide a combined book marketing and distribution service for a limited number of high profile trade publishers including Element Books, Rough Guides, Which Consumer Guides and Wisden cricket handbooks.

Plymbridge Distributors
http://www.plymbridge.com
Established in 1985, Plymouth-based Plymbridge Distributors now provides a comprehensive national and international distribution service for almost 100 British and American publishers.

Turnaround
http://www.ytd36.dial.pipex.com/
Turnaround provides a sales, distribution and marketing service for independent publishers from the UK, USA and Europe.

Turpin
http://www.turpin-distribution.com
Based in Letchworth, Turpin provides a range of global fulfilment and distribution services for research and scholarly publishers in the area of print and electronic publications. It has been trading for over thirty years and numbers amongst its clients Arnold, the British Library, IP Publishing, Woodhead Publishers, and the Royal Society of Chemistry. The site includes publisher links, an online bookshop and other features.

Vine House Distribution
http://www.vinehouseuk.co.uk
Vine House's aim is to provide an efficient, personal, promotion-minded and cost-effective distribution service for small and medium sized pub-

lishers, from both the UK and overseas. Its web site provides a summary of services including warehousing and distribution, order processing, cash collection, sales representation and marketing, and mail order fufilment.

World Leisure Marketing
http://www.map-guides.com/
WLM is a distributor of a wide range of UK and imported maps and guides.

Publishers A to Z

Addison Wesley Longman
http://www.awl-he.com
AWL is a global leader in higher education publishing, trading under the Pearson brand name. This is its international home page which contains a site search, a subject resource centre, and a developing section on online learning. A useful feature is the addition of 'companion web sites' which are available to support Pearson Education textbooks. These offer lecturers support materials and students opportunities to carry out online learning and self-assessment. There are also links to AWL offices, subsidiaries and operating divisions worldwide. These include Addison Wesley, Prentice Hall, Longman, Financial Times, Prentice Hall, Allyn & Bacon, and Benjamin/Cummings.

Adlard Coles – see A & C Black.

Aerospace Publishing
http://www.airpower.co.uk
Aerospace is an aviation publisher based in west London, England, and has been producing fact-filled, densely illustrated aviation titles for over 20 years. It publishes the colour illustrated quarterlies *World Air Power Journal* and *Wings of Fame*, plus a number of aviation books.

African Books Collective
http://www.africanbookscollective.com
ABS is a self-help initiative established in 1989 by a group of African publishers to market and distribute their books in Europe, North America, and in Commonwealth countries outside Africa. It currently has 42 member publishers from 12 African countries. More than 1,500 titles are available from its UK warehouse.

Aidan Ellis
http://www.demon.co.uk/aepub/index.htm
Based in Salcombe, Devon, Aidan Ellis is an independent literary trade publisher established in 1971. French literature is among its specialisms. Its authors include Pierre Androuet, Alan Bloom, Roy Lancaster, Patrick McCabe, Jose Miguel Roig, Françoise Sagan, Josephine Saxton, Henri Troyat, and Marguerite Yourcenar. Its non-fiction topics include gardening, tall ships, cheese, and more.

Airlife Publishing
http://www.airlifebooks.com/
Airlife is a general trade publisher specialising in titles of aviation, military and nautical interest.

Ian Allan
http://www.ianallan.com
Ian Allan titles are aimed at railway enthusiasts interested in steam, preservation and lost or forgotten lines. Ian Allan Publishing Ltd recently acquired the established railway imprint, OPC, and also publishes titles on road transport, maritime, aviation subjects and military matters. Its Dial House imprint encompasses football and cycling books.

Allens: The Horseman's Bookshop
http://www.allens-books.com
JA Allen is an established publisher by Royal Appointment of books, videos, cards for country life and country sports. Here you can find out about everything from equestrian anatomy and farriery to saddlery, to showing, instructorship, eventing, and more.

Allison & Busby
http://www.allisonandbusby.ltd.uk
Founded in 1967, the company publishes biography, fiction, travel, writers' guides, crime and history titles. You can read the first chapter of selected titles online. You can also enter its online competition for poets. Customers can order online via a link to the Book Pl@ce and to Hammicks.

Architectural Press
http://www.architecturalpress.com/
Publications in the fields of architecture, construction, engineering and continuing professional development. See also Butterworth-Heinemann.

Arnold Publishers
http://www.arnoldpublishers.com
Established for over 100 years, Arnold is an international book and journal publisher for students, academics and professionals. This web site provides full details of over 1,000 titles. Online order and inspection copy request forms are also available. You can search the web site by subject or keyword (including author, title or ISBN). The company produces subject catalogues covering medicine, nursing and health sciences, engineering, construction, technology, statistics, history, geography, environmental science, cultural, media and literary studies, language, linguistics, and psychology. Arnold is part of the Hodder Headline group.

Art Attack
http://www.artattack.co.uk/
This web site was under development when reviewed.

Publishers: UK and Ireland

Ashgate
http://www.ashgate.com
Based in Aldershot, Hampshire, Ashgate is an international publisher of scholarly studies and collected essays. It publishes around 600 new titles a year across the whole spectrum of humanities and social sciences. There is a site search facility, information for prospective authors, plus an extensive well-organised selection of links to sites of associated interest. The site offers a 15% discount for all online orders, plus secure server ordering.

Aslib
http://www.aslib.co.uk/
Aslib, the Association for Information Management, was founded in 1924 and is now a global corporate membership organisation with over 2,000 members in some 70 countries. It promotes best practice in the management of information resources. It provides consultancy and information services, professional training, conferences, recruitment, and publishes journals, conference proceedings, directories and monographs, much of it online.

Automobile Association
http://www.theaa.co.uk/
The AA is the leading UK motorists' organisation. Here you can find full details of the AA's ever-expanding range of illustrated travel guides, maps and atlases. Online ordering is available for selected titles. Transactions are in pounds sterling and are charged at current rates of exchange. US$ prices are shown for guidance. The AA offers other online services including insurance, hotel booking, a driving school competition, job vacancies, motor finance and personal loan quotes.

Barefoot Books
http://www.barefoot-books.com
Barefoot Books is an independent children's publisher with an emphasis on original, high-quality full colour picture books from traditional cultures all over the world. The two publishing principals combine work and family responsibilities, working from their respective homes in London and Bath. The Barefoot list includes Barefoot Beginners, Barefoot anthologies, poetry collections and picture books.

Batsford
http://www.batsford.com/
Batsford is a London-based general diversified publisher of illustrated trade titles covering chess, craft, art, graphics, gardening, architecture and other subjects.

BBC
http://www.bbc.co.uk/education/bookcase/
'Bookcase' is part of the massive and impressive if somewhat chaotic BBC web site, where you can explore some of its in-depth book information for adults and children. There is an enormous number of book-related

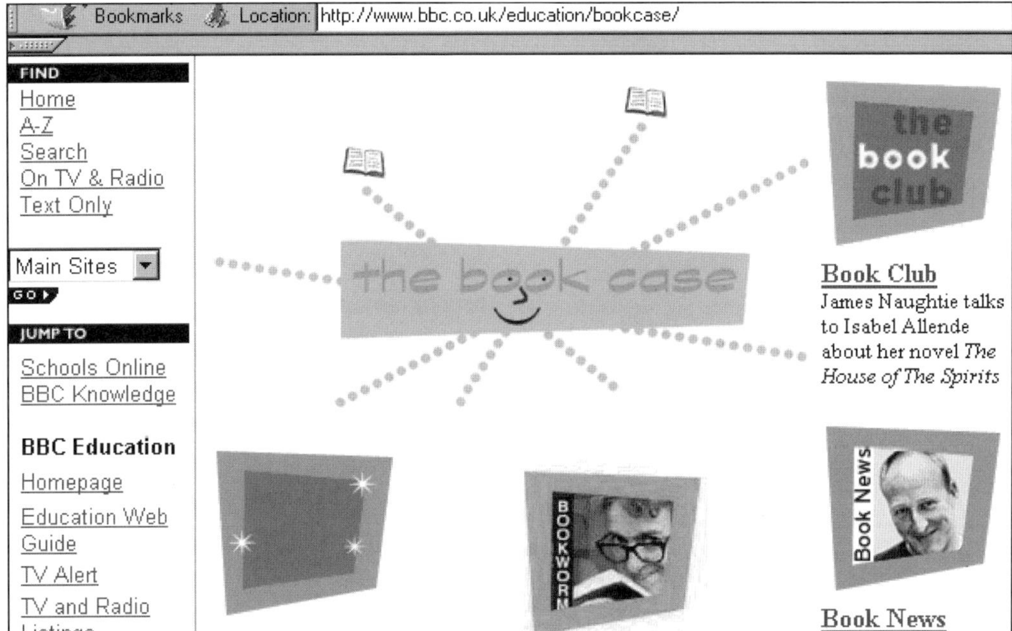

Fig. 36. The BBC Bookcase web site, a magazine-style web site containing information about books and writers featured on BBC television and radio programmes.

links here, some in the form of drop down menus. In its search engine we input the word 'books' which yielded over 4,000 results. You can find a list of hundreds of authors and poets who have been featured within BBC Education's book and literary sites including the Bookworm, National Libraries Week and National Poetry Day.

Beaconsfield Publishers
http://www.beaconsfield-publishers.co.uk
Formed in 1978, Beaconsfield Publishers is a small publisher specialising in medicine and nursing titles. It maintains an additional commitment to alternative medicine, and has a list of books on homeopathy. You can order its titles online (non-secure server) or by traditional means.

Berg Publishers
http://www.berg.demon.co.uk/
Berg is an independent publisher of academic textbooks and monographs spanning cultural studies, social anthropology, dress and fashion studies, European history and politics and film studies.

Bernard Babani Books
http://www.kantaris.com/babani/win95.htm
Babani are well-known publishers of specialist computer, radio and electronics pocket books.

BIOS Scientific Publishers
http://www.bios.co.uk/
BIOS was founded in 1989 as a specialist publisher in biology and medicine. It publishes 30 to 40 new titles each year from its Oxford offices, with a focus on genetics, anaesthesia, plant science and molecular biology. Its list includes textbooks for undergraduates, practical manuals and reference guides for postgraduates and professionals.

A & C Black
http://www.acblack.co.uk/
Black is active is children's book co-production, sports, ceramics, theatre, writing, reference, including *Who's Who*, travel, nautical, ornithology, art and design. The site was under construction when reviewed.

Blackstone
http://www.bpp.co.uk/blackstone/index.htm
A subsidiary of the publicy-quoted BPP, Blackstone Press publishes a wide range of study guides and handbooks for both the student and practitioner markets. It titles include degree course books and support material, texts for Law Society and Bar exams, and a rapidly expanding practitioner list.

Blackwell
http://www.blackwellpublishers.co.uk
Founded in Oxford in 1926, Blackwell claims to be the world's largest independent academic publisher of books, journals and educational software. As you would expect, the rather sober-looking site gives very comprehensive information about its books, journals and various electronic products. A good starting point it its excellent online catalogue subject index. If you choose to order by credit card, its secure server software encrypts all of your personal information.

Blackwell Science
http://www.blacksci.co.uk/
With offices throughout the world, Blackwell Science publishes about 125 journals and 160 new books each year with a backlist of some

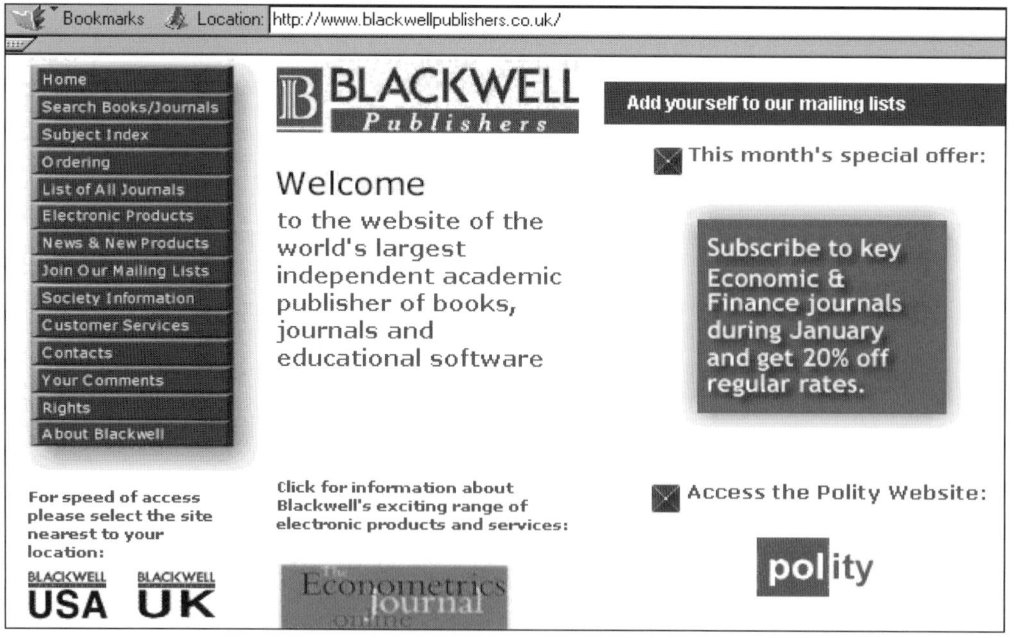

Fig. 37. Blackwell has made a substantial investment in its online bookselling operation. You can explore a vast and well-organised catalogue of books, journals and educational software. You are invited to register.

2,000 titles. It specialises in medicine (including veterinary medicine), nursing and allied health, life sciences, earth sciences, construction and engineering, and agriculture and fisheries. Its publications include primary research journals, textbooks for undergraduates and reference and handbooks for professionals. A rapidly growing proportion are available electronically as well as on paper. The site offers secure online ordering.

Bloodaxe Books
http://www.bloodaxebooks.demon.co.uk
With over 400 titles in print and more than 250 poets published, Bloodaxe has revolutionised poetry publishing in Britain during the last twenty years. Its authors and books have won virtually every major literary award for which the genre is eligible, including the Nobel Prize for Literature (with three Nobel laureates). The site contains useful links to other interesting poetry sites.

Bloomsbury
http://www.bloomsbury.com
Bloomsbury is an independent literary UK publisher dedicated to publishing the best in fiction and non-fiction. You can browse its 'shelves' on this attractively presented web site for fiction, fiction classics, poetry classics, non-fiction, reference, biography, film, health and lifestyle, gardening, cookery, music, and children's books. The site includes a secure shopping trolley.

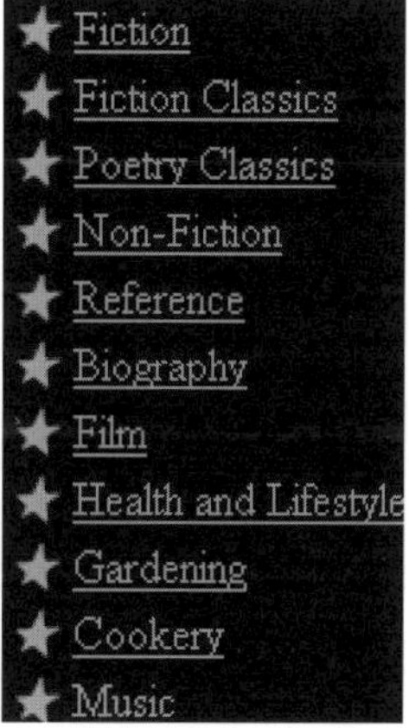

Bodley Head – see Random House.

Book Guild
http://www.bookguild.co.uk
Founded in 1982, the Book Guild is a small independent publishing house of sponsored books based in Lewes, East Sussex. It carries a diverse list covering fiction, biographies, autobiographies, military histories and human interest. It also has an expanding mainstream list. You can order by traditional means.

Booth-Clibborn
http://www.booth-clibborn-editions.co.uk
Booth-Clibborn is a publisher of popular culture and contemporary art. This is a small but stylishly designed site. You need a level 4 browser to view all the sometimes slow-loading graphics successfully.

Bowker-Saur
http://www.bowker-saur.co.uk/service/
Bowker-Saur is a professional and reference publisher across a range of media. Its products encompass bibliographies, contact, professional and business directories, abstracting and indexing services, historical and contemporary biographical reference and library and information science titles in book, journal, microform, CD-rom, and online formats. As well as publishing under the imprints Bowker-Saur, Headland Busi-

ness Information and Hans Zell Publishers, it distributes titles from leading reference imprints R.R. Bowker, Martindale-Hubbell, Marquis *Who's Who* (UK and Europe), K.G. Saur (UK only) and D.W. Thorpe (UK and Europe). It is a part of the Reed Elsevier group.

Boydell & Brewer
http://www.boydell.co.uk/
Based in Woodbridge, Suffolk, Boydell & Brewer are history publishers. Their catalogues cover medieval history, literature, music, and include a trade catalogue, Camden House catalogue, Tamesis catalogue, and Early English Text Society catalogue. The rather spartan site includes details of their sales representatives. Customers are invited to post or fax their orders.

BPP
http://www.bpp.co.uk/
London-based BPP has over a few years grown into one of Europe's leading professional education groups. Its well-regarded professional training publications and courses cover accountancy, banking, law and languages, providing information on exam preparation and career development. Its divisions include Blackstone Press (law books).

Brasseys see Batsfords.

Nicholas Brealey
http://www.nbrealey-books.com
Here you can browse the complete illustrated catalogue of titles from one of the UK's leading specialist business book publishers. The site has an attractively clean and functional design, and is quick to load. It plans to include a discussion forum, news pages and extracts from forthcoming titles. The site includes a title index, author index, and order form. Full details of a large number of titles can be viewed.

Brimax – see Reed.

Brinnoven
http://www.brinnoven.demon.co.uk/
Brinnoven offers Scottish pre-press and publishing services, concentrating on local history, place names, dialects, languages, and traditional and folk music.

British Council
http://www.britcoun.org
The British Council's publishing promotion team publicises British books and multimedia through participation in international book fairs and staging specialised exhibitions in areas such as science, technology, management and the arts. It aids the development of local book-trade capacity and showcases British expertise through consultancies, training courses for booksellers and publishers, and support to book trade visitors to Britain.

British Film Institute
http://www.bfi.org.uk/
BFI Publishing issues books and other educational materials for a variety of audiences – from primary school pupils studying media for the first time to undergraduates who have chosen to study the moving image at an advanced level. Many of its titles are also aimed at the general reader with an interest in cinema and television – for example its BFI Film Classics series featuring writers such as Salman Rushdie and Melvyn Bragg. As for online ordering, you can email the online form stating your credit card details, or print the form and post it. The site does not currently provide encrypted data transmission.

British Museum Press
http://www.britishmuseumcompany.co.uk
British Museum Press is one of the most successful museum and gallery publishers in the world, publishing lively and authoritative titles for the general, scholarly and academic reader. It also publishes a highly regarded children's list for the under 12s; a stimulating range of printed guides for the Museum visitor; popular books-as-merchandise for adults and children; postcards and postcard sets; CD-ROM and audio guides.

Brown, Son & Ferguson
http://www.skipper.co.uk/
This Glasgow-based firm has been a nautical publisher since 1832. If you are interested in books about the sea, historical books, old sailing ships, how to build model ships, how to pass your exams, this is the place for you.

Burns & Harris
http://www.burns-harris.co.uk/
Burns & Harris are specialists in advertising-backed publications for public bodies, local authorities and private companies in Scotland.

Business Monitor International
http://www.businessmonitor.com/
BMI publishes key news, data, analysis and forecasts on economic and political developments in global emerging markets. Yearbooks and newsletters are available in print, CD and electronically.

Butterworth-Heinemann
http://www.bh.com/
Part of the giant Reed-Elsevier publishing group, B-H is an international publisher of books, open learning materials and electronic products for students and professionals in technology, medicine and business. From its offices in the UK, USA and Australia it publishes over 500 titles per year. It also has offices in South Africa, New Zealand, Japan and India. It embraces imprints such as Focal Press, Digital Press, Newnes, Pergamon Open Learning, Inkata Press, Wright, and Architectural Press. The ordering facilities are designed primarily for the book trade, schools, colleges and universities.

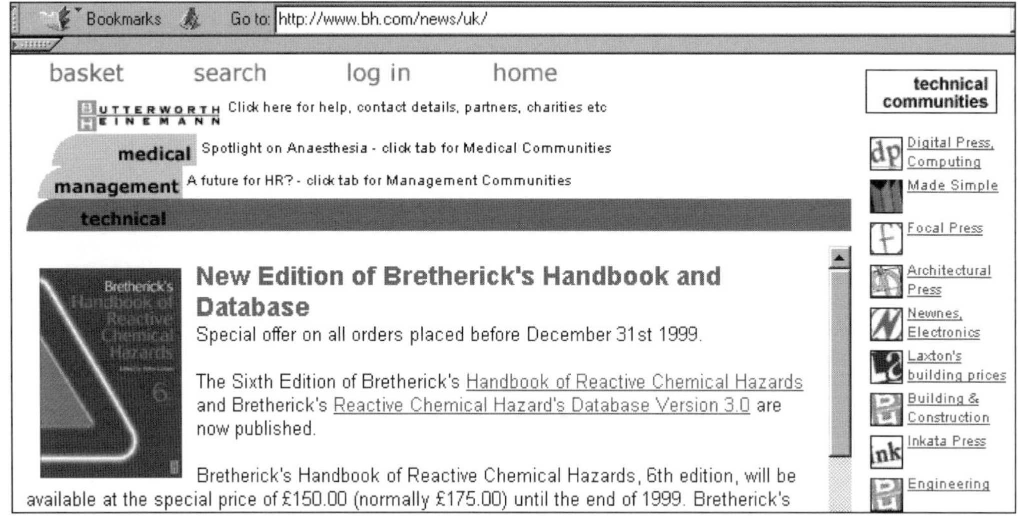

Fig. 38. The web site of Butterworth Heinemann is a good place to locate key publications in the fields of science, technology and medicine.

Butterworths Publishers (UK)
http://www.butterworths.co.uk/

Cadogan Books
http://www.cadogan.demon.co.uk
Cadogan Books began life in the mid 1970s as a small general nonfiction publishing house in a basement just off Cadogan Square in London. It developed a varied list encompassing car books, a plant hunting series, and literary anthologies, as well as the travel guides for which is now best known. Cadogan works in partnership with Globe Pequot, to whose web site you are directed. You can order Cadogan titles online via Globe Pequot's secure server using a Visa or Mastercard.

Calmann and King
http://www.calmann-king.com/
C&K is a publisher and producer of books on art, design, architecture, history and religion, for both the professional and student markets. The company was founded in 1976.

Cambridge University Press
http://www.cup.cam.ac.uk/
CUP is the printing and publishing house of the University of Cambridge. Founded in 1534, it is the world's oldest press. Today it is one of the largest educational and academic publishers, producing more than 2,000 titles a year in print and electronic form. The Press is an international publisher, drawing authors from more than 100 countries and distributing its products to almost 200. Its web site includes a searchable catalogue, online ordering facilities, news, extracts, features and detailed guidelines for prospective authors. Its main products include bibles and prayer books, ELT, humanities, medical, science, reference, social sciences, and textbooks, plus CD-rom and online publishing.

Cameron May
http://neon.airtime.co.uk/C-May/
Founded in 1992, Cameron May specialises in books, journals and semi-

nars on international environmental law. Its prices are show in sterling and US dollars. Secure online ordering was in preparation when we reviewed this London-based site.

Canongate
http://www.canongate.co.uk/
Canongate Books has been in existence for almost twenty-five years and is one of Scotland's leading publishers with strengths in fiction, both Scottish and general, children's books, history, biography, and art. It has two subsidiary imprints, Payback Press and Rebel, specialising in Black American fiction and music and counterculture. It also has a Scottish audio imprint. It has secure online ordering.

Capstone
http://www.capstone.co.uk
Oxford-based publisher Capstone produces a range of inspirational books on issues in the modern business world, ranging from leadership, to doing business in Asia. Its online ordering routes you automatically to the Internet Bookshop (WH Smith Online).

Carcanet Press
http://www.carcanet.co.uk
Based in Manchester, Carcanet has established itself as a leading publisher of fiction, poetry, memoirs and biographies. Its web site gives readers throughout the world access to over 500 of its in-print books, with recent publications described and illustrated. It publishes between 50 and 70 titles a year. A simple search function allows readers to browse or to zero in on specific areas, authors or titles. The online Carcanet bookshop includes a secure payment page.

Carfax
http://www.carfax.co.uk/
Established for more than 25 years, Abingdon-based Carfax publishes journals in the fields of area studies, economics, business and law, education, geography, planning and development, humanities, sociology and gender studies, media, communication and cultural studies, medicine and healthcare, politics and international relations, science and technology. See also Taylor & Francis.

Carlton Group
http://www.carlton-group.co.uk/
Carlton is one of the UK's leading publishers of information and reference books on British government. Its publications deal with Westminster, Whitehall, the House of Commons and House of Lords, executive agencies, public bodies, quangos, the European Community, public affairs, trade and law.

Cass, Frank
http://www.frankcass.com
Cass is a publisher of academic books and journals in the fields of history,

politics and international relations, military studies (including strategic studies), middle eastern studies, African studies, slave and post slave societies, development studies, economics and business, law. The web site is informative and easy to navigate if basic in appearance.

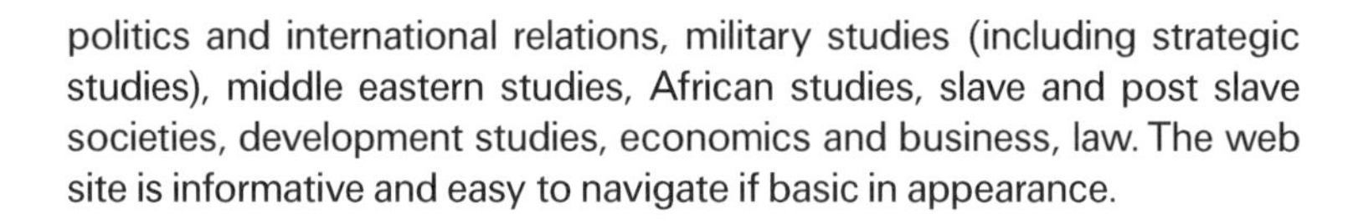

Cassell
http://www.cassell.co.uk
Cassell is one of the most famous names in publishing, with a history stretching back to 1854. This cheerful looking site features its four main book divisions, Cassell Academic, Cassell General, Cassell Reference and Victor Gollancz. You will also find *Inside Cover*, a monthly magazine featuring its latest and forthcoming releases, author interviews, book extracts, reviews and more. There is a secure online ordering facility. Cassells is part of the Orion group.

Castle Hill Press
http://www.castle-hill-press.com
Castle Hill Press is a Hampshire-based publishing and information service to those interested in the life and work of T. E. Lawrence ('Lawrence of Arabia').

Cavendish
http://www.cavendishpublishing.com
Cavendish publishes a range of brightly presented UK law texts and study guides, and the periodical *The Student Law Review.*

Centre for Alternative Technology
http://www.cat.org.uk
CAT is an educational charity striving to achieve co-operation between the natural, technological and human worlds. The site appeared to be relocating its server at the time of our review, so some of the web site could not be viewed.

CCH Editions
http://www.cch.co.uk/
CCH Editions Limited is a business unit of Croner Publications Limited, part of the Wolters Kluwer Group. It publishes bound books, loose-leaf reporting services, newsletters and electronic products on UK and European topics for distribution worldwide. These cover law, human resourcing, company secretarial, audit and accountancy, tax and business. The site map offers a handy information tree. The CCH web site is an essential bookmark for business and professional advisers.

Chadwyck Healey
http://www.chadwyck.co.uk/
Chadwyck Healey is an international group of publishing companies with offices in the UK, Spain and the USA. It publishes reference and research publications for the academic, professional and library markets, using electronic, microform and print media. Its titles include *Literature Online, History Online, UKOP Online, International Index to Music Periodicals*

(IIMP), Archives USA, and *International Index to the Performing Arts.* The site allows you to sign up for a free trial to search a database (available to an institution considering a subscription).

Chanterelle
http://www.medIndex.co.uk/
Chanterelle publishes *Medindex Electronic,* a specialist directory of suppliers of healthcare equipment and services. Copyright for all data contained in these files is the property of the publishers, but it is made available on this web site to enable users to identify and contact providers of equipment and services, and may be downloaded in a 50K zipped file and browsed off line for this purpose.

Chapman & Hall – see Wolters Kluwer.

Chivers Press
http://www.chivers.co.uk
Based in Bath, Chivers Press produces large print books and unabridged audio books. Its expanding range runs to some 8,000 titles, encompassing a wide range of best-selling authors and catering for all tastes. It also publishes hardcover crime novels under the Black Dagger imprint and Westerns under the Gunsmoke and Five Star Westerns imprints, all in standard print. This is rather a plain-looking web site but it does benefit from secure transaction processing (SSL), accepting a range of credit cards.

Churchill Livingstone
http://www.churchillmed.com/
Churchill Livingstone is a global publisher of health and medical information in a variety of media, including books, journals, CD-roms, online, and seminars and conferences. Its most famous title is *Gray's Anatomy,* first published in 1858. Formerly a Pearson company, it is now a division of Harcourt. This web site gives an overview of its multimedia products and its other titles. Some of its books, journals and electronic media should be available for downloading from this site. If you get lost, there is a user-friendly site map. The site is an essential bookmark for medical and health professionals.

CIB Publications
http://www.cib.org.uk
The Chartered Institute of Bankers publishes a range of training and reference materials including a range of over thirty A4 self-study manuals for students geared towards the CIB Associateship, Banking Certificate and Professional Investment Certificate qualifications, *The CIB Directory of Corporate Banking in the UK* and other banking publications.

CIT Publications
http://www.telcoms-data.com/
CIT is a business information publisher focusing on the telecoms and media industries. It publishes a range of yearbooks, data files, special

market reports and competition reports and a fortnightly telecommunications newsletter. It also provides its publications in electronic format. Its client list includes all the major telecommunications equipment manufacturers and service providers as well as consultancy firms, media corporations and financial institutions from around the world.

Class Publishing
http://www.class.co.uk
Class is an independent UK publisher of consumer health information. The site includes a secure shopping cart link.

Peter Collin Publishing
http://www.pcp.co.uk
Started in 1985, the company publishes more than fifty English and bilingual dictionaries and glossaries covering many different languages and specialist subjects. This web site includes sample pages in Adobe Acrobat and GIF graphics file formats so that you can see what the books contain. If you are a teacher of English or any modern language, you can visit the Teacher Resource area. Teachers wanting to add a link to their own language web page, or having information about forthcoming events or publications, are invited to pass on details.

Compass Equestrian Publishing
http://www.users.globalnet.co.uk/~compbook
Compass Equestrian is a newly established publishing company. Its aim is to produce original books on popular equestrian topics for young people at realistic prices without sacrificing quality. There are a few appealing colour pictures of horses which you can download.

Computational Mechanics
http://www.cmp.co.uk
CM is an American publisher of engineering research. Its substantial list of titles include monographs, edited volumes, books on disk, and software in areas such as: acoustics, advanced computing, architecture and structures, biomedicine, boundary elements, earthquake engineering, environmental engineering, fluid mechanics, fracture mechanics, heat transfer, marine and offshore engineering and transport engineering. It works in partnership with the Wessex Institute of Technology, based in Southampton, UK.

Computer Bookshops Birmingham
http://www.compbook.co.uk
Computer Bookshops is Europe's largest wholesale trade distributor of computer books, CD-roms, videos, and training accessories. You can use this site to keep up to date with the latest computer book titles, browse through its extensive catalogue and search the database, but it does not sell direct to the public.

Computerstep Books
http://www.computerstep.com/
Computerstep Books produce some excellent practical illustrated books on computing and internet topics. They include the *In Easy Steps* series and *The Complete Guide* series. You can order your books safely online via a secure server using your credit card (currently Mastercard and Visa only). A small shipping charge is made for delivery.

Constable Publishers
http://www.constable-publishers.co.uk/
Constable's rather functional-looking site features Catherine Cookson, Dover Technical publications, mountaineering, self-help and other titles, with new book information updated monthly.

Crambeth Allen Publishing Ltd
http://www.capable.co.uk
The publications of this specialist technical publisher include *Petroleum Technology Quarterly* and *Asia Steel.*

Croner Publications
http://www.croner.co.uk/
Croner Publications is a top UK provider of management information on subscription. Professionals everywhere rely on Croner materials to help them manage their organisations. These materials comprise more than 100 loose-leaf reference books, newsletters, magazines, electronic media, bound books, telephone advisory services, public seminars and in-company training services. They cover employment law, health and safety, education management, export and transport law. On its web site, its publishing areas have been divided into Information Channels, each containing a full list of packages with their individual products. Croner is a part of the international Wolters Kluwer group.

Current Biology
http://biomednet.com/cbiology/
Current Biology publishes research journals, review journals, books and databases right across the biological sciences. Since its formation in 1990, it has sought to make scientific literature more efficient, accessible and informative. After pioneering the use of full-colour in many of its journals in 1995, Current Biology became the first major biological publisher to put the full text of all its journals on the internet. In 1997 the company became part of Elsevier Science, London. The site contains detailed instructions for authors wishing to submit proposals electronically.

Dalesman
http://www.yorkshirenet.co.uk/dalesman/
The Dalesman is a magazine of the Yorkshire Dales, and publisher of Dales guide books and videos.

Dance Books
http://www.dancebooks.co.uk/
Dance Books is possibly the only company in the world completely dedicated to the publishing and retail selling of books, CDs, and videos on dance and human movement. It carries approximately 2,000 items sold through its London shop, by mail order and via the world wide web. This is a good example of a niche publisher likely to do well from the possibilities of the internet.

David & Charles
http://www.davidandcharles.co.uk/
Based in Newton Abbot in Devon, D&C is a publisher of illustrated non-fiction titles, specialising in interiors, crafts, gardening, art techniques, equestrian and photography.

Debrett's Peerage
http://www.debretts.co.uk/
Debrett's is a specialist reference book publisher and an authoritative guide to traditional social custom in the UK. The enterprise was founded in 1769 (when George III was on the throne) and first took the name Debrett in 1802. Debrett's is best known for its reference book *Peerage and Baronetage*. Now published every five years under licence by Macmillan, the latest edition is January 2000. The firm also publishes *Debrett's People of Today* and guides on aspects of social etiquette. Its web site is fittingly presented in royal blue and gold.

Derwent Information
http://www.derwent.co.uk/
Derwent is one of the world's leading providers of patent and scientific information. It is a subsidiary of Thomson.

Andre Deutsch – see VCI.

Digital Press – see Butterworth-Heinemann.

Do-Not Press
http://www.thedonotpress.co.uk
Founded in October 1994 by rock music journalist and promoter, Jim Driver, The Do-Not Press exists to 'put the pub back into publishing and the friction back in to fiction. We scorn true romances, we sneer at royal biographies and we laugh at just about anything.' The site shows a view from the firm's tent at Glastonbury in 1998.

Dorling Kindersley
http://www.dk.com/
DK is a large and successful publisher of illustrated educational books and CD roms for children. Its appealing in-depth web site offers a range of freely available webzines on topics such as science, nature, geology, inventions, dinosaurs, animals, history, health and fitness, cartography. It also features a Kid's Guide to the Web, competitions, and corporate infor-

Fig. 39. Dorling Kindersley is well up to speed with its online bookstore. The home page includes a handy store guide, and a drop-down menu containing links to everything from arts and crafts to sports and hobbies, study and learning.

mation. There are currently two DK Online Stores where you can obtain your books. The UK store stocks UK editions (sold in UK pounds sterling).

Martin Dunitz
http://www.dunitz.co.uk
Established in 1978, Martin Dunitz Ltd produces medical books, slide atlases and journals, and is a major independent medical and dental publisher in the UK. The site includes journal news and subscriptions. Its areas of interest encompass cardiology, dentistry, dermatology, gastroenterology, haematology, neurology, oncology, ophthalmology, orthopaedics, pathology, plastic surgery, psychiatry, radiology and similar topics. You can email the company but there was no online ordering facility when reviewed.

Dutton – see Penguin Putnam.

Earthscan
http://www.earthscan.co.uk
Earthscan Publications Ltd is a UK publisher of books on environment and sustainable development. It has a backlist of over 200 titles, and publishes some 50 new books each year. In 1991 it became a subsidiary of Kogan Page. It has published in partnership with numerous national and international institutions. The web site features highlights, course texts, catalogue search by subject or title, shopping basket, order form, further information, trade customers, academics, NGOs, authors, useful links, and feedback.

Edinburgh University Press
http://www.eup.ed.ac.uk/
EUP is an independent publisher of academic books, journals and general books for a worldwide readership. Founded fifty years ago, the

press underwent a major change in 1992, becoming an editorially and financially self-determining company whilst remaining closely linked to its owner, the University of Edinburgh. It publishes titles on archaeology, history, Islamic studies, language and linguistics, literary theory, media and cultural studies, philosophy and legal theory, politics and political theory, religious studies, gender studies, humanities and social sciences journals. The press shares marketing with Blackwell Publishers.

Egmont Children's Books
http://www.egmont.com/
Egmont produces children's books under the imprints Dean Children's Books, Hamlyn Children's Books, Heinemann Young Books, Mammoth, and Methuen Children's Books.

Eland Books
http://www.travelbooks.co.uk
Eland specialises in travel literature and associated topics, but its list also includes biography, fiction, and oral history.

Element Books
http://www.eastwest.com/Element/
Based in Shaftesbury, Dorset, Element Books is well known for its output of titles on religious traditions, alternative health, and psychology. Recent sample titles include *Original Jesus: Buddhist Sources Of Christianity*, and *The Complete Illustrated Guide To Feng Shui*.

Edward Elgar Publishing
http://www.e-elgar.co.uk
Edward Elgar Publishing was founded in 1986. It is a privately owned scholarly publisher with a focus on economics. It publishes monographs, reference works and advanced textbooks by leading scholars in North America, Europe, Asia and Australia. It has over 1,000 books in print and adds over 200 new titles a year. The site includes a useful collection of links to economics associations worldwide, and guidelines for prospective authors. Its online shopping basket was under development when reviewed. There is a search facility and drop down menu of main subject categories to explore.

Elliot Right Way Books
http://www.right-way.co.uk
Based in Tadworth, Surrey, Elliot Right Way Books are established publishers of very affordable how-to books on a host of popular mass market topics. These range from cookery, winemaking and driving to indoor and outdoor hobbies, drawing, quizzes, fishing, business, speaking, family reference, personal finance, horses, and pets.

Ernest Press
http://www.ernest-press.co.uk
Ernest Press are UK publishers of mountaineering books and mountain bike guides.

Euromoney
http://www.euromoney.com/
The site is a project of the London-based *Euromoney* magazine, which offers in-depth comment, opinion and analysis of international capital markets, global investment and similar topics. Most of the site is free to access but you must become a registered user. Once registered you can take out a six-week free trial of *Euromoney Confidential. Euromoney* is a market leader in its field, and a publicy quoted company.

Euromonitor
http://www.euromonitor.com/
Established for over 25 years, Euromonitor is a top business information publisher. It provides off-the-shelf research, issues over 200 new titles each year, and provides consultancy in consumer market intelligence. In recent years, emphasis has been put on the electronic delivery of information with the launch of CD-roms and the web site. You can search its database to identify the industry publication you want. You then click on a chapter title to view the details. To purchase the entire chapter, click on the checkbox next to the chapter title, then click 'Purchase Marked Chapters'. The dollar amount next to the chapter title represents the price for the entire chapter.

Europa
http://www.europapublications.co.uk
For over seventy years, London-based Europa has published a series of regularly-revised reference books covering international affairs, politics, and economics. Its key titles are *The Europa World Year Book, The World of Learning,* and *The International Who's Who*. Most of the publications are compiled in-house by team of over thirty editors and researchers. There is an order form you can download, complete and post or fax to Europa.

Everyman Library – see Random House.

Exley Giftbooks
http://tanutech.com/exldir.html
Here you can find details of Exley's *Illustrated Notebook Series, Mini Address Books, To Give and To Keep Series, Art Notebooks*, and *Illustrated Notebooks.*

Express Publishing
http://www.expresspublishing.co.uk
Express Publishing is an EFL publishing house established in 1987. It produces a series of course books on writing skills, grammar, usage and exam practice. It has offices in Swansea and Athens.

Faber & Faber
http://www.faber.co.uk
Faber and Faber Ltd is a famous literary publisher of poetry, drama, film and fiction. The original firm of Faber and Gwyer was founded in 1925, and Faber and Faber in 1929. Its early catalogues included books by Ezra

Pound, Jean Cocteau, Herbert Read, George Rylands, John Dover Wilson, Vita Sackville-West and many other famous names. Today it publishes art, biography, children's books, culture and social studies, drama, fiction, film, food and wine, general non-fiction, literary studies, music, poetry, science, sport and travel. There is guidance on manuscript submission for authors, and you can register online if you want to receive information on forthcoming Faber books. The site includes secure online ordering.

Falmer Press
http://www.tandfdc.com/Falmer/Falmhome.htm
Falmer began publishing books for the education community in 1976. Its list covers education research, education leadership and management, education policy, schools and schooling, curriculum, further and higher education, gender and education, childhood and adolescence, and subject studies. The company is a division of Taylor & Francis Publishers.

Postgraduate Courses
Certificate Page
Course Details
Inquiry Form
Diploma Page
Course Details
Inquiry Form
Masters Page
Course Details
Inquiry Form
MBA Page
Course Details
Inquiry Form
Site Map

Financial Times Management
http://www.ftmanagement.com
The FT brand provides a range of information-based materials and services focused on helping managers to make the right decisions. Its products include directories, management briefings, manuals, journals, and electronic management information, and cover accountancy, law, marketing, finance, and public sector management. There is a good site map. You can search the catalogues, order online, and subscribe or receive inspection copies. The company also distributes computer books from Sybex and Manning Publications.

Findhorn
http://www.findhorn.org/findhornpress/
For 27 years Findhorn Press has been publishing books of spiritual inspiration, healing, humour, guidance and transformation, arising out of the Findhorn Community. The site includes a preview of forthcoming titles, audio tapes, videos and greetings cards.

Focal Press
http://www.bh.com/focalpress/
For over 60 years Focal has published books on photography and the media for professionals and students. Its list encompasses photography and imaging, film, TV and video production, broadcast and communication technology, lighting, audio, broadcast management and theory, multimedia and graphics, radio, journalism and writing. The company is a division of Butterworth-Heinemann.

Folens
http://www.folens.com/
Folens produces educational material for both teachers and for children up to age 16. Their product range includes atlases, maths and language materials, English dictionaries and grammar books. The site contains a book search, an IT works section, events, contact and secure online

ordering facilities.

Footprint Handbooks
http://www.footprintbooks.com/
Footprint produces guidebooks for independently minded travellers, with a particular emphasis on the Caribbean, Africa, southeast Asia, and Latin America. Its 'flagship' is the famous annual *South American Handbook*, said to be the longest running guide in the English language.

Gaia Books
http://www.gaiabooks.co.uk/
Gaia publishes books about health, spirit, natural history, and books on the environment and ecology. It has a vision of the future in which the relationships between people, plants, animals and the planet may be better understood. Its web site offers a bookshop, useful links area, and environment news. Ordering is either by traditional means, or there are links to Amazon and the Internet Bookshop.

Gee Publishing
http://www.gee.co.uk
Gee is a long-established name in UK accountancy and business publishing. Today, Gee Business Network (GBN) offers an online business compliance information service, covering human resources, company administration, payroll and health and safety issues. GBN is built around FactFinder, a comprehensive database of reference information for busy executives. FactFinder provides practical guidance through the ever-growing jungle of law and regulations affecting all UK organisations. Online registration is required.

Gill & Macmillan
http://www.gillmacmillan.ie
Gill & Macmillan is a prominent educational and trade publisher in Ireland. It produces a wide range of textbooks for secondary school, colleges and universities. Its list includes history, current affairs, biography, reference, cooking, tourism and guide books. Under the Newleaf imprint, books are published on popular psychology, counselling, health and healing, complementary medicine and mind body spirit. Gill & Macmillan also distributes for other Irish publishers.

Ginn
http://www.ginn.co.uk/
Ginn & Company's educational publishing spans all areas of the UK curriculum. You can choose from the 'stars in the galaxy' to find out about the wide range of its resources and the latest materials to help you keep up with new teaching ideas and strategies. You can visit its interactive areas and register for the Maths Megastore and the Science Investigators Club. Ginn is a division of Reed Elsevier.

Gollancz
http://www.gollancz.co.uk/
Victor Gollancz Ltd has been publishing and non-fiction since 1928. Its distinguished authors include Daphne du Maurier, George Orwell, Ivy Compton-Burnett, Dorothy L. Sayers, Franz Kafka, A. J. Cronin and H. G. Wells. More recent authors have included Arthur C. Clarke, Kingsley Amis, J. G. Ballard, Angela Carter, John Irving, D. M. Thomas and Terry Pratchett. The company is now part of Cassell/Orion.

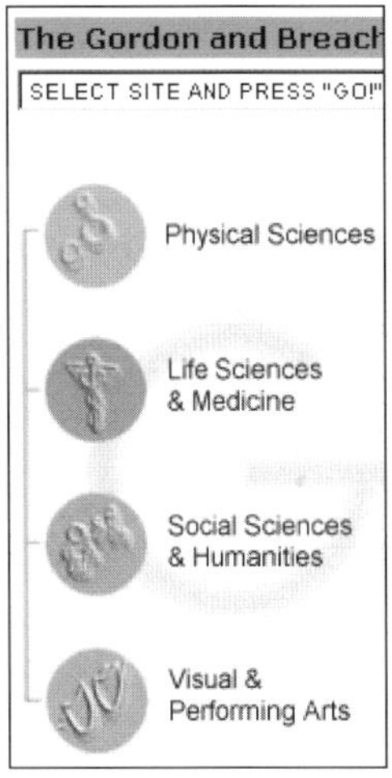

Gordon & Breach
http://www.gbhap.com
Founded in 1961, Gordon & Breach is a worldwide group of publishing companies concerned with science, technology, medicine, the arts and humanities. The group today publishes nearly 300 journals, as well as books, magazines, reviews, monographs, videotapes, and CDs serving a broad range of academic and scientific disciplines. You can check out a complete listing of over 4,000 titles in print, view details of the latest and forthcoming titles, and consult its online journal schedule.

Gothic Image Publications
http://www.isleofavalon.co.uk/gothic/gi.pub/start.html
Gothic Image produces material in the fields of earth mysteries, sacred landscape, and consciousness studies.

Gower
http://www.gowerpub.com
Based in Aldershot, UK, Gower is a leading publisher on management and business practice. Its books range from 1,000-page handbooks to practical manuals and popular paperbacks, covering all the main functions of management. Gower also produces training videos and activities manuals, and books on library and information management. You can add your name to Gower's mailing list, view author guidelines, search its catalogue, and use its shopping cart facility.

Granta Books
http://www.granta.com
Granta offers a limited but stylishly produced online magazine of new writing. It has recently launched an ambitious new line of books in the UK, covering contemporary fiction, reportage, travel, and more. These titles were not yet available online when the site was reviewed, but promised soon, together with a complete interactive guide. You are invited to register to receive updates on the progress of the site.

Green Books
http://www.greenbooks.co.uk
Green Books is a small independent publishing company seeking to inform and inspire the general reader about ecological, spiritual and cultural issues. It produces books on organic and forest gardening, renewable energy and ecological building, native American, politics, local economics, and more.

Greenhill Books
http://www.greenhillbooks.com
Based in London, Greenhill publishes military books and distributes for other military book publishers. Founded in 1984, its authors are mainly British and American, but include German, Russian and some from other countries. Greenhill Books is a venture of the military publisher Lionel Leventhal, founder of Arms & Armour Press.

Grub Street
http://www.grubstreet.co.uk/
Grub Street produces illustrated non-fiction titles covering military, aviation, cookery, wine and health subjects.

Guinness
http://www.guinnessrecords.com/
This is the home of *The Guinness Book of Records.* Using an attractive magazine-style format, this well-designed site tells you all you want to know about the activities of Guinness publishing. You can read the latest news on amazing record attempts, check out the latest schedules for its TV show, and meet the contestants, search its official records, visit its club area and join in the fun, and test your knowledge on its quiz.

Gulf Publishing
http://www.gulfpub.com/books.html
Founded in 1916, Gulf has well over 400 titles in print, focusing on scientific and technical, human resource development, and management.

David Hall
http://www.davidhall.co.uk/
David Hall is the UK's largest independent publisher of angling magazines. These pages explain how to subscribe to the best magazines in the sport. All its titles are produced by practising anglers. 'That's what makes us better than the rest, we understand your angling problems, we'll solve them.'

Hamish Hamilton – see Penguin.

Hanson Cooke
http://www.hcooke.co.uk/
Hanson Cooke, based in London, is part of the publicly quoted Columbus Group. Sample titles include *The Commonwealth African Investment Almanac, The Commonwealth Yearbook, The Commonwealth Trade & Investment Almanac, The Commonwealth Banking Almanac, Global Communications*, and *Global Aid.*

Harlin Quist
http://www.manning-partnership.co.uk/hq.html
Harlin Quist is a small independent UK childrens' books publisher. Their list is marketed by the Manning Partnership and distributed by Littlehampton Book Services.

HarperCollins
http://www.harpercollins.co.uk/
This UK page links you automatically to the international HarperCollins 'Fire and Water' book publishing web site.

Hart Publishing
http://www.hartpub.co.uk/
Hart is an independent and privately owned law publisher founded in Oxford in 1996. The site includes guidelines for authors, and secure online ordering facilities. Recent sample titles include *Tortious Liability of Statutory Bodies* and *Privacy and Employment Law.*

Harvey Miller Publishing – see Gordon and Breach Publishers.

Harvill Press
http://www.harvill-press.com
This UK firm, independent since 1995 after some years in the Collins stable, continues to publish fiction, biography, literary criticism, travel, poetry, philosophy and religion. A feature of the list is its international cultural links and translations of Russian, European and other works. The site includes a link to worldwide writing where you can 'explore the Harvill atlas and find books from over 70 countries.'

Haynes
http://www.haynes.com
Based in Yeovil, this UK company is a market leader in the production and sale of automotive and motorcycle repair manuals. Each one is based on a tear-down and rebuild of the specific vehicle. Hundreds of photographs are taken to accompany the step-by-step instructions written from actual experience. It also has titles on decorating and home DIY, cycle repair and maintenance, mountain biking and ride guides. The firm has offices in the USA, France, Sweden and Australia.

Hayward Medical Communications
http://www.hayward.co.uk
With offices in Newmarket and London, Hayward as a publisher of specialist online and traditional journals on medical topics. Sample titles include *The British Journal of Dermatology Nursing, The International Journal of Gastroenterology, The Journal of Nursing Care,* and *The Medical Microbiologist.* You can apply online for details of subscriptions.

Healthworks Online
http://www.healthworks.co.uk
Based in Leeds, Healthworks' CD-rom shop features over 700 medical CD-rom database and multimedia titles. It also publishes a range of newsletters including *Health on the Internet, The Medical Computing* and *Disabilities Informer.* You can obtain a free sample email newsletter on request.

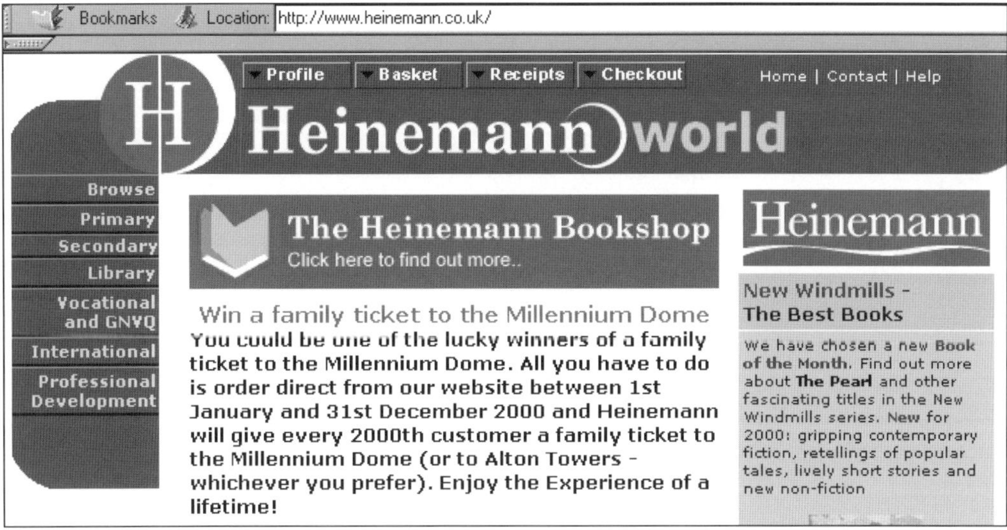

Fig. 40. Heinemann Educational is a key resource for primary, secondary, vocational education. The site also offers professional development services for teachers.

Heartland Publishing
http://www.heartland.co.uk
Heartland is a small independent general book publisher based in Kent.

Heinemann Educational
http://www.heinemann.co.uk
Heinemann Educational is the largest educational publisher in the UK, producing materials for the 4 to 19 age range. This appealing-looking site has a magazine-style look, with links to lots of topics and resources of interest to teachers, parents, pupils and authors. For example, the clearly laid out business and economics section offers a series of free case studies, with expert advice and study skills materials which the student can use. Its catalogues, which you can request online, cover English, science, drama, geography, history, music, learning support, politics, school management, and more.

Helicon Publishing
http://www.helicon.co.uk
Based in Oxford, Helicon is a pioneer of electronic and multimedia educational products. It was the first British company to publish a multimedia encyclopedia and the first to publish a British encyclopedia online. Its subject areas are general reference, arts, history, biography, science and computing, and military history. It continues to publish in book, CD-rom, and online form. Helicon was acquired by W H Smith in 1998.

Hobsons Careers Publishing
http://www.hobsons.co.uk/
Hobsons has long experience of publishing educational and recruitment guides for students. It began in 1974 as an outgrowth of the Careers Research and Advisory Centre (CRAC), a charitable organisation based in Cambridge. Today it offers details of thousands of career and educa-

tional opportunities in the UK and around the world. The company is owned by the Daily Mail and General Trust plc.

Hollis Directories
http://www.hollis-pr.co.uk
Hollis produces public relations and business entertainment directories. Its titles include *The Hollis UK Press & Public Relations Annual, Hollis Europe, Hollis Sponsorship & Donations Yearbook, Hollis Sponsorship Newsletter, Hollis Sponsorship Awards, Hollis Business Entertainment, Hollis Database, Willings Press Guide, Advertisers Annual, The Marketing Handbook* and *Handy Hollis.* The site includes extensive links to public relations consultancies.

Horizon Scientific
http://www.horizonpress.com
Located in Norfolk, Horizon Scientific produces specialist books and journals on molecular biology and microbiology. Full chapter abstracts and book reviews are available online. The site offers fully secure online ordering. The company also has offices in Portland, Oregon, USA. Sample titles include *The Journal of Molecular Microbiology and Biotechnology, The Internet for the Molecular Biologist* and *Gene Cloning and Analysis.*

How To Books
http://www.howtobooks.co.uk
Oxford-based How To Books publishes a large range of self-help paperback titles in the areas of careers, personal development, business and other life skills.

C. Hurst & Co
http://www.hurstpub.co.uk/
Hurst is a publisher of contemporary history, politics and sociology with particular reference to Eastern Europe, Africa, Asia and the Islamic world.

IBC (Informa)
http://www.ibc-uk.com/
International Business Communications is a leading UK conference and publishing group. It provides market information for a wide cross section of business and industry. It forms part of the Informa Group created when IBC merged with LLP Group in 1998. With offices in 16 countries, Informa offers 'must have' business-to-business information through 3,500 conferences and seminars and 750 print and electronic publications.

IM Publications
http://www.impub.co.uk/
IM Publications is an independent publishing company, specialising in spectroscopy. As well as its own journals and books, it has links with *Spectroscopy Europe*, the controlled circulation magazine for spectroscopists in Europe, and NIR Publications, a specialist publisher of

information on NIR spectroscopy and technology. The company is based in Chichester, West Sussex.

Imperial College Press
http://www.icpress.demon.co.uk
ICP produces authoritative books and journals in both printed and electronic formats. It is a joint venture between Imperial College of Science, Technology & Medicine and World Scientific Publishing. Sample titles include *Introduction to Stochastic Calculus with Applications* and *Dynamics of Complex Fluids.* Copies of its textbooks are available for lecturers to evaluate for class use.

Inkata Press – see Butterworth-Heinemann.

Institute of Directors
http://www.iod.co.uk/
The IoD is the top UK organisation representing individual company directors. It has 47,000 members, including directors on the boards of three-quarters of *The Times* Top 1,000 companies, as well as 65 per cent of members who are directors of small and medium-sized enterprises. It publishes *The Director* magazine, a series of *Director's Guides* and *Pocket Books*, and a range of business books such as its *Corporate Governance Series* which can be purchased online.

Institute of Management
http://www.inst-mgt.org.uk/
The mission of the Institute of Management is to promote the art and science of management. It offers a range of materials and services to support managers, including CD-rom databases of useful information for desktop use. The IM Management Information Databases form the one of the largest collections of resources on management in Europe, focusing on all aspects of management principles, theories, techniques and practices.

Institute of Personnel & Development
http://www.ipd.co.uk
The IPD has over 90,000 members and is the leading UK professional institute for those involved in the management and development of people. This is a substantial and well- organised web site. It is an established commercial publisher of books and materials in the human resources field. Sample titles include *Competing for the Future, Decision Making and Problem Solving,* and *Ethical Leadership*. You can order through bookshops or direct from its distributor, Plymbridge. IPD members ordering books from Plymbridge can claim a 10 per cent discount on most titles by quoting their IPD membership number.

Institute of Physics
http://www.iop.org/
The UK-based Institute of Physics is an international learned society and professional body for the advancement and dissemination of physics,

pure and applied, and promotion of physics education. Its books range from large-scale reference works, specialist monographs, and student textbooks to popular science books suitable for a range of readerships.

Intellect
http://www.intellect-net.com
Exeter-based Intellect publishes books and journals of both scholarly and general interest. It tracks the newest developments in digital creative media such as art, film, television, design and the web. It examines theories in education, language, gender study, and international culture. It also publishes in AI, computer science and human-computer interaction. This site contains Intellect's publication lists, sub sites of general interest, and sample journal articles.

Intermediate Technology
http://www.oneworld.org/itdg/
Intermediate Technology is a development agency and British registered charity that works with rural communities in Africa, Asia and Latin America.

International Maritime Organisation
http://www.imo.org
The IMO is a specialised United Nations agency responsible for improving maritime safety and preventing pollution from ships. Its publishes the numerous texts – conventions, codes, regulations, recommendations, guidelines – prepared by the Organisation as part of its work programme. Today, IMO has about 250 titles available in English, some in electronic formats. They are translated into French and Spanish and many also into Arabic, Chinese and Russian. The web site itself can be viewed in English, French and Spanish.

Internet Handbooks
http://www.internet-handbooks.co.uk
Internet Handbooks are designed to help all kinds of people explore the possibilities of the internet. The illustrated paperbacks are aimed at householders, students, job hunters, people at work, business managers and professional people throughout the private and public sectors. Sample titles include *Using Email on the Internet, The Internet for Students,* and *Personal Finance on the Internet.*

IPC Magazines
http://www.ipc.co.uk/
This is a leading UK consumer and trade magazine publishing group. With its readership surveys and market analyses, the web site appears to be mainly directed towards advertisers and business users.

Irish Academic Press
http://www.iap.ie
Irish Academic Press is a long established Dublin-based publisher of books of Irish interest. It publishes early and modern Irish history, legal

history, military history, social history, local history, women's studies, famine studies, genealogy, Irish literature, arts and architecture, music, education, and Italian studies.

Jane's Information Group
http://www.janes.com/
A hundred years ago Fred Jane, the son of a Surrey vicar, began to annotate the details of the world's fighting ships. In 1898, the first edition of *Jane's All the World's Fighting Ships* (later shortened to *Jane's Fighting Ships*) was released and soon became an authoritative guide to ship recognition and naval intelligence. Today, Janes is widely regarded as the ultimate reference for defence, aerospace and transportation information. Its titles include *Jane's Defence Weekly, Jane's Fighting Ships* and *Jane's All the World's Aircraft.*

Janus Publishing Company
http://www.januspublishing.co.uk
Formed in 1991, Janus publishes about 70 titles a year in categories ranging from poetry to psychology, and memoirs to religion, many written by first time authors. It is a 'subsidy publisher'. In other words the author is required to make a substantial investment in the costs of publishing but then shares in any benefits.

Jordans
http://www.jordanpublishing.co.uk
The name of Jordans has been long associated with new company formations, company searches, administration, property services, trade marks and names. It is also an independent legal publisher, producing titles on such varied legal subjects as health and safety law through to charity law.

Michael Joseph – see Penguin.

Kegan Paul
http://www.demon.co.uk/keganpaul/
Kegan Paul International has around for over a hundred years and remains independent. From its London offices, it continues to build a reputation for scholarship and quality. The list remains strong in its traditional subjects – Africa, Arabic linguistics, art, architecture, archaeology, Asian studies, China, Egytpology, environmental studies, natural science, international studies and law, Islam, Japan, Korea, literature and poetry, the middle east, oriental philosophy and religion, the Pacific, photographic and travel books. It is distributed in the UK by John Wiley & Sons.

Jessica Kingsley
http://www.jkp.com/
Jessica Kingsley publishes books for professionals and academics across the social sciences, specialising mainly in social work, psychiatry, therapies, regional studies and higher education policy. It also publishes books on autism and Asperger Syndrome. It welcomes proposals for books in these areas.

Kogan Page
http://www.kogan-page.co.uk
Kogan Page is a leading independent business book publisher, and this detailed and well-structured web site reflects this. Formed by Philip Kogan in 1967, the company publishes key business information and practical guidance at affordable prices. It also produces books on education and training, careers, personal development and – through Earthscan – the environment. The list comprises over 3,500 books, journals, cassettes and CD-roms, and about 300 new titles and new editions are published each year.

Ladybird
http://www.penguin.co.uk/ladybird/index.html
Ladybird publishes a large range of pocket-size illustrated books for very young children. The imprint is part of the Penguin Group (which also publishes the Puffin titles).

Law Pack
http://www.lawpack.co.uk
The web site promotes a range of DIY legal publications enabling users to handle their own straightforward legal transactions at a fraction of the cost of going to a solicitor. These include legal books, legal form packs, legal kits, and legal software featuring user-friendly pull-down menus, point-and-click mouse controls, and the ability to customise type fonts. They cover such topics as making a will, setting up a limited company, collecting a debt, and letting residential property. You can complete its ready-to-use forms or modify them for your own needs.

Publications
The Law Society publishe
key areas such as proper
marketing and client com
View our catalogue
- Accounts, Cost and Fe
- Criminal Law
- Directories
- Employment Law
- Environmental Law
- Family and Social We
- Financial Services
- Information Technolo
- Litigation
- Marketing and Client

Law Society Publishing
http://www.publishing.lawsociety.org.uk/
Law Society Publishing produces books, directories, CDs and other information products for solicitors, designed to help develop their professional expertise and commercial practices.

Learned Information
http://info.learned.co.uk/
Part of the multinational VNU Group, Learned Information is a publisher

and conference organiser, serving the library community. It produces an extensive range of journals, books, CD-roms, newspapers, conferences and exhibitions for many industry sectors. Its titles include *Information World Review, Online & CD-Rom Review, The Electronic Library, The Online Manual, Digital Publishing Technologies* and *Knowledge Management*. It also publishes a series of database directories such as *Datasite* and *Computer Software & Services, The Computer Users' Year Book* and *The Software Users' Year Book.* The company runs the annual Online Information fair in London.

Learning Matters
http://www.learningmatters.co.uk/
Exeter-based Learning Matters publishes books and online materials for trainee teachers, and for newly qualified teachers embarking on their careers.

Leckie & Leckie
http://www.leckie-and-leckie.co.uk
This Scottish publisher has developed a range of study guides to help students pass their Standard Grade and Higher Grade school exams. These titles are also useful for GCSE exams. Subjects offered include art and design, biology, chemistry, computing studies, craft and design, drama, French, geography, history, maths, office and information studies, physical education, physics, science, computing studies, physics. The company is based in St Andrews.

Letts Educational
http://www.lettsed.co.uk
Letts is a market leader in the publication of study and revision materials for British children and young people. Its titles cover the needs of pre-school, National Curriculum key stages 1 to 4, and post-16 students. The clear and well-designed web site provides book information, sample pages, and free online revision notes for students. It also offers education news updates, and forums.

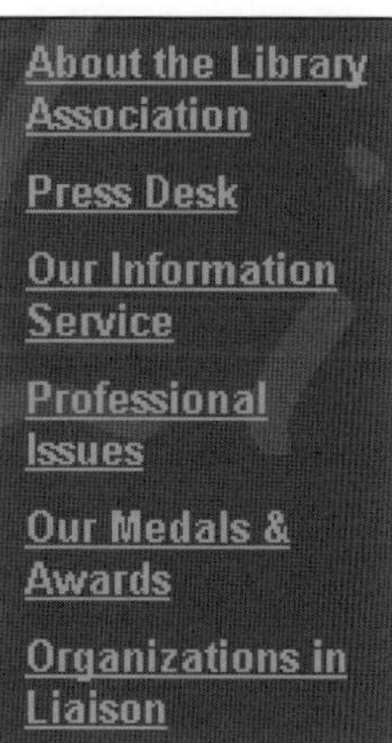

Library Association Publishing
http://www.la-hq.org.uk/lapublishing
Books and materials for librarians and information management professionals and students.

Lion Publishing
http://www.lion-publishing.co.uk
Founded in 1971, Lion is an independent book publisher based in Oxford. Its speciality is books relating to Christianity, and these range from major illustrated reference books to gift-style anthologies, and from children's bibles to contemporary social issues. The site brings you interviews with authors, extracts from new books, background news and articles. Check out its online magazine *Roar* each month for the latest updates.

Frances Lincoln
http://www.frances-lincoln.com/
Frances Lincoln is a publisher of illustrated adult and children's books designed for the international co-edition market. The firm specialises in board and novelty books, fiction and non-fiction picture books, gardening, health, interior design, and photographic baby books.

Liverpool University Press
http://www.liverpool-unipress.co.uk/
LUP focuses on archaeology, art history, current affairs, English, French and Hispanic literature, history, primary science education, science fiction criticism, urban and regional planning, and veterinary science.

Lonely Planet
http://www.lonelyplanet.com/
Lonely Planet is known worldwide for its practical, reliable and no-nonsense travel guides. Its books contain streetwise travel information, maps, photos, and background historical and cultural information. It has every continent covered – even Antarctica – with a burgeoning list of travel guides, atlases, phrasebooks and travel literature. This must be one of the best travel publishing web sites on the internet, packed with good design, customer-friendly content and innovative features. Visit the Postcards area, where you can 'swing on the traveller's grapevine', and don't miss the Thorn Tree, a kind of newsgroup area.

Luath Press
http://www.luath.co.uk
Edinburgh-based Luath Press takes its name from Robert Burns. It publishes a diverse range of material, primarily but not exclusively focusing on Scotland. Sample titles include *Blind Harry's Wallace, Rum: Nature's Island*, and *The Bannockburn Years.*

Lutterworth Press
http://www.lutterworth.com/
Lutterworth is an old-established publisher of adult general titles, religious and children's titles. It can trace its origins back to the Religious Tract Society in Georgian London, with its headquarters just off Fleet Street. Today its imprints also include James Clarke & Co (academic and religious titles) and Acorn Editions (local and minority interest titles).

Macdonald Young Books – see Wayland Publishers.

Macmillan
http://www.macmillan.com
Macmillan was founded in 1843 and has published such greats as Lewis Carroll, Tennyson, Hardy, Kipling, Yeats, and Keynes. Now its academic, educational and literary publishing spans college texts, scientific journals, and large scale reference works such as *The New Grove Dictionary of Music and Musicians, Dictionary of Art,* and *Encyclopedia of the Life Sciences*. This substantial and professional-looking site also includes links to the home pages of some of its academic and technical authors.

Macmillan is part of the German publishing conglomerate Holtzbrinck.

Macmillan-Heinemann ELT
http://www.helt.co.uk/
Macmillan Heinemann ELT is the education division of Macmillan Publishers, publishing educational textbooks and supplementary materials in every subject for the international market. It is particularly well known for its English LanguageTeaching materials. It publishes primary, secondary and adult course books, exam texts, reading and language development materials. With over 40 companies and offices world wide, the division comprises a network of local publishing operations, each focused on the curriculum needs of the country in which it operates. You can register online to obtain free classroom posters.

Made Simple Books
http://www.madesimple.co.uk/
Recognisable for many years by its distinctive orange, black and yellow cover designs, the paperback Made Simple series has been an imprint of Butterworth-Heinemann since 1968, and now has its own dedicated web site. Here you can find out about the latest developments, especially in the areas of computing and business titles.

Mayfield Books
http://www.btinternet.com/-mayfield/
Mayfield are publishers of books on horology. Sample titles include *Kent Clocks and Clockmakers* and *Restoring Musical Boxes & Musical Clocks*. A useful feature of the site is its link to 'The horology index: the complete guide to horological information on the internet' which contains a massive 3,000 horology links, sorted by category.

MCB University Press
http://www.mcb.co.uk/
Based in Bradford, UK, MCBUP is an independent and privately owned company. It was founded in 1967 by a group of senior Business School academics dissatisfied with the publishing outlets then available. Today it is a leading publisher of journals, books and electronic media in business and management. It covers economics, education, finance, health and environment, library and information services, logistics and purchasing, management, marketing, materials science and technology, and training and development.

McGraw-Hill UK
http://www.mcgraw-hill.co.uk/
This is the European web site of McGraw-Hill, whose UK offices are in Maidenhead, Berkshire. It contains a searchable and browseable product catalogue with details of nearly 30,000 in-print titles covering business and economics, computing, engineering, sciences, health care and more. It also offers an online inspection copy requesting service for university lecturers.

Mehring Books
http://www.mehringbooks.co.uk
Mehring is a specialist Sheffield-based firm which publishes socialist books and pamphlets in the English language, ranging from history and philosophy to culture and contemporary politics. The imprint is named after Franz Mehring, a writer and historian of the Second International, the Marxist movement before World War One.

Mercier Press
http://www.mercier.ie/mercier
Mercier is a publisher of general trade books, based in Dublin. It produces books on cookery, poetry, fiction, travel, literature, history, archaeology, folklore social issues, mind, body and spirit, biography, Irish language and other topics.

Metal Bulletin
http://www.metalbulletin.co.uk/
Metal Bulletin issues books, directories, and global news journals for the iron, steel and non-ferrous metals industries. You can use this site to find out more about its products, order online, and download free sample copies or selected pages of selected products, and go to the pages of individual products for more information. Sample titles include *The World Mining Directory and Iron*, and *Steel Works of the World CD-Rom.*

Microform Academic
http://www.microform.co.uk
Microform Academic Publishers are located near Wakefield, in West Yorkshire. This site contains a complete and up-to-date listing of all the microfilms and microfiches currently available in its extensive catalogues, which cover African, American, Caribbean, Irish and Slavonic studies, literature, history and education.

Military Press
http://www.militarypress.co.uk
Based in Milton Keynes, the Military Press is a specialist imprint for books on war and warfare, especially dealing with the history of the British army in India, and the Second World War.

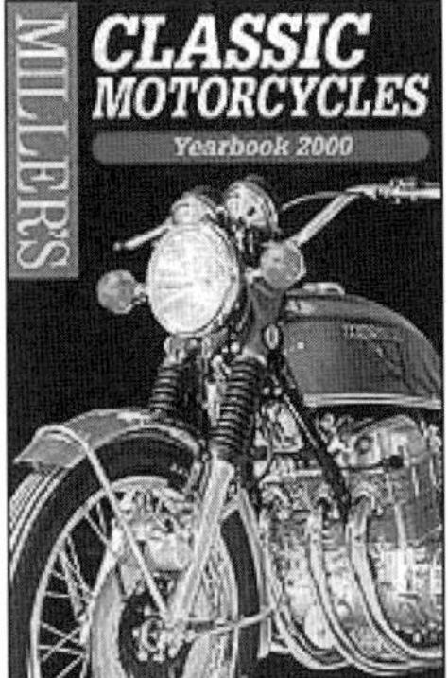

Miller's Antiques Price Guides
http://www.millers.uk.com/
Miller's leads the field in antiques publishing, including the annual best-selling *Miller's Antiques Price Guide.* The web site features a new Miller's Collectors Forum where you can buy, sell and make contact with other collectors online. Miller's is now published by Mitchell Beazley, an imprint of Octopus Publishing Group.

Minerva Press
http://www.minerva-press.co.uk
Minerva Press is an independent 'subsidy publisher', producing a range of

titles in many different categories, but specialising in the publication of books by new authors.

Mitchell Beazley
http://www.mitchell-beazley.co.uk
A division of the Octopus Publishing Group, Mitchell Beazley is one of the leading illustrated reference book publishers in the UK, especially known for titles on antiques, art and design, interiors and craft, gardening, general reference, and wine and food. Its titles include the Miller antique price guides, and Hugh Johnson's books on wine.

Multilingual Matters
http://www.multilingual-matters.com
Based near Bristol, Multilingual Matters produces books and journals on all aspects of multilingual and multicultural education, including second language learning. Sample titles include *Dyslexia: A Parents' and Teachers' Guide*, and *Literacy for Sustainable Development in the Age of Information.* The functional-looking site includes guidelines for prospective authors.

National Trust
http://bookshelf.nationaltrust.org.uk
The National Trust produces a wide range of books to promote its work and the enormous variety of properties in its care. If you would like to know more about what the Tudors ate, how the Victorians washed their clothes, and who was responsible for running some of the biggest houses in the land, then look no further than its 'Bookshelf' web site. The Trust has over 60 titles in which you can find the answers to these questions and more.

Natural History Museum
http://www.nhm.ac.uk/info/publications/
Founded in Victorian London, this famous Kensington Museum is an established publisher of illustrated books on art, botany, entomology, history of science, mineralogy, palaeontology and zoology.

Newnes – see Butterworth-Heinemann.

No Exit Press
http://www.noexit.co.uk/
No Exit Press is a small independent UK publisher of crime fiction. The site includes some links to crime authors and crime magazines web sites.

Nottingham University Press
http://www.nup.com
NUP publishes and books and journals in the fields of agronomy, animal science, English language, food science, forestry, information technology, law, medicine, psychology, sport and general interest.

O'Brien Press
http://www.obrien.ie
The O'Brien Press was formed in 1974, evolving out of a family-run printing and type house. Located in Dublin it has published a diverse trade list of over 600 books, some 250 of which remain in print. These cover fiction, architecture, travel, humour, the environment, history, biography, classic literature, autobiography, guides, reference, and business books. Rather functional in appearance, the web site nevertheless contains detailed information on most of its titles, together with thumbnail cover pictures which download quickly.

Octagon
http://www.clearlight.com/octagon/
For 30 years, London-based Octagon has been a primary source of information by and about the Sufis, past and present. The thirty and more works by Idries Shah (1924-1996) published in that period present his experiential psychology in the Sufi manner, ranging between studies of traditional psychologies, anthropology, travel, literature, philosophy and Sufi thought.

Octopus
http://www.reedbooks.co.uk/opg.htm
Originally founded by Paul Hamlyn, the Octopus Publishing Group is one of the world's leading publishers of colourful books for the consumer market. Its mainly non-fiction list covers mass market areas such as cookery, travel, gardening, sports, and illustrated history. Its imprints include Octopus, Hamlyn, Bounty Books, Brimax and Mitchell Beazley. A management buyout from Reed Books in August 1998 saw the company once more become an independent business, based in London's docklands.

Omnibus
http://www.omnibuspress.com/
Omnibus Press is one of the world's best known publishers of books about music and musicians. Its catalogue covers everyone from Guns N' Roses, The Velvet Underground and The Cranberries to Bach, Purcell and Beethoven. Each year it produces some 600 new music publications and products including MIDI-files, CD-roms and new media products, single sheets, choral works and children's publications, and illustrated books. Omnibus is part of the Music Sales Group of companies.

Open University Press
http://www.openup.co.uk
The Open University Press is an independent academic press – independent, because in 1988 the University sold the press to its senior management. Its publications support students, academics and professionals in the fields of education, health and social welfare, counselling and psychotherapy, management, sociology, women's studies, politics, psychology, literature and cultural studies, higher education and crimin-

ology. Sample titles include *Research Methods for Nurses and the Caring Professions, Counselling Skills in Social Work Practice*, and *Black Students and Higher Education.* Secure credit card ordering is available over the internet via its distributor, Marston Book Services.

Orbit Books
http://www.orbitbooks.co.uk
Established a generation ago, Orbit is a publisher of science fiction and fantasy titles. Its authors include Terry Brooks, Iain Banks and Robert Jordan. The site has a secure ordering system. Orbit is an imprint of Little Brown.

Ordnance Survey
http://www.ordsvy.gov.uk
OS is the UK's national mapping agency, producing and marketing maps, computer data and other information for business, leisure, educational and administrative use. Its database records over 200 million features of the British landscape right down to telephone boxes and private garages. It is effectively a seamless map of Great Britain, replacing the need to separately maintain around 230,000 individual paper maps. The site includes some free downloadable mapping. Maps at up to 1:250 000 scale for the whole of Great Britain are provided free for users to print for personal and internal business use. In addition, a small number of images can be captured for use in your own web pages.

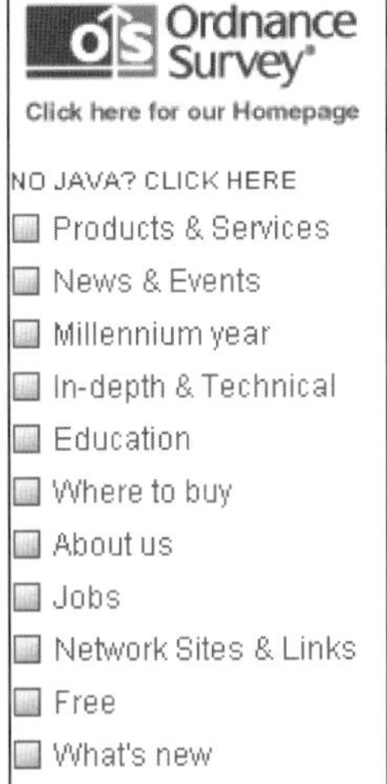

Osborne Books
http://www.osbornebooks.co.uk
Osborne Books, based in Worcester UK, is a business education publisher. It produces business finance texts both for GNVQ Business and for accountancy titles, which are widely used both in the UK and overseas. Sample titles include *Payroll Accounting, Financial Accounting* and *Costing, Reports and Returns*. You can download its TestMaster demo software. The firm has also diversified into historical publishing, with the Osborne Heritage imprint. Authors can telephone to obtain a free author pack. Book ordering is by traditional methods.

Osprey Publishing
http://www.osprey-publishing.co.uk
Based in near Oxford, Osprey is a leading international publisher of illustrated books in the military, aviation, and automotive fields. Its series include *Men-at-Arms, Campaign, Order of Battle, Aircraft of the Aces, Combat Aircraft, Colour Car Classics, Car Restoration and Maintenance, Elite, Warrior, Classic Aircraft, New Vanguard, Civil Aircraft, Aircraft Cutaways, Motorcycles, Automotive Histories* and others. The Osprey Military Club is open for an annual membership fee of £10. The benefits include the quarterly magazine *Osprey Military Messenger* and various concessionary offers. The site offers links to other sites of military, automotive, and aviation interest.

Overseas Development Institute
http://www.oneworld.org/odi/
The ODI is Britain's leading independent think-tank on international development and humanitarian issues. It publishes an extensive range of books in association with leading publishers, *Special Reports, Development Policy Studies* (in association with Routledge). *Research Studies, Working Papers*, and other materials. Available on its web pages are *Briefing Papers* on contemporary development issues, *Natural Resource Perspectives Papers*, and *DFID Key Sheets* for development in the natural environment.

Oxbow Books
http://www.oxbowbooks.com
Oxbow publishes around twenty specialist monographs a year, mainly on archaeology, but also in related historical and scientific fields. It also distributes books for a number of learned societies and organisations. On the web site you can look through thousands of archaeology, classics and medieval titles, including its own publications and those it distributes for other publishers. Books can be searched for and ordered online, or you can request a free paper catalogue.

Oxfam Publishing
http://www.oxfam.org.uk/
Oxfam publishes and distributes books and other resource materials for development practitioners, academics, schools, children and young people, and the general public, as part of its programme of advocacy, education, and information.

Oxford Academic
http://www.ool.co.uk/oxac/
Oxford Academic is an offshoot of Oxford Open Learning, established in 1989 as an adult education publishing and teaching organisation. Oxford Academic itself is a new publishing house whose aim is to disseminate original scholarly research mainly by electronic means. Its particular interest lies in the electronic publication of doctoral theses that bear significant intellectual value, but which are likely to be rejected by conventional academic presses. It aims to publish 1,000 monographs by the end of 2001 – the answer to the prayers of many academic researchers.

Oxford University Press
http://www.oup.co.uk/
OUP is the world's largest university press. It publishes a staggering 3,000 new titles a year, operates in more than fifty countries, and employs some 3,000 people worldwide. It has become familiar to millions through its diverse publishing programme ranging from scholarly works in all subject areas, to bibles, music, textbooks, children's books, English language teaching materials, business books, dictionaries, reference books, journals, and electronic publishing. OUP is an integral part of the University of Oxford, incorporated by royal charter, and governed under university statute by the Delegates of the Press, who are appointed

Fig. 41. This is the impressive web site of Oxford University Press, packed with information and services for English language learning and teaching, children's publishing, journals, dictionaries, international contacts and more.

from the academic staff of the University. This is a large and well-organised web site, which also offers secure online ordering.

Palladian Law Publishing
http://www.palladianlaw.com/
Palladian is a law publisher specialising in European trade and technology law and international commercial law.

Pavilion Publishing
http://www.pavpub.com/
Based in Brighton, Pavilion is a British publisher of training materials and a conference organiser in the health and social care sector. It publishes and distributes 200 titles and five journals, organises over 80 conferences per year and manages around 30 events for other organisations. It works in partnership with many voluntary organisations. Its web site offers you information on publications and staff training materials, journals including abstracts and related articles, plus conferences where you can find a listing of forthcoming events. You can download previews of its publications.

Pearson Publishing
http://www.pearson.co.uk/
Based in Cambridge, this company produces and distributes educational resources across the curriculum for primary, secondary and further education, designed to give practical help and guidance to teachers, and administrative support. A useful feature of this clear and well organised site are the A-Z links to hundreds of schools web sites, sixth form college web sites, and a searchable database of educational sites from around the UK and worldwide.

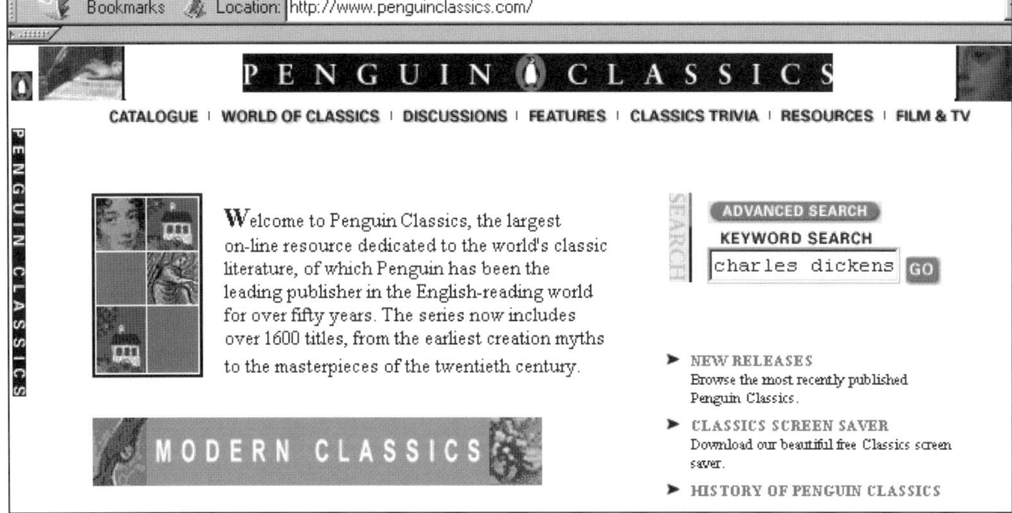

Fig. 42. Penguin has developed this web site specially to promote Penguin Classics, a publishing division which now runs to some 1,600 titles reflecting the literature of the world.

Penguin UK
http://www.penguin.co.uk/
Founded by Allen Lane in 1935, at a time when there was little in the way of cheap entertainment, Penguin pioneered its famous range of sixpenny paperbacks that brought classics and contemporary literature to a much wider reading public. The distinctive orange, white and black homepage leads you into a large, stylish and impressive site which will tell you everything you want to know about this famous publisher, its history and current publishing, and its huge list of titles and authors. There is an online magazine called *Read-Me*, features, competitions, job opportunities, and a searchable database of some 11,000 titles. Penguin's online ordering facility is naturally a fully secure service, where your credit card transaction is encrypted for privacy.

Pentland Press
http://www.pentlandpress.co.uk/
Pentland is a publisher of fiction, poetry, military, aviation, maritime, memoirs, biography, children's, religion, philosophy, travel and literature. The site deals with self-publishing, co-operative publishing, joint-venture publishing and subsidy publishing.

Pergamon Open Learning – see Butterworth-Heinemann.

Perpetuity Press
http://www.le.ac.uk/CWIS/AD/PO/CP/RE/cppp.html
Based at Leicester University, Perpetuity Press specialises in titles relating to crime, security, criminal justice and law. Each of the publications listed has been edited or written by lecturers at the Scarman Centre for the Study of Public Order.

Phaidon Press
http://dbooks.hypermart.net/phaidon-3.html
At the time of writing Phaidon Press did not appear to have its own web site, but you can explore its highly regarded list of art books and purchase here through Amazon.com, mostly at a discount.

Pharmaceutical Press
http://www.pharmpress.com
The Pharmaceutical Press is the publications division of The Royal Pharmaceutical Society of Great Britain. The site contains details of its major reference works, annual publications, and journals. Sample titles in its searchable catalogue include *International Pharmacopoeia, Pharmacy Practice* and a *Handbook of Nonprescription Drugs.* The site includes a secure ordering facility.

George Philip
http://www.philips-maps.co.uk
The London-based firm has been publishing maps since 1834. On its site you can explore a wide range of titles, including atlases of the world, Ordnance Survey road atlases of Britain, encyclopedias, and many other reference materials including maps ands globes. You can view samples of the high-quality digital data that Philips offer for a whole range of applications, review available business gifts and incentives, find out about foreign rights sales, and obtain a list of key contacts including email addresses. The site enables you to complete an order form, but you then have to print it out and send it by fax or post.

Piatkus
http://www.piatkus.co.uk
Piatkus is an independent publisher, publishing 200 books a year. Its subject areas include fiction, health, mind body and spirit, self-help, parenting, business, popular psychology, biography and history. When reviewed the site offered a 25% discount on all titles and free postage on orders of two books or more (UK only).

Pickering & Chatto
http://www.pickeringchatto.com
Bloomsbury-based Pickering & Chatto publishes definitive editions of major historical figures, thematic collections of original texts and cleaned up reproductions of important journals and magazines. Its online catalogue is organised under literature, romanticism, history of economic thought, 18th century studies, history of political thought, women's writing, history of science, and British history. You can print out an online order form and order by fax or mail, or order on line using a credit card.

Pimlico – see Random House.

Pinter & Martin Publishers
http://www.pinter.dircon.co.uk
The London-based company issues a small number of fiction and non-fiction titles. You are invited to order its titles via the Internet Bookshop, or by fax or post. The firm is not to be confused with (Frances) Pinter Publishers.

Pluto Press
http://www.plutobooks.com/
An independent publisher in political, labour movement and current affairs, Pluto's list covers anthropology, black studies, cultural studies, economics, environment, gender studies, history, international studies, Irish studies, law, media studies, Middle East studies, politics and political theory, and social issues. Its secure server software (SSL) is the industry standard for secure online ordering.

Policy Press
http://www.bristol.ac.uk/Publications/TPP/
The Press is an editorially independent publisher located at the Faculty of Social Sciences, University of Bristol. It produces books, journals, reports and practice guides for the academic and policy communities. Its subject areas include community care, criminal justice, race and ethnicity, family policy, child welfare, labour markets, urban and regional policy and similar topics. Book ordering is by traditional means.

Polity Press
http://www.polity.co.uk
Polity is a social science and humanities publisher in the fields of sociology, politics, media and cultural studies, gender studies, philosophy, history, geography, psychology, linguistics, literary theory, anthropology, and religion. You can register on its mailing database or to request its subject and new books catalogues. You can print out its order form and fax or mail your order to its offices in Oxford. The site includes 'resource centres' in a number of key subject areas. It also gives information for prospective authors, details of rights contacts, a directory of agents and representatives, plus distribution and customer services information.

Polygon – see Edinburgh University Press.

Portland Press
http://www.portlandpress.co.uk/
Portland Press is the wholly owned publishing subsidiary of the UK Biochemical Society. It is a not-for-profit publisher of electronic and hard copy journals and books in the cellular and molecular life sciences. The surplus from the sales of its publications are returned to the scientific community via the activities of the Biochemical Society. There is a useful and detailed site map.

PRC Publishing
http://www.interreach.com/prc
London-based PRC offers a range of colour-illustrated mass-market titles on topics ranging from Harley Davidson motorcycles to beer and World Cup football.

PricewaterhouseCoopers
http://www.pwcglobal.com/uk/
This giant global accountancy and management consulting group publishes a range of professional materials on national and international

finance, taxation, business practice, economics and law.

Pulp Faction
http://www.pulpfact.demon.co.uk
Pulp is a north London publisher of underground and contemporary fiction. Customers are referred for ordering to traditional bookshops, to Amazon, or direct from the publisher.

Puffin Books
http://www.puffin.co.uk/
This delightful site for young children is presented in the form of a colourful house, with a bedroom, games room, library, living room and bathroom. Each part of the house features something different in the way of current book news and features. The site includes information for prospective writers, as 'Unfortunately Penguin Children's Books is no longer able to accept unsolicited manuscripts. This is due to the enormous amount of manuscripts we receive.'

Ragged Bear
http://www.ragged-bears.co.uk/
Based in Andover, Hampshire, Ragged Bears are publishers and distributors of children's books from a number of different imprints. The site contains submission guidelines for authors and illustrators.

Random House
http://www.randomhouse.co.uk/
This is the UK page of Random House, the world's largest English-language general trade book publisher. The site offers a search facility, online ordering and email updates about forthcoming titles. Its authors

Fig. 43. The home page of Random House UK, which describes itself as the UK's biggest selling book publisher.

include Ian McEwan, Maeve Binchy, Louis de Bernières and Sebastian Faulks, John Grisham, Ruth Rendell, Margaret Forster, Toni Morrison, Iris Murdoch, Margaret Atwood, Bruce Chatwin, Roald Dahl, and George Orwell. You can also explore job vacancies, academic support, FAQs, a children's area, bestsellers, and more.

Reaktion Books
http://www.reaktionbooks.co.uk
Based in London, Reaktion publishes material on global art, culture, and topography. Books are listed by series, with extended details of new titles available. An ordering form and contact details are provided. The site includes details of its international representation, and a traditional style order form to fax or post.

Reed Books
http://www.reedbooks.co.uk/
This page directs you to the consumer and mass market publications of Octopus (see above).

Reed Business Information Ltd
http://www.reedbusiness.com/
This is a division of Reed Elsevier plc, which publishes more than fifty business newsletters, directories, reference books, electronic products, and online services covering markets in the UK, United States and Asia.

Reed Elsevier
http://www.r-e.com/
Reed Elsevier is one of the world's leading publishing and information businesses, employing in excess of 25,000 people worldwide. Its two parent companies are Reed International and Elsevier NV, listed on the Amsterdam, London and New York Stock Exchanges. Its publishing franchises are founded on its strength in the ownership of 'must have' scientific, professional and business information, including law. It publishes in both in print and electronic form, and its services include conferences, journals, seminars, reports, reference publishing, magazines and event organising.

Ripping Communications
http://www.ripping-pub.co.uk/
Ripping Communications aims to create the types of adventurous books, images and artwork designed to get the blood coursing. Its web site incorporates a virtual bookshop selling science fiction, sport, aviation, motorbike and other titles.

Rough Guides
http://www.roughguides.com/
Rough Guides publishes music and travel reference guides both on paper and online. There are links to travel, internet, music and news. To access the 600-site web directory from the guide, you can browse any of the categories shown on the web site. *Rough News* brings you reports from

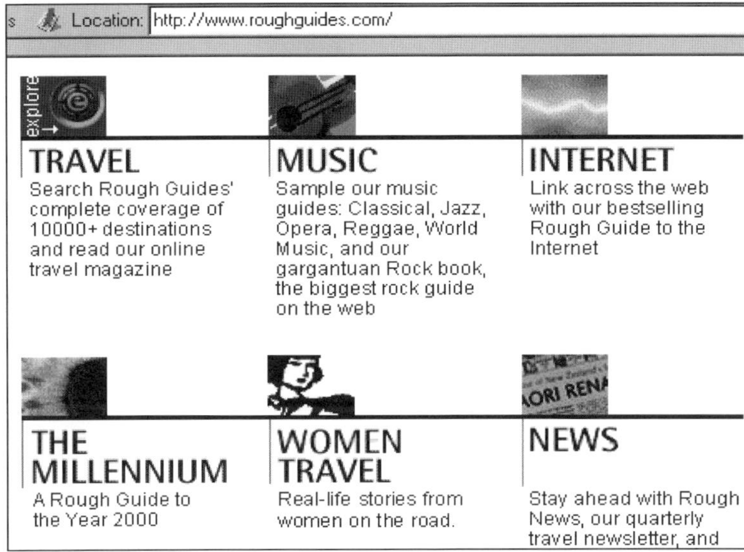

Fig. 44. The Rough Guides web site. One of its titles, *The Rough Guide to the Internet*, has been a runaway bestseller, distributed through computer shops as well as the traditional book trade.

Rough Guide writers on the road, interesting snippets from readers and news, views and debates about all things travel, music and internet. One of the firm's current best-sellers is *The Rough Guide to the Internet*.

Routledge
http://www.routledge.com/
Routledge is an old-established UK academic, trade, professional, and reference publisher. This page offers you a choice of viewing its New York web site, or its London-based web site (Taylor & Francis Group). The site includes details of its publications in the fields of classics, history, language, linguistics and philosophy, and offers some useful resource centres for particular subject areas online. Prospective authors can download a PDF file of guidelines.

Royal Society
http://www.pubs.royalsoc.ac.uk/
Based in London, the Royal Society is the principal UK academy of science. Founded in 1660, its mission is to recognise excellence in science; to encourage research and its application; to further the role of science, engineering and technology in society and to promote the public understanding of science. This is the Society's publications page containing details of its proceedings, transactions, notes and records, biographical memoirs and other items.

Sage Publications
http://www.sagepub.co.uk
Founded over 30 years ago and privately owned, Sage Publications is a leading international publisher of books, journals, and electronic media ranging right across the humanities and social sciences. Its list extends from anthropology, biology, business to urban studies, and women's studies. It produces reference books, professional books, textbooks, text supplements, workbooks, newsletters, videos, and electronic media.

WB Saunders & Baillière Tindall
http://www.hbuk.co.uk/wbs/
Founded in Philadelphia in 1888, WB Saunders Company is a leading international publisher of health science books and periodicals. Baillière Tindall's long publishing history began over 150 years ago as the English branch of a French publishing house that specialised in medicine. Today their combined list of over 2,500 titles contains major textbooks, reference works and periodicals in all medical specialities, from undergraduate textbooks to major reference works; nursing; health-related professions; veterinary medicine and dentistry. The company is a division of the American group Harcourt International.

Scholastic
http://www.scholastic.co.uk
Scholastic UK is a leading publisher of children's books and teacher's resources in the UK. Through the site you can check to see the latest issues of its magazines or look through the titles in its teacher's resource list. There is also a forward publishing list for Scholastic children's books which displays covers. You will also find information on school book fairs and school book clubs which it runs in schools throughout England, Scotland, Wales and Northern Ireland each year.

School Government Publishing Company
http://www.schoolgovernment.co.uk/
Established in 1871, SGP is a leader in UK education database compilation and management, and a publisher of standard reference works for education the UK including *The Education Authorities Directory and Annual, The Primary Education Directory* and *Special Education Directory.*

Science History Publications
http://www.shpltd.co.uk/
SHP is an academic publishing company established in 1971 and based in Cambridge. It specialises in journals in the fields of history of science, astronomy and archaeoastronomy. Its journals include *History of Science, The Journal for the History of Astronomy,* and *Archaeoastronomy.* The site offers secure online ordering.

Serpent's Tail
http://www.serpentstail.com/
The site was under reconstruction when reviewed.

Sheen Publishing
http://www.sheen-pub.co.uk
Based in Buckhurst Hill, Essex, Sheen publishes trade and technical magazines in engineering construction worldwide and for the refurbishment and restoration sectors of the UK building industry. Their titles include *Machinery World, Refurbishment Projects* and *Plant World.*

Sheffield Academic Press
http://www.shef-ac-press.co.uk/
Founded in 1976, Sheffield Academic Press specialises in academic books and journals in the humanities (especially biblical studies, archaeology and literature) and in biomedicine, science and technology. The web site contains details of over 1,000 titles published by SAP. You can search the database by author, keyword, subject or series. The site includes information for prospective authors.

Shire Publications
http://www.shirebooks.co.uk/
Shire publishes a well-known series of non-fiction budget paperbacks on a wide range of subjects, often found in bookshop counter spinners or floorstands. If you are looking for the obscure, the unusual, the collectable or the historical, this is a good place to come. The pocket guides cover everything from archaeology and ceramics to rural crafts, toys and games.

- Archaeology
- Ceramics
- Egyptology
- Garden History
- Horse Power
- Maritime
- Music
- Railways & Steam

Sidgwick & Jackson – see Macmillan.

Sigma Press
http://www.sigmapress.co.uk
Located in Wilmslow, Cheshire, Sigma is an independent UK publisher started in 1980. Its list covers dance and music, football and golf, cookery, towns and villages of Britain, local heritage, postcards from the past, murder and mystery, popular science, cycling and mountain biking, climbing and mountains, walking guides, regional UK walking guides, themed UK walking guides, and long distance UK route guides

Silver Link
http://www.slinkp-p.demon.co.uk
Based in Kettering, Silver Link Publishing and Past & Present Publishing specialise in illustrated nostalgia. Its Nostalgia Collection includes books covering railways, towns and cities, daily life, the counties of Britain, road transport including trams, buses and commercial vehicles, the rivers and waterways of Britain and Ireland.

Siren Books UK
http://www.slicc.mcmail.com
The site gives details of a small number of magazines and books on music, historical literature, photography and the performing arts. SLICC in its address stands for the St Leonard's Internet Communications Company.

E & FN Spon
http://www.efnspon.com
Based at New Fetter Lane in London, the firm was founded in 1834 as a scientific and technical bookseller and publisher. Today, it is an imprint of Routledge, and an established publisher in four professional market segments in the United Kingdom: civil engineering, the built environment,

architecture, and sports and leisure management. Its publishing programme includes books and subscription-based journals. The web site includes guidelines for authors, as well as for prospective suppliers and distributors.

Springer Science London
http://www.springer.co.uk/
This is the UK web site of Springer Verlag, a German-based company which publishes books and journals in the fields of computing, engineering, mathematics, medicine and astronomy. The site includes catalogues, electronic publications, support materials, and information for authors.

The Stationery Office
http://www.tsonline.co.uk/
The Stationery Office has a long history of publishing statutory, parliamentary and governmental information. The current enterprise emerged from the privatisation of HMSO in October 1996. It has been the UK's official publisher to Parliament for more than 200 years. It is also the UK's largest publisher by volume, developing some 11,000 books, CDs and web sites every year. Its best-known titles include *The Highway Code, British Pharmacopoeia* and *Whitaker's Almanack.* You can order by phone, by post, by fax, or online. All online credit card transactions are carried out over a secure encoded link. The site also includes job vacancies.

Stockton Press
http://www.stockton-press.co.uk
Stockton Press publishes medical and scientific journals for an international audience. It is a division of Macmillan Press, itself now part of the Holtzbrinck Group. The group publishes internationally renowned journals, such as *Nature* and *Scientific American*. The site contains complete details of Stockton Press journals, instructions to authors, editor information and free access to tables of contents. To see abstracts you are asked to register. To see the full text of articles you are also required to register using your subscriber number. The company operates from Basingstoke, UK, and New York, USA.

Studymates
http://www.studymates.co.uk
Studymates publishes a series of popular paperback study and revision guides for students taking examination courses in further and higher education. Sample titles include *Macroeconomics, Organic Chemistry, Studying Literature, Studying Psychology, The English Legal System,* and *Understanding Maths.* The web site includes guidelines for prospective authors, and free curriculum links to help students with coursework.

Sweet & Maxwell
http://www.smlawpub.co.uk/
1999 marked the 200th anniversary of UK legal publisher Sweet & Maxwell. Today, the firm offers more than 1,100 titles ranging from

books, periodicals and loose-leaf publications, to titles on CD-rom and online information services. Its products are designed to meet the needs of the legal profession and law students at college or university. The site includes a *What's New* section featuring a daily current awareness service and information on key cases. It also includes a directory of barristers, online inspection pages, and guidance for authors on making a publishing proposal and submitting journal articles.

Tarquin Books
http://www.tarquin-books.demon.co.uk
Gerald Jenkins, the founder of Tarquin in 1970, had been a maths teacher and so most of the company's earlier books were based on mathematical ideas. Its first books were the *Make Shapes* series of innovative mathematical models to cut out, glue together and decorate. The Suffolk-based firm now produces books for children about paper engineering, science, optical illusions, mirror reflections, costume and history as well as do-it-yourself pop-up books and collections of colourful mobiles and gift boxes.

Taschen UK
http://www.taschen.com/
Taschen is a publisher of highly illustrated pocket books on art, architecture, interiors, sex and photography.

Tate Gallery Publishing
http://www.tate.org.uk
TGP is wholly owned by the Trustees of the Tate Gallery in London. It publishes a wide range of books, postcards, posters and prints, slides, greetings cards, stationery and gifts. These are available by mail order through this web site for each gallery (London, Liverpool and St Ives) and in the general fields of modern art and British art.

Taylor & Francis
http://www.tandf.co.uk/
Taylor & Francis plc has grown rapidly over the last two decades and emerged as a leading international academic publisher. With offices in London, Brighton, Basingstoke and Abingdon in the UK, New York and Philadelphia in the USA and Singapore and Sydney in the Pacific Rim, the group publishes a broadly-based list of about 450 journals and 1,500 new books each year. Its imprints include Carfax Publishing, E & FN Spon, Europa Publications, Falmer Press, Garland Publishing (New York), Routledge, University College of London Press, and others.

Art Nouveau
Klaus-Jürgen Sembach
Hardcover, 240 pages

Thames & Hudson
http://www.thameshudson.co.uk/
Thames & Hudson is the best known British and trans-Atlantic art book publisher. It has the largest list of books in the English language relating to art, architecture, design, photography, decorative arts, history and music. The firm now has over 1,000 books in print including the famous World of Art series in its distinctive glossy black covers – and publishes over 150

new titles each year, covering everything from Etruscan art to Francis Bacon. Book ordering is by traditional means. The site includes details of new digital products.

Thistle Press
http://www.thistlepress.co.uk
Founded in 1992, Thistle Press produces guidebooks to the highlands, islands and north-east Scotland. The site includes author guidelines, and a Scotland book store. The firm is a member of the Scottish Publishers Association.

Thomson Learning
http://www.thomsonlearning.com/
'Whether it is in the traditional education setting, the corporate training room, the career school or the virtual classroom: if you are a student, an instructor or trainer, an administrator, a concerned parent, or a bookstore, this site will send you to a rapidly growing list of services, products and information.' In over 100 countries around the world, Thomson provides learning materials in a wide variety of subjects and disciplines. Formerly known as ITP, it publishes for schools, higher education, career and vocational/technical institutions. It is also a growing presence in the world of business, industry and government training.

Thomas Nelson & Sons
http://www.nelson.co.uk/
Nelson is one of Britain's leading and oldest-established publishers of educational materials, with best-selling books and resources across the subject areas and at all levels from nursery to further education. The site is categorised by age and subject to help you find what you are looking for, whether as a teacher, or parent. Nelson publishes The Arden Shakespeare. The company has recently been acquired by Wolters Kluwer.

Thornes Education
http://www.thorneseducation.com
Stanley Thornes is a leading educational publisher in the UK, established in 1972 and now part of the huge Wolters Kluwer Group, which also owns Nelson, Croner and other imprints in educational and professional publishing worldwide. Thornes produces educational resources for the full learning range, from pre-school to university level. The efficient web site includes a site search, members area, jobs section, news, site tour and site map, shopping basket facility, and links to useful web sites for educational and professional development.

Thorsons
http://www.fireandwater.com/imprints/thorsons
Thorsons publishes a popular range of mind, body and spirit books. The imprint is part of HarperCollins. The Thorsons web page was still under development when reviewed.

Time Out
http://www.timeout.com/
The Time Out Group is the publisher of *Time Out Magazine* and the *Time Out City Guides* which now cover many of the world's major cities.

Tolley
http://www.tolley.co.uk/
Founded in 1916, Tolley Publishing is a leading publisher of tax, legal and business publications in the UK. It publishes in a variety of formats including loose-leafs, textbooks, journals, newsletters, magazines and CD-roms. It aims to meet the needs of legal, tax and accountancy practitioners, directors, managers, administrators, in-house professionals and corporate officers in the commercial and local government sectors. It also manages training events and conferences, and produces personalised publications. The company is now a part of Reed Elsevier.

Trentham Books
http://www.trentham-books.co.uk
Stoke-on-Trent publisher Trentham issues a wide range of titles along with seven professional journals, mainly in the field of education and social policy and including law, media studies and women's studies. The site includes a complete catalogue of its publications, arranged alphabetically by titles or authors' names, or numerically by ISBN number, with links to review pages.

Trident Press
http://www.tridentpress.com
From its offices in London, Trident Press mainly publishes material of Arabian interest – natural history, wildlife, travel, history, archaeology, social history, culture, heritage, current affairs and national development. Its material is available in printed and electronic formats (including DVD), together with brochures, booklets and posters. English, French and Arabic editions are available.

Trotman Publishing
http://www.trotmanpublishing.co.uk
Trotman is an established independent UK careers and educational publisher. It produces a large and well-regarded range of books and materials on careers options, education, UCAS, higher education, university entry, skills focus, getting into university, and degree course offers. The site includes guidance on how to submit your publishing proposal, and even a web cam offering constantly-refreshed views of nearby Richmond Green in Surrey.

Careers UK
CAREERS PORTAL
Order Master

Publishing Schedule
Enclosed is Trotman's publications programme for
This will be regularly updat throughout the year to keep informed how each publicat progressing.

Twelveheads Press
http://www.twelveheads.demon.co.uk
Twelveheads has been publishing books about transport, industrial and social history, mainly in Cornwall and the south west of England, since 1977. It also publishes the *Heritage* series of guidebooks to Cornwall and the Isles of Scilly. The company is based in Truro.

Ulverscroft
http://www.ulverscroft.co.uk
Ulverscroft is a leading UK publisher of large print books, producing 40 brand new titles in large print every month. Begun by FrederickThorpe in 1964, the original company has grown considerably, and now encompasses FA Thorpe Publishing, Ulverscroft Large Print Books, TJ International and Magna Large Print Books. Almost 6,000 titles are available from stock.

University of Exeter Press
http://www.ex.ac.uk/uep/welcome.htm
The UEP list embraces history, literature, philosophy, dictionaries, geology, European studies, middle eastern studies and religious studies. Titles can now be securely ordered online. Editorial enquiries are welcomed.

University of Wales Press
http://www.swan.ac.uk/uwp/home.htm
The UWP list ranges from art and architecture, classical studies, archaeology and early history, history, literature, dictionaries, language and linguistics, gender studies, law, politics and social sciences, theatre and media studies, music, theology, biblical studies, philosophy, science and journals. The site includes a catalogue of Welsh-language titles.

Usborne Publishing
http://www.usborne.com
Usborne is an UK-based international publisher of illustrated fiction and non-fiction books for children. The firm was founded over 20 years ago by Peter Usborne. Today its books are sold throughout the English-speaking world, as well as in the French, Dutch, Italian and Spanish languages. If you are interested in helping them sell their books, you can check out the details of the Usborne direct home sales network on this site.

Vacation Work Publishers
http://www.vacationwork.co.uk/
Oxford-based VW publishes a popular series of summer and winter job directories for Britain, Europe and the USA, and a number of established travel survival kits to living and working in individual countries abroad. It also produces directories on careers and voluntary work, au pair work, kibbutzim and gap years. Books purchased online have a £2 reduction on the bookshop price.

Vallentine Mitchell
http://www.vmbooks.com
Vallentine Mitchell publishes works of mainly Jewish interest ranging from philosophy, history and heritage to literature, biography, cookery and travel. The company has offices in Ilford, Essex, and Portland, Oregon.

VCI
http://www.vci.co.uk/
Video Collection International is a leading UK publisher and distributor of home entertainment formats including video, music and audio, and books. VCI are proprietors of the publishing imprint of Andre Deutsch, offering 500 or so titles covering biography, essays, eclectic fiction and photographic titles, plus popular offerings in music, humour, sport, entertainment and children's titles.

Verso Books
http://www.versobooks.com/
Verso ('the left-hand page') was founded in 1970 by the London-based *New Left Review*. It is a publisher of critical works that represent authors in the social sciences and humanities, including politics, cultural studies, history, philosophy, sociology and literary criticism. Among them are Noam Chomsky, Terry Eagleton, Stuart Hall, Eric Hobsbawm, E.P. Thompson, and Raymond Williams. Verso is perhaps the largest radical publisher in the English-language.

Virgin Publishing
http://www.virgin.co.uk/entertainment/virgin_publishing.shtml
This is the publishing arm of Richard Branson's Virgin Group. It produces original hardbacks and paperbacks in the area of popular culture, predominantly music, film and TV books. Its imprints include Virgin, Black Lace, Nexus and Target.

Waterlow Legal Publishing
http://www.waterlow.com/
Waterlow has served the professional information market for over 150 years. Today, it is one of the largest legal and company services agents in the UK. With a client base of over 10,000 companies, it helps some 4,000 solicitors' and accountants' practices each year, as well as commercial businesses, government bodies, public organisations, and individuals. The Waterlow Legal Bookfinder Service lists and classifies about 2,500 law books currently in print on around 190 subject areas of practical interest to lawyers and their staff.

Wayland
http://www.wayland.co.uk/
Based in Hove, Wayland is an established publisher of illustrated educational titles for primary and secondary school libraries. Its list covers most areas of the curriuculum. The company also works on co-productions with educational publishers overseas. Along with its sister company Macdonald Young Books, it was recently acquired by the high street retailer WH Smith.

Weidenfeld & Nicolson – see Orion.

Winslow Press
http://www.winslow-press.co.uk/
Winslow publishes books and resources for educational special needs, learning disabilities, health, elderly care and all aspects of social care.

Witherby & Co
http://www.witherbys.com/
Established for over 75 years, the City of London firm of Witherby specialises in insurance and shipping titles both as publishers and booksellers. Its web site enables you to search over 250 titles by subject, category, title or author.

Women's Press
http://www.the-womens-press.com
The London-based Women's Press publish books by and for women, specialising in fiction, non-fiction, lesbian writing, black women's studies, and younger women. It offers 10% discount on books ordered through its web site, which also features a book club and book extracts.

Woodhead Publishing
http://www.woodhead-publishing.com
Woodhead produces books and videos on welding and joining, materials engineering, textile technology, finance and business, and operations management. The firm is situated on the site of the Welding Institute near Cambridge. Information for authors is available online.

Wright – see Butterworth-Heinemann.

Writers and Readers
http://www.writersandreaders.com/
Writers and Readers produces the Beginners' Guides, a series of popular documentary comic books, and Black Butterfly children's books. Sample titles include *Brecht for Beginners, London for Beginners* and *Orwell for Beginners*. Its web site includes various special offers, and the chance to contribute reviews of its books.

Wyvern Crest
http://www.wyvern.co.uk/
Wyvern Crest is a direct mail publisher of practical business and management books, newsletters and software, designed to save you time, boost your profits and achieve your personal goals.

Yale University Press
http://www.yaleup.co.uk
The site was under construction when reviewed.

Zed Books
http://www.zedbooks.demon.co.uk/
'21 years of radical independent publishing.' Zed was originally founded in 1977 and is based in London. Today it publishes about forty books a year on international and Third World topics, largely aimed at college and

university students and lecturers. Zed is managed co-operatively by its worker directors. Recent sample titles include *In The Net: A Guide for Activists* and *The Third World in the Age of Globalisation.*

Zero Press
http://www.zero.dircon.co.uk
Founded in 1948, the London-based Zero Press publishes books on literature and art, and has done so over the years from Paris, Tangier, Mexico City, New York, London, Philadelphia and Dublin. Its authors include James Baldwin, Samuel Beckett, Paul Bowles, Christopher Isherwood, Federico Garcia Lorca, Jean-Paul Sartre and William Carlos Williams.

7 European Publishers

In this chapter we will explore:

- *European publishers' associations*
- *book fairs in Europe*
- *major European publishing groups A-Z*

The development of web sites by publishing firms across Europe is still at a relatively early stage. This section focuses in providing online contacts for the leading European publishing and media groups. Not all these organisations yet made it possible to view all the content in English.

European publishers' associations

European Association of Directory Publishers
http://www.eadp.be/
Founded in 1966, the EADP was the outcome of the aspirations of several European reference publishers. Today it has 194 members in 37 countries. The site is in English.

France Edition
http://www.franceedition.org/
Developed by its 240-odd publisher members and supported by French government authorities (primarily the Ministry of Culture and Communication), France Edition is responsible for the international promotion of French books abroad. This is a very handy place to explore French pub-

Fig. 45. France Edition. This site contains a handy guide to French publishers, plus a guide to international rights sales, newsletter, forum, catalogues and other features.

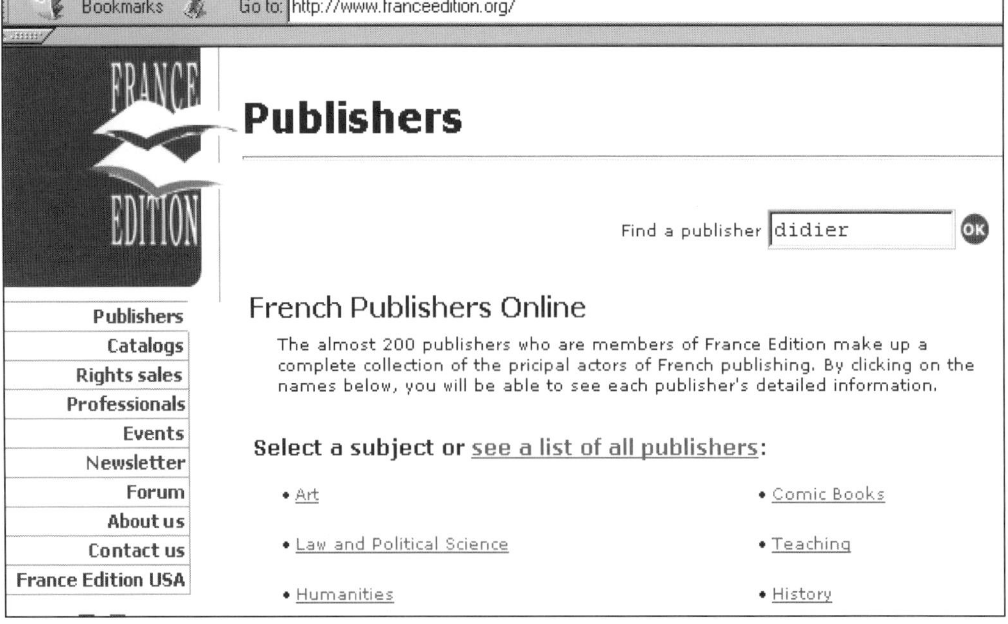

lishers online. You will find a fairly complete collection of the main players in French publishing. The site can be viewed in both French and English.

Software Publishers Association
http://www.spa.org/
This is a trade association of software publishers in the USA and Europe. This site provides access to press releases, anti-piracy information, research, and publications. The site is in English.

World Intellectual Property Organisation
http://www.wipo.org/
WIPO is an intergovernmental organisation with headquarters in Geneva, Switzerland. It is one of the 16 specialised agencies of the United Nations system of organisations. It is responsible for the promotion of the protection of intellectual property throughout the world through cooperation among States, and for the administration of various multilateral treaties dealing with the legal and administrative aspects of intellectual property. The site can be read in English, French and Spanish.

Book fairs in Europe

Bologna Children's Book Fair
http://www.smart.it/BookFair/welcome.html
Held for four days each March/April, the Bologna Children's Book Fair in Italy is the biggest trade event of its kind in the world. The exhibitors and visitors include publishers, illustrators, designers, book packagers, authors and agents from all over the world. The site is presented in English but can also be read in Italian.

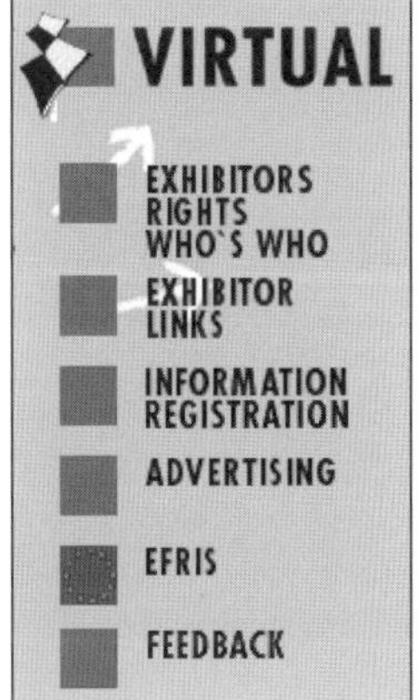

Frankfurt Book Fair
http://www.frankfurt-book-fair.com/
The Frankfurt Buchmesse today is the most important annual trading event in the international rights and licences business within the publishing industry. Founded directly after the Second World War, it has become the symbol of modern internationally oriented book trading. For six days each autumn, it showcases 360,000 books published by more than 6,800 individual exhibitors and 80 national exhibitions. It is attended by publishers and multimedia producers from 100 countries, as well as by 300,000 visitors from all over the world. The site is presented in English but can also be read in German.

Leipzig Book Fair & Antiquarian Fair
http://www.leipziger-messe.de
This is eastern Europe's best known and longest established book fair, held in March each year. The site is presented in German and English.

Liber
http://www.liber.ifema.es
Alternating between Madrid and Barcelona, Liber is Spain's annual Feria Internacional del Libro, a major book trade exhibition organised by Reed. The site is presented in Engish and Spanish.

Paris Book Fair
http://salondulivre.reed-oip.fr
Established for about twenty years, the Paris 'Salon du Livre' is held each year in March at Paris Expo, an attracts about 35,000 professional visitors ranging from booksellers and librarians to publishers, software developers and printers. The site can be viewed in French or English, and you can download an application for admission.

Major European publishing groups

Addison Wesley Longman (Europe)
http://www.awleurope.com
AWL publishes a range of programs and materials for primary and secondary school students and teachers. It also produces teaching materials and textbooks for the further education sector, along with higher education textbooks and multimedia in every major academic subject. It publishes books and multimedia for business professionals, practising engineers, programmers and software developers, plus ELT/ESL/EFL programs and materials for students of all ages to learn American or British English.

Anaya
http://www.anaya.es/
This is the impressive web site of one of Spain's leading educational and general publishing groups, founded in 1959. Using an attractive magazine-style format, the site includes catalogues, detailed book listings, a search engine, and an online store for books and CD roms. The text is in Spanish only.

Fig. 46. The Bertelsmann international web site. The post-war growth of this German-based publishing and media group has been enormous. This page leads you to a network of related Bertlesmann sites in throughout the USA and Europe.

Bertelsmann AG
http://www.bertelsmann.de/
This is the main corporate web site of the giant German-based global publishing and communications conglomerate. You can read it in German or English. Bertelsmann is the third largest media company in the world with annual sales of some DM 26 billion, and is associated with AOL Time Warner. The company has major interests in all media areas including book, magazine and newspaper publishing, music, television, online, film and radio. With more than 600 individual companies, Bertelsmann employs 60,000 people in 53 countries. About 100 of these companies have their own sites on the internet, for example Bantam Doubleday Dell and Random House.

Bonnier
http://www.bonnier.se/
Based in Sweden, the long-established firm of Bonnier AG is Scandinavia's leading media company, with publishing operations in 17 countries. It produces books, daily newspapers and magazines, and produces and distributes music, film, radio, television and business data. Its web site can be viewed in English as well as Swedish.

Elsevier Science
http://www.elsevier.com/
Established a century ago, Elsevier Science has grown into a global information provider. It publishes almost 1,200 English-language journals containing core scientific research articles. Its fields of interest are agriculture, biological sciences, chemistry and chemical engineering, clinical medicine, computer science, earth and planetary sciences, economics, business and management, engineering, energy, environmental studies, life sciences, materials science, mathematics, physics and astronomy and social sciences. To find particular publications of interest, you select a subject area to enter the first level of the classification hierarchy. At each level, you can refine the subject of interest by browsing deeper into the hierarchy until you reach the publication listing level. The site's many features include an alerting service, customer support, electronic publishing services, and author information.

European Union
http://europa.eu.int/
This is the European Union's server which will tell you all you want to know about activities of the Parliament, Council, Commission, Court of Justice, Court of Auditors and the huge array of ever-expanding agencies and bureaucracies of the European Union. You can access a virtual mountain of official documents, legal texts, publications, databases, and other sources of information.

Folium
http://www.folium.ru
The Moscow-based Folium Publishing Company specialises in producing scientific books and periodicals in Russian and English, including

the translation and preparation of camera-ready copies and runs. There is no online ordering, and customers are invited to use phone, fax or post.

Hachette
http://www.hachette-livre.fr/
This is the substantial web site of France's best known general trade and educational publishing house: 'Éditeur de livres répondant aux besoins d'éducation, de connaissance, de culture et de loisirs pour un large public en France et à l'étranger.'

Hatier
http://www.editions-hatier.fr
Hatier is a leading French children's and educational publisher. 'Éditeur scolaire de Bescherelle, Annabac, Profil, Ratus, propose aux élèves, enseignants, parents et libraires, des exercices et corrigés, des concours, des forums, ses catalogues.'

Kluwer Academic Publishing
http://www.wkap.nl/
Netherlands-based Kluwer Academic is a leading international academic and professional publisher. Formed by a series of mergers in recent years, it is active in many fields - science and technology, biological, agricultural and environmental sciences, medicine, business and economics, humanities and social sciences and law. It publishes English-language books, journals, loose-leaf publications, and electronic publications. KAP is a division of the Wolters Kluwer publishing empire and operates worldwide from offices in Dordrecht, Boston, and London.

Michelin
http://www.michelin.com/
The company is almost as well known for its well-established travel guides and maps as for its tyres, and on this web site you can also find out about route-planning and personalised itineraries through Europe's cities.

Mondadori
http://home.mondadori.com/
This is the substantial web site of Italy's biggest general publishing group. Its activities encompass books and book clubs, consumer magazines and newspapers, trade and reference publishing and printing. The site can only be viewed in Italian.

Munksgaard International Publishers
http://www.munksgaard.dk
The Danish firm of Munksgaard is one of Europe's leading and oldest-established publishers of scientific, medical, dental and educational publications.

Reed Elsevier
http://www.r-e.com/
See the entry under UK publishers.

Springer Verlag
http://www.springer.de/
The Germany company Springer is one of the world's foremost science publishers, with a huge output of material each year in both traditional and electronic formats. In October 1999 Bertelsmann Professional Information Group and Scientific Publishing Group Springer merged into a new entity, Bertelsmann Springer.

Wolters Kluwer
http://www.wolters-kluwer.com
The Dutch company Wolters Kluwer has emerged in recent years as one of the dominant professional and educational publishing groups in the world. Its many operating subsidiaries include Kluwer Academic Publishers, CCH, Croner Publications, and Lippincott Williams & Wilkins. Its core activities are legal and tax publishing, business publishing, medical and scientific publishing and educational publishing and professional training. Wolters Kluwer has annual sales of some Dfl. 6 billion and more than 16,000 employees.

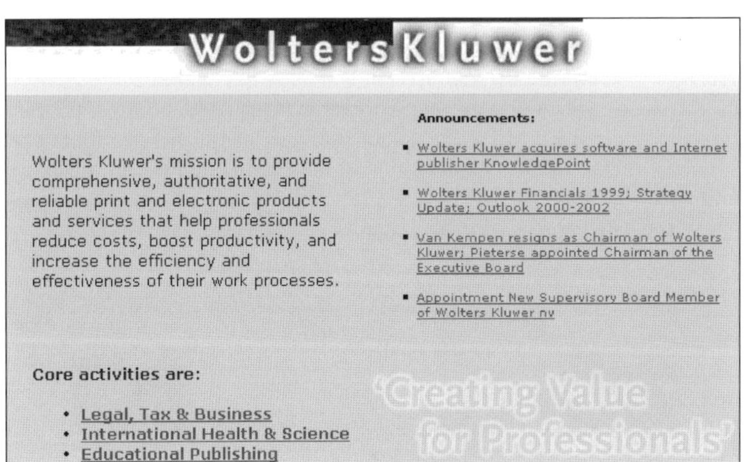

8 Publishers: American & Canadian

In this chapter we will explore:

- *publishers' associations*
- *book fairs*
- *publishers A-Z*

Publishers' associations

American Association of University Presses
http://aaupnet.org/
The AAUP is a cooperative, non-profit organisation of university presses. It promotes the work and influence of university presses, provides marketing support, and helps its members respond to the changing economy and environment. It is headquartered in New York City. The site includes guidelines for submitting traditional and electronic manuscripts to publishers, and details of job opportunities with the member organisations.

Association of American Publishers
http://www.publishers.org/
The AAP has some 200 member firms across the United States. These publish hardcover and paperback books in every field, audio and video tapes, computer software, looseleaf services, electronic products and services, maps, globes, filmstrips, and testing materials. With its news and features, this in-depth web site contains a wealth of resources about the American publishing scene.

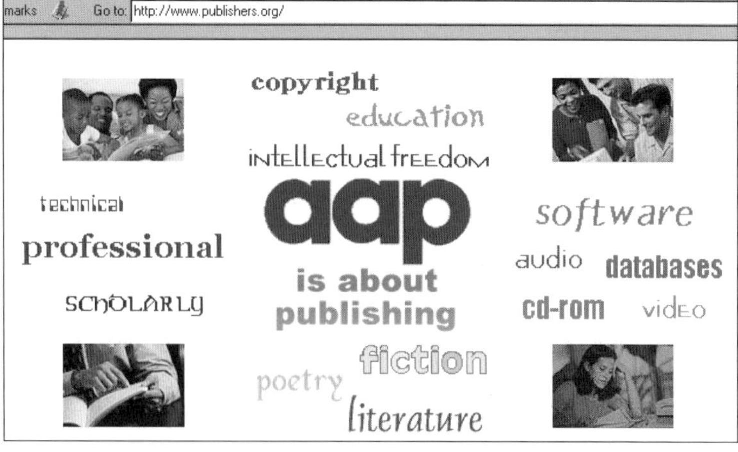

Fig. 47. The web site of the Association of American Publishers. In addition to providing extensive trade information and links, the AAP is noteworthy for its support of intellectual freedom in the face of moves by governments and pressure groups to censor the internet.

Association of Canadian Publishers
http://www.publishers.ca/
The ACP represents over 135 Canadian-owned book publishers, with members from all provinces and across the literary, general trade, educa-

tion, and scholarly sectors. It aims to encourage the writing, publishing, distribution and promotion of Canadian books. The site contains information about affiliates, committees, government relations, marketing, members and membership, research and staff.

Audio Publishers Association
http://www.audiopub.org/
This US site presents an online resource designed for both audiobook listeners and industry professionals.

Freelance Editorial Association
http://www.tiac.net/users/freelanc/
This is an American non-profit organisation staffed by volunteers, which works to promote the interests of freelance editors, illustrators, indexers, production specialists, proofreaders, translators, and writers. The site includes a directory of freelancers by subject, news, links, a skills index, and a bulletin board. The Association is based in Cambridge, Masschusetts.

The Editorial Freelancers Association
http://www.the-efa.org
This is a New York based non-profit, professional organisation of self-employed workers in the publishing and communications industries. The site gives information about courses, events, history, membership, a job phone, and other services.

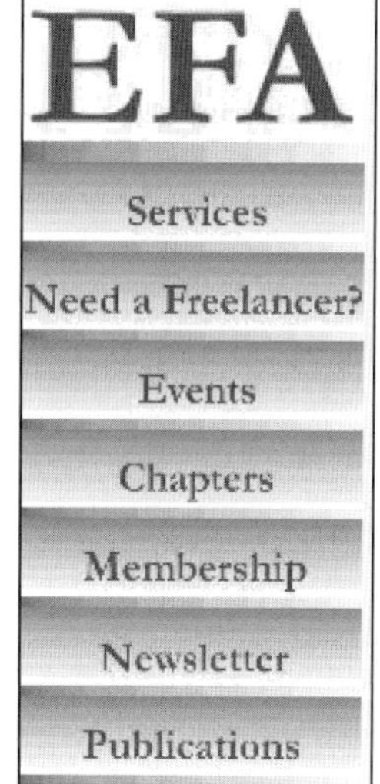

Publishers Marketing Association
http://www.pma-online.org/feedback.html
The PMA is a US-based non-profit trade association representing independent publishers of books, audio, video and CDs.

Publishing Triangle
http://www.publishingtriangle.org
Founded in 1988, The Publishing Triangle works to create support and a sense of community for lesbian and gay people in the publishing industry. Its members include book and magazine writers, editors, agents, marketing, sub-rights, publicity and sales people, booksellers, designers, librarians, and general book lovers. The association is run from New York. Membership is $30 a year.

Small Publishers Association of North America
http://www.spannet.org/
SPAN is a recently (1996) formed non-profit professional trade association that aims to show you how to make, and save, money. Its members are independent presses, self-publishers, and savvy authors who realise if their books are to be successful, they must make them so.

World Intellectual Property Organisation
http://www.wipo.org/
WIPO is an intergovernmental organisation with headquarters in Geneva,

Switzerland. It is one of the 16 specialised agencies of the United Nations system of organisations. It is responsible for the promotion of the protection of intellectual property throughout the world through cooperation among States, and for the administration of various multilateral treaties dealing with the legal and administrative aspects of intellectual property.

Book fairs

American Booksellers Association Convention
http://bookexpo.reedexpo.com
The annual ABA Convention and Book Expo is the largest trade event in the United States serving the entire book publishing industry. It is a major forum for publishers, authors, agents, illustrators, manufacturers and distributors from all over the world.

Fig. 48. The American Booksellers Association Convention is a key date in the international publishing calendar. Publishers, authors, librarians and booksellers from around the world attend each year.

Publishers

Abacus
http://www.myglobalmall.com/rpd/rpd.htm
Based in Glendale, Arizona, Abacus are publishers of books, software and videos specialising in self-help subjects mainly for citizens of the United States. It covers topics such as estate planning, financial planning, retirement planning, legal forms and information, make your life easier software, medical information and personal safety.

Abbeville Press
http://www.abbeville.com
The site of this New York children's and general trade publisher was under

construction when reviewed.

Academic Press
http://www.apnet.com/
Originally founded in Leipzig, Germany, in 1906, AP is a major publisher of academic journals and textbooks, and one of the largest commercial publishers in the USA for scientific information. Its associated imprints include Morgan Kaufmann (computer and engineering) and Scivision (scientific application and modelling software). Today, AP is a division of Harcourt Science and Technology. The site explains how to submit a book proposal to its various acquisitions editors.

ABC-CLIO
http://abc-clio.com/
For more than 40 years, ABC-CLIO has been an industry leader in the creation and publishing of research and reference materials. With headquarters in Santa Barbara, California, and offices in Denver, Colorado, and Oxford, England, the company produces both print and electronic reference products. History, sports, literature, mythology and global issues are among the subjects you will find among the firm's reference books, CD-rom products, and research publications.

Acadian House Publishing
http://www.acadianhouse.com
Acadian publishes regional and Cajun recipe books from its base in Lafayette, Louisiana.

Active Training
http://activetraining.com
AT produces books and workshops on business training and classroom techniques. The company is based in Princeton, New Jersey.

Adamant Press
http://www.adamantpress.com
Founded in 1971, Adamant publishes books in education, progressive education, social thought, and creative expression in art, literature and the sciences.

Adams Media Corporation
http://www.adamsmedia.com
AMC is a diversified publisher of print and electronic products. It is a leading North American publisher of career titles including JobBank books (more than one million copies sold) and the Knock 'em Dead series (more than two million copies sold). It publishes about 100 new books annually, and is now a $10 million company with 65 employees, and worldwide distribution.

Agora Publishing
http://www.agoraworldwide.com/
Based in Baltimore, Maryland, Agora is an international publisher of

financial, health, travel, and special interest information. Its list comprises more than 300 books and 40 newsletters. It produces French and German language versions of several of its titles. The company has affiliated offices in Florida, New Mexico, London, Paris, and Germany.

Akadine Press
http://www.akadine.com/
Akadine is a mail order publisher and distributor of books, videos and CDs. The subjects in its 'common reader' catalogue include art, photography, music, science, food, children's humour, mysteries, essays and literature, fiction, biography, history, the classics, and travel. It also sells a selection of British imports.

Allyn & Bacon
http://www.abacon.com/
Part of Pearson Education, Allyn & Bacon is a leading USA publisher of college textbooks in education, social science, and the humanities. Through its Longwood Professional Division it publishes materials in the fields of career development, communication, communication disorders, contemporary issues, education, health and physical education, the helping professions, parenting, the performing arts, psychology, and student success. The site includes a student centre, faculty centre, and catalogue. It also features a 'web gallery' where you can click on selected disciplines to see its complete listing of companion web sites.

Amadeus Press
http://www.amadeuspress.com
Amadeus Press is a music book publisher founded by Richard Abel in 1987. Its mission is to publish books that would appeal to a wide audience of discerning music lovers yet maintain their scholarly integrity. The list contains more than 100 titles on everything from piano technique to master classes, famous musicians, and opera.

American Management Association
http://www.amanet.org/books/
Established for 75 years, AMACOM is the world's largest training organisation for managers and executives. It also publishes practical, solution-oriented books offering both classic and innovative approaches to current business concerns. This is a magazine-style web site with lots of features, from seminars and conferences to a job shop, membership section, press room, and more. You can browse and search its extensive, well-organised and detailed catalogue, and order its titles online.

Arsenal Pulp Press
http://www.arsenalpulp.com
Arsenal Pulp Press is a book publisher in Vancouver, Canada with 135 titles in print, ranging from fiction and poetry to cultural, gender and multicultural studies, westerns, romances, new age, literary and art studies, political and sociological studies, and more. The company began life in 1971 as Pulp Press Book Publishers, founded by a collective

of university students and associates disenchanted by what they perceived to be the academic literary pretensions of Canadian literature at the time. Run as a co-operative, Pulp printed its first publications on a Gestetner machine.

Atlantic Publishing
http://www.atlantic-publishing.com/index.htm
Based in Florida, Atlantic publishes information on food service, restaurant, and hospitality industry topics, plus a range of books, videos, tapes, tools, and posters. The site contains a search facility, and secure online ordering.

Avon Books
http://www.avonbooks.com/
Avon Books was founded in 1941 and acquired by The Hearst Corporation in 1959. It is the second oldest paperback publishing house in the United States. It publishes mass-market titles for adults and young readers, mainly romance, and mystery. The company does not accept book orders on its web site.

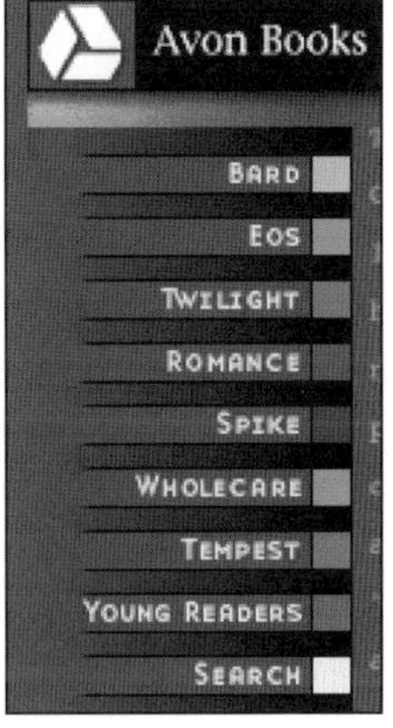

Ballantine
http://www.randomhouse.com/BB/
Ballantine is a New York based general trade publisher, and a division of Random House. This informative and reader-friendly site includes features on its current books, a searchable catalogue of titles in print, lots of sample chapters to try, category newsletters, and publishing news, plus special sections for teachers and librarians. There are also some helpful and wide-ranging FAQs covering everything from authors' guidelines to employment in the company. It also offers free links to the web sites of famous authors, such as Ken Follett, Margaret Atwood, Michael Crichton, and lots of other top names. If you want to order titles online, you are routed via Random House to individual bookstores with online ordering facilities.

Bantam Doubleday Dell
http://www.randomhouse.com/
Bantam, Doubleday, Dell and Broadway are now part of Random House. Information about all books published by the Random House groups (including those previously found on BDD Online) can now be found on this official web site of Random House.

Barrons Educational Series, Inc
http://www.barronseduc.com
Barrons is a leading USA trade and educational publisher. It publishes more than 1,800 titles on business topics, pets, children's interests, college guides, foreign languages, cooking, art, and test preparation books for numerous exams. This attractively presented web site is presented as 'Barronsville', a virtual town complete with town hall, book emporium, news stand, fast food joint, movie theatre, school house and other stopping-off points. It includes a search engine, author chat,

featured titles, email, and offline ordering information (which includes zip code links to online bookstores).

SPIRIT
ART
JUSTICE
KNOWLEDGE
ABOUT BEACON
ORDERING
PERMISSIONS AND OTHER BUSINESS
READING AND DISCUSSION GUIDES
JOBS & INTERNSHIPS
MAILING LIST
SEARCH

Beacon Press
http://www.uua.org/Beacon/
Based in Boston, Massachusetts, Beacon Press has been an independent publisher of serious non-fiction books since 1854. Its publishes on such issues as freedom of speech, religious pluralism, anti-racism, and respect for social diversity. Its authors include James Baldwin and Herbert Marcuse. Its current publishing program includes African-American studies, anthropology, essays, gay, lesbian and gender studies, education, children and family issues, nature and the environment, religion, science and society, and women's studies. For ordering you are asked to follow links to selected online bookstores.

Belltowne Publishing
http://www.belltowne.com
Based in Houston, Texas, Belltowne is a small independent publisher of assorted mass market titles for adults and children. There is an email link but no online ordering.

Bend Press
http://www.bendpress.com/
This Californian youth publishing site was under construction when we reviewed it. Its original contents featured skateboarding and music.

Matthew Bender
http://www.bender.com/
The company offers more than 500 publications in print and electronic formats to subscribers in more than 160 countries. It publishes legal information in every major practice area authored by the leading experts in the legal community. Its standard titles include *Attorney's Textbook of Medicine, California Forms of Pleading and Practice, Collier on Bankruptcy, Current Legal Forms, Damages and Tort Actions, Moore's Federal Practice, Products Liability* and *Immigration Law and Procedure*. This in-depth site includes a search facility, meet the experts, and shopping cart. Part of its published information requires registration.

Bergin & Garvey – see Greenwood.

Berkeley Books – see Penguin Putnam.

Berkeley Hills Books
http://www.berkeleyhills.com/
This is a small general trade publisher based in Berkeley, California.

Berkshire House Publishers
http://www.berkshirehouse.com
Berkshire is a publisher of travel guides, cook books, and woodworking books with strong connections to New England and the north-eastern US. These include historic interest, travel, and a range of topics from

Shaker antiques and Edith Wharton, to Red Lion Inn recipes and Hudson Valley farm foods.

Berlitz
http://www.berlitz.com/
With a history going back over 120 years, Berlitz is the world's premier language services company, providing a vast range of language instruction, translation, and publishing services. You can order its world-famous phrase books, complete language courses, travel guides, CD-roms and other products here, choosing from more than 1,000 titles in multiple languages.

Beyond Words
http://www.beyondword.com
Founded in 1984, Oregon-based Beyond Words is a publisher of coffee table and illustrated books on personal growth, new age, and children's interests. It has about 100 titles in print and sold more than 1.5 million books in over thirty languages.

Biddle Publishing Company
http://www.maineguide.com/biddle/biddle.html
Biddle is a small press located on the Maine coast. It specialises in self-help, personal history, social concern and poetry books.

Bison Publishing
http://www.bison.com/index.html
Bison publishes CDs of songs and stories celebrating spirituality.

Blackbirch Press
http://www.blackbirch.com/
Based in Connecticut, Blackbirch Press is a publisher of illustrated books for kids and young adults. It has about 160 titles in print, which include everything from biography to animals and nature to American history. Its online ordering is linked to Amazon and Barnes & Noble.

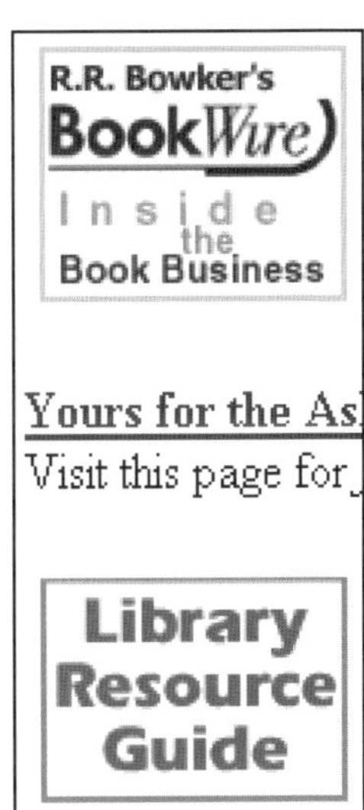

Bowker
http://www.bowker.com/
Bowker are leading publishers of standard and substantial reference products for the library and bookselling communities. These products include *Publishers Trade List Annual, The Reader's Adviser, Literary Market Place*, as well as other core professional resources. The site includes a search facility.

Bowker-Saur
http://www.bowker-saur.co.uk/service/
Bowker-Saur is a professional and reference publisher across a range of media. Its products encompass bibliographies, contact, professional and business directories, abstracting and indexing services, historical and contemporary biographical reference and library and information science titles in book, journal, microform, CD-rom, and online formats.

As well as publishing under the imprints Bowker-Saur, Headland Business Information and Hans Zell Publishers, it distributes titles from leading reference imprints R.R. Bowker, Martindale-Hubbell, Marquis *Who's Who* (UK and Europe), K.G. Saur (UK only) and D.W. Thorpe (UK and Europe). It is a part of the Reed Elsevier group.

Braille International
http://www.gate.net/-braille
Located in Florida, Braille is a not-for-profit organisation dedicated to enhancing the independence and quality of life for blind persons everywhere. It publishes a range of literary braille material.

Butterworths Canada
http://www.butterworths.ca/
This is the home page of the Canadian affiliate of the world's foremost legal publisher. The links include: company profile, online catalogue, new releases, electronic products, book reviews, academic titles, special promotions, sales amd marketing, associates, and legal links. There is also guidance for prospective authors and employees.

C&M Online Media
http://www.cmonline.com/
C&M publishes electronic books under the imprint Boson Books. Its books can be downloaded from this web site in Adobe Acrobat format.

Camino Books
http://www.caminobooks.com
Philadelphia-based Camino Books was founded in 1987 to publish nonfiction books of regional interest to people in the mid Atlantic states. Its list focuses on cooking, travel, gardening, and history, but it also publishes biographies, local reference books, and books on parenting and important health issues. It publishes about ten new books a year.

Carswell Publishing
http://www.carswell.com/
Canadian publisher Carswell describes itself as a national resource for information and legal interpretations, for law, accounting, tax and business professionals. Its extensive list is well cross-referenced and supported by a search facility. Carswell is a division of Thomson Professional Publishing. Using a Carswell password you can order through its secure online ordering system.

Chartwell
http://chartwellinc.com/
Chartwell is an Atlanta-based independent publishing company serving the utility industry (electric, gas and water) with books, newsletters, conferences and other information products. These range from brief collections of case studies to full-scale research reports.

Chatham House Publishers
http://www.chathamhouse.com/
Established in 1979, Chatham House publishes materials in the fields of political science, philosophy and public affairs. It is a division of Seven Bridges Press, and based in Chatham, New Jersey.

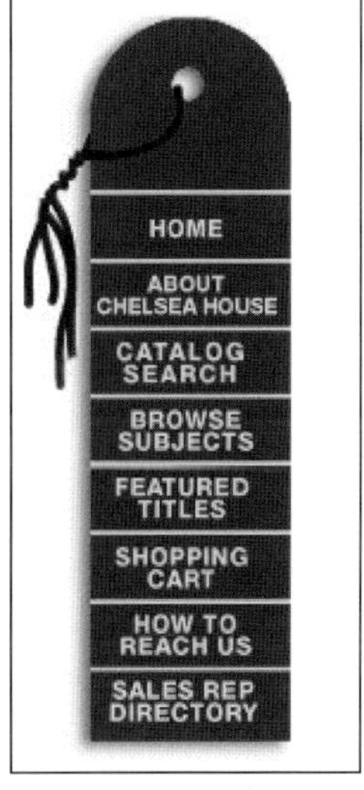

Chelsea House Publishers
http://www.chelseahouse.com/
Chelsea House publishes non-fiction for children and young adults. These include biographies, histories, multicultural studies, and hundreds of volumes of literary criticism and references for older readers. Its complete list is now online. You can browse subjects, look at featured titles, use the catalogue search with keywords (author name, or set topic), use the shopping cart system to collect all the titles you need, then check your order and check out any time. The site includes a sales reps' directory. The company is represented in the UK and Europe by the Roundhouse.

Chronicle Books
http://www.chronbooks.com
This zesty American publisher's titles include cookbooks, fine art, design, photography, and architecture, and children's books. You can search for specific books by author, titles, or subject; stroll through the 'Playhouse' for excerpts, recipes, art, travel tips, design ideas, wacky animal facts, and even send an electronic postcard using images from its books. The FAQ page gives information on employees, online ordering, new book proposals, job openings, and more. Its children's section has a complete list of children's titles, plus book reviews, educational guides for the classroom, creative ways to keep kids entertained on rainy days, and more.

Clark Boardman Callaghan
http://www.cbclegal.com/
CBC is a leading USA law publisher. It is now part of West Group, joining together with Bancroft-Whitney, Lawyers Cooperative Publishing, Westlaw and West Publishing to offer an integrated professional law research system.

Cliffs Notes
http://www.cliffs.com/
Cliffs Notes is a popular series of inexpensive literary study guides established in the USA and other markets for 40 years. In its distinctive yellow and black covers, the series now covers more than 200 authors from Achebe to Wright. You can order securely online. The site – which makes rather heavy use of frames – includes a 'teachers' lounge' plus some educational and fun links for students.

Coach House Books
http://www.chbooks.com
Coach House Books is a small literary publisher based in Toronto,

Canada. Founded in 1997, it has already published a wide range of poetry, visual and concrete poetry, fiction, and artist books in finely crafted editions. It offers all its texts online. Using the shareware 'try before you buy' model, all titles are available to the public free of charge, and print titles are available to order by secure server. You are also asked to 'Tip the author' – that is, pay the author a small royalty when you have enjoyed a title online.

CATALOGUES
SERIES INFORMATION
NEW RELEASE BULLETINS
CD-ROM & Y2K INFO
CONTACT US

Columbia University Press
http://www.cc.columbia.edu/cu/cup/
Based in New York, CUP is a major academic publisher and the web site does justice to its range and depth. Indexes take you A to Z from African Studies and anthropology, architecture and art right through to technology, transportation, urban studies and women's studies. You can also find information about submitting a manuscript, requesting a title for review, and getting a job at the Press. The site contains detailed ordering instructions for private individuals, librarians, booksellers and wholesalers, and for different parts of the world. Private customers are encouraged to order through bookstores, for which hyperlinks are given.

Combined Publishing
http://www.combinedpublishing.com/
CP is a Pennsylvania publisher and distributor which represents a number of well known imprints specialising in military history and illustrated book publishing. These include Leo Cooper, Pen & Sword, Chatham Publishing, Salamander Books, Windrush Press and the Wordsworth Military Library.

Community Communications
http://www.gotocommunity.com/index.html
CC is an Alabama-based publisher of books for commercial, civic, historical, and trade purposes. Its projects include American and Canadian Enterprise Series.

Cornell University Press
http://www.cornellpress.cornell.edu/
Located in Ithaca, New York, Cornell has the oldest university press in the USA. From its beginnings in 1869, it has grown to be a major scholarly publisher offering 150 new titles a year. Its titles reflect many disciplines – anthropology, classics, cultural studies, history, literary criticism and theory, medieval studies, philosophy, politics and international relations, psychology and psychiatry, and women's studies. Life sciences and natural history are published under the Comstock imprint, and industrial and labour relations under the ILR Press imprint.

Crown Publishing Group – see Random House.

Disney Books
http://disney.go.com/DisneyBooks/
This is the place to come for everything you want to know or buy concerning all those famous Walt Disney cartoon characters.

Dow Jones
http://www.dowjones.com/
Dow Jones publishes one of the world's leading business and financial publishing services. Its flagship publication is *The Wall Street Journal*, the largest paid circulation subscription site on the web, with more than 250,000 paid subscribers. Most of its publishing is in the form of periodicals, and these are increasingly available in electronic form. The site is an essential bookmark for anyone requiring global investment or financial information.

Dun & Bradstreet
http://www.dnb.com/
Dun & Bradstreet is the leading American and international publisher of corporate and financial information used mainly for the purpose of commercial credit checks and cash flow management. Its products today comprise electronic data, software, specialist financial reports, risk and payment reviews, country profiles and other financial information.

Dutton – see Penguin Putnam.

East View Publications
http://www.eastview.com
Based in Minneapolis, East View offers information gleaned from Russia and the Newly Independent States (NIS) of the former Soviet Union. It provides news on current events and the changing political winds, updates on new legislation, elusive market data and financial figures, official standards, industry directories and new advertising opportunities. The site's services include books and databases, newspaper and journal subscriptions, online publications, and microform products and services.

ECW Press
http://www.ecw.ca/Press/
ECW is a Canadian publisher of a broad list of trade books ranging from contemporary celebrity biographies, to books about the people, places, phenomena and issues that shape our lives, and from politics to pop culture, poetry and perversity.

Elsevier Science
http://www.elsevier.com/
Established a century ago, Elsevier Science has grown into a global information provider. It publishes almost 1,200 English-language journals containing core scientific research articles. Its fields of interest are agriculture, biological sciences, chemistry and chemical engineering, clinical medicine, computer science, earth and planetary sciences, economics, business and management, engineering, energy, environmental studies, life sciences, materials science, mathematics, physics and astronomy and social sciences. To find particular publications of interest, you select a subject area to enter the first level of the classification hierarchy. At each level, you can refine the subject of interest by browsing deeper

into the hierarchy until you reach the publication listing level. The site's many features include an alerting service, customer support, electronic publishing services, and author information.

Encyclopaedia Britannica Online
http://www.eb.com/
The famous encyclopaedia was first published in 1768, and has now been reborn on the internet. It is a subscription service, available from $5 a month, by which you can explore its 32 volumes, 72,000 articles and 12,000 images. Britannica Online offers a variety of subscription programs for individuals and institutions. It's still far cheaper than buying the back-breaking set of books – and think of the space you'll save. Payment is by credit card, using secure online payment technology, or you can phone or fax your details. You then access the site using a password of your own choosing.

Fig. 49. Encyclopaedia Britannica. This famous and old-established publisher has reacted aggressively to the rise of the internet, abandoning much of its traditional publishing in favour of new online services.

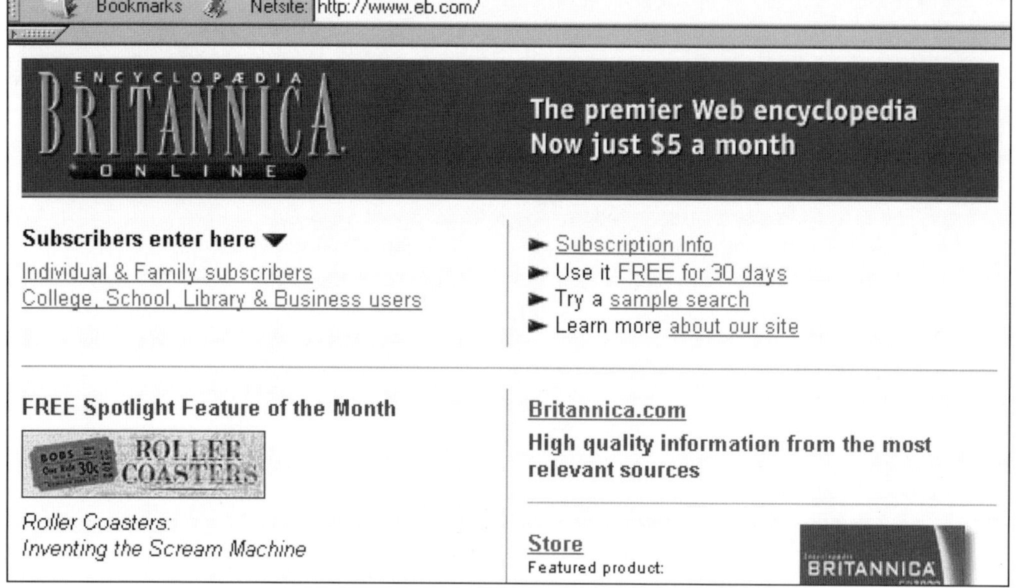

Facts on File
http://www.factsonfile.com
This is a New York publisher of reference, school and library titles, and material in other media. Its subjects include anthropology and archaeology, art and architecture, biographies, CD-roms, contemporary issues, education, health and medicine, history, language and literature, law, music and entertainment, pop culture, religion and mythology, science, sports and leisure. The site does not have secure online ordering.

Feral House
http://www.feralhouse.com/
Feral offers books and media on conspiracy, true crime, and underground culture.

Fisher Books
http://www.fisherbooks.com/
Based in Tucson, Arizona, Fisher Books is a publisher of books on pregnancy, childcare, cooking, business, motoring, self-help, nature and gardening. Established in 1987, its catalogue features all of its 80 or so titles in print. It also offers about 100 titles from other publishers. You can browse its catalogue by category, title, author, new books and bestsellers.

Fitzroy Dearborn Publishers [Reference]
http://www.fitzroydearborn.com/
Fitzroy Dearborn is an international publisher of encyclopaedias and reference books for libraries. It has offices in Chicago and London. Its subjects include the arts, humanities, business, and the sciences. Complete reviews of its more recent titles can be viewed. The site lacks online ordering facilities.

Franklin Watts – see Grolier.

Funk & Wagnalls – see Primedia.

Gale
http://www.gale.com/
Gale is a pre-eminent international publisher of academic, educational, and business research references serving libraries, educational institutions, and businesses in all major markets worldwide. Its hundreds of directories, reference materials, online services, and educational, academic and business information products, are available in CD-rom, microfilm, print, and online formats. The company is among the most successful publishers delivering subscription-based information services through the web. It is a subsidiary of the Thomson Corporation, a foremost group of professional information businesses in library and business reference, scientific, and other vertical markets worldwide.

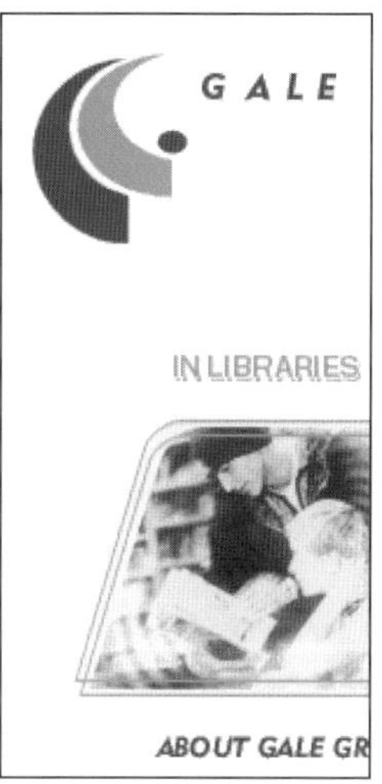

Gateway Books
http://www.gatewaybooks.com
Gateway believes in a free exchange of information on the changes that are happening in the world. It publishes books about free energy and alternative science, cosmic questions, conspiracies, spirituality and self-empowerment.

Gay Sunshine Press
http://www.gaysunshine.com/
Gay history, sex, politics, and culture are the focus of the titles published by San Francisco's Gay Sunshine. Founded in 1970, its list includes work by such writers as Gore Vidal, Christopher Isherwood, Tennessee Williams, Jean Genet, and Allen Ginsberg, as well as work by younger American writers, and gay literature in translation from other cultures including Japan, China, Latin America and Russia.

General Publishing
http://www.genpub.com/
GP is a leading Canadian general publishing group and book distributor. It also represents the catalogues of many UK and other overseas publishers in the Canadian market, as listed on this rather uninspired web site.

Globe Pequot Press
http://www.globe-pequot.com/
Globe Pequot is an old-established US publisher of travel books, guides and maps as well as popular outdoor recreation and language books. It is now among the top three sources for travel books in the United States, issuing some 250 new, distributed and Globe-published titles annually. It claims to offer the broadest selection of travel titles of any vendor in this market.

Greenwood Publishing Group
http://www.greenwood.com/
Based in Westport, Connecticut, Greenwood publishes academic, reference, trade, general interest, and professional books. Its imprints include Auburn House, Bergin & Garvey, Greenwood Press, Praeger, and Quorum. The subject areas include academic reference books, education, women's studies, religion and philosophy, military studies and international security, art and architecture, performing arts and popular culture, library and information science, literature, general interest and trade, history, politics and law, communications, African studies, economics, anthropology and sociology, and psychology. The site includes an author's page, ordering information, and career opportunities.

Grey House Publishing
http://www.greyhouse.com
Based in Connecticut, Grey House is a publisher of reference directories covering direct marketing, health care, disabilities, international trade, education and learning, and the food industry.

Grolier
http://www.grolier.com/
Grolier is a leading and very old-established American publisher of illustrated encyclopaedias and other educational reference materials, in print and electronic form. Its Kids' Club markets some of the most popular children's book clubs in the world; its publishing team provides schools and libraries with children's books and reference materials; while its interactive group develops and markets reference multimedia and online products. The international group brings Grolier's range of encyclopaedias, reference sets, children's books, and electronic products to the Asia Pacific region. The company is located in Danbury, Connecticut. It employs 800 people in Danbury and 2,000 worldwide.

Groves Dictionaries
http://www.grovereference.com
The famous Grove's Dictionaries cover art, music, science, politics, eco-

nomics, and history. Groves is part of the Macmillan Publishing Group in the UK, itself now part of the German Holtzbrinck publishing group. This worldwide family of companies includes book publishers, scientific, technical and medical magazines and journals, business publications, daily and weekly newspapers, television and radio broadcasting companies, and multimedia publishers. Grove's Dictionaries uses industry standard secure socket layer (SSL) encryption to ensure security for purchases over the internet. If you are a bookseller, distributor or wholesaler, you are invited to view its bookseller's pages.

Gryphon House
http://www.ghbooks.com/
Gryphon House Books Inc was founded in 1970 in Washington, DC. Its mission is to provide teachers and parents with quality materials to aid the development and education of young children. Its books are used widely throughout the United States, and have been translated into twelve languages for use by educators and nurturers throughout Eastern and Western Europe, the Americas, the Near and Far East, and Australia. A feature of the site is the 'wonder room' which offers links to a range of early childhood education sites across the internet.

Gulf Publishing Company
http://www.gulfpub.com/
This Texas-based company undertakes specialised publishing for the oil and gas industry.

Hammond
http://www.hammondmap.com/
Four generations ago, Caleb Stillson Hammond believed he could produce a better map, and in 1901 founded the American company that bears his name. The world has changed dramatically since that time. Today Hammond produces cutting-edge computer-based maps and atlases. Here you can find out about the Hammond digital collection – an extensive library of thousands of maps, charts and flags available for the multimedia developer. Hammond's digital maps feature highly accurate physical terrain detail, and 3D realism. The geographic data is complemented with thematic data and almanac information for all countries of the world.

Hampstead House Books
http://www.hhbooks.com
Situated outside Toronto in Canada, Hampstead House is a family publishing business founded twenty years ago. It publishes popular trade books, videos, gift items and calendars. You can apply online for its free 32-page catalogue featuring over 250 titles.

Harcourt Brace
http://www.harcourtbrace.com/
The American publisher Harcourt owns some of the world's most prestigious publishing imprints, serving educational, scientific, technical,

medical, professional and trade markets worldwide, and you are invited to browse their individual sites. These include Harcourt Brace School, College and Trade Publishers, Holt Rinehart Winston, the Psychological Corporation, National Education Training Group, the Steck-Vaughn Publishing Company, Archipelago, and International Correspondence Schools. Many of them now have online catalogues and some process orders securely online.

Harlequin Enterprises
http://www.romance.net/
Harlequin is a North American publisher of mass-market romance titles, and this web site is aimed squarely at the reader of books of this genre. Presented in various pastel shades, it includes such features as school of romance, contest, best-sellers, reading room, recipe for romance, women's health, food and fitness, author appearances, what's new, horoscopes, silhouette quiz, electronic love letters, readers' polls on marriage, silhouette, worldwide mystery, famous families, and more. There are also editorial guidelines for prospective authors. The company has links with Mills & Boon in the UK.

Harper Collins
http://www.harpercollins.com/
http://www.fireandwater.com
Part of Rupert Murdoch's News International, Harper Collins are high profile general trade publishers in the UK and worldwide, strong in fiction, biography and autobiography – and covering everything from romance to religion, and Dylan Thomas to Dilbert. They also publish children's books (see below). On its well-designed web site you can subscribe to HarperLine and get a monthly email detailing their new and

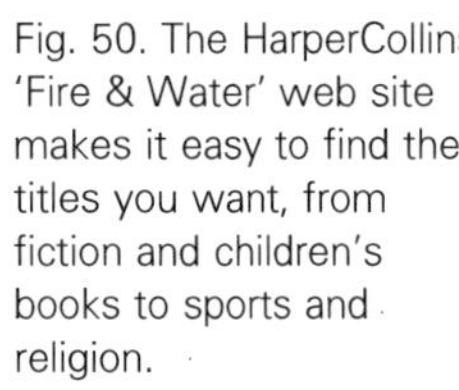

Fig. 50. The HarperCollins 'Fire & Water' web site makes it easy to find the titles you want, from fiction and children's books to sports and religion.

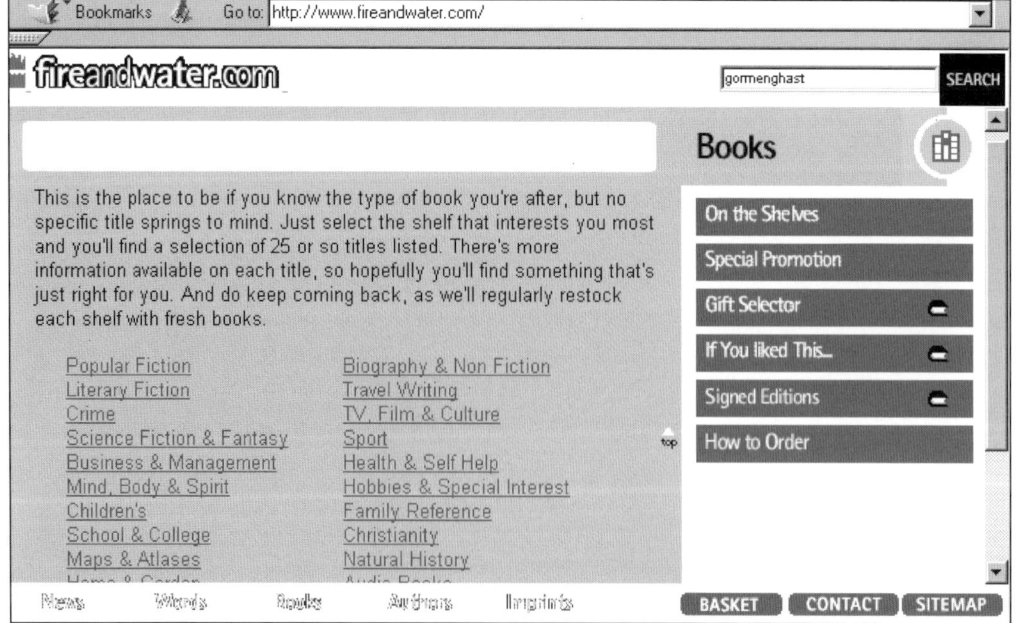

noteworthy titles and events, for example upcoming author tours. Assuming your computer has speakers, you can also hear an online sample from the Harper Audio library, such as Ernest Hemingway's *The Old Man and the Sea* read by Charlton Heston. The company is also developing a new web site Fire and Water, as a resource for book lovers. All internet orders on these sites are fully secure so you can shop with confidence.

HarperCollins Children's Books
http://www.harperchildrens.com/
This is another attractively designed web site from Harper Collins: here you can visit the world of Narnia, or obtain free teachers' guides at the big schoolhouse. There is news about forthcoming books, book features, details of how a book is made, awards, games, links to individual authors and illustrators, and more. There are loads of things for kids to do and explore on the site.

Harry Abrams
http://www.abramsbooks.com/
Harry Abrams is a leading publisher of fine art and illustrated books. It also distributes exhibition catalogues for many of the world's great museums, including the Museum of Modern Art, the Metropolitan Museum of Art, the Guggenheim, and the Whitney Museum of American Art. The web site gives details of its catalogue of more than 1,100 titles, which covers a broad spectrum of visual subjects, from art history to popular culture. The company has also started a new programme of books for young readers.

Harvard University Press
http://www.hup.harvard.edu/
HUP is located in Cambridge, Massachusetts. On its impressive web site you can sign up to receive free email notification of forthcoming books in your areas of interest. You can search the site, view a books menu containing current and backlist titles, see an awards listing, check out featured books, and explore the Loeb Classical Library. You can order titles, read newsroom press releases, request review copies, and enquire about foreign and translation rights. Titles are listed by language, publisher and expected publication date. Explore the history of the Press, view its current editorial program, find out about manuscript submissions, exam copies, permissions policy, and more. There are also links to other web sites of interest to the publishing community and to academic researchers.

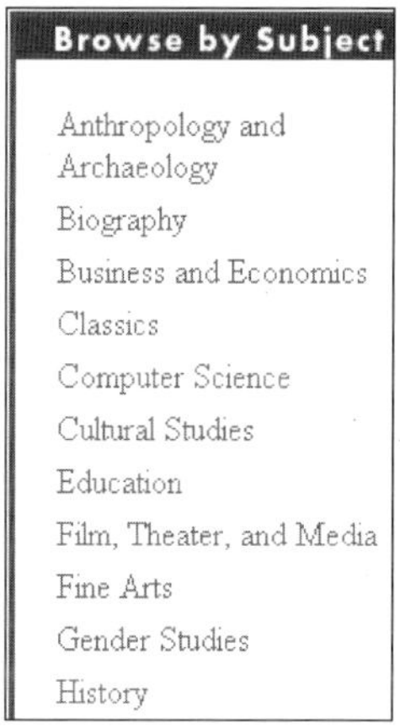

Heinemann USA
http://www.heinemann.com/
Heinemann is one of the world's leading international educational and children's publishers. The site includes a search facility, special offers, 'college connexion', and news of exhibitions. It also offers online 'HeinemannU' English courses, for which a free demo is available online.

Heyeck Press
http://www.heyeckpress.com
Based in California, Heyeck has been printing and publishing both fine limited editions and paperback editions of contemporary poetry and books on paper marbling for over two decades. All of the books are printed letterpress by Robin Heyeck, using metal type and a hand-fed platen press. Fine edition books are printed on dampened handmade paper and then bound in hand-marbled paper or silk.

Hippocrene Books
http://www.hippocrenebooks.com/
New York-based Hippocrene has published over 200 foreign language dictionaries in over 100 different languages. Over the years, it has developed dictionaries for students, travellers and business people. It also publishes cook books, love poetry, history, militaria, titles of Polish and Jewish interest, and children's books.

Holt, Rinehart and Winston
http://www.hrwcollege.com/
Since publishing its first foreign language textbook in 1866, this well-known imprint has developed a large and popular list of instructional language materials. Today it uses the latest in multimedia and CD-rom technology. The company is a division of Harcourt.

John Hopkins University Press
http://www.press.jhu.edu
Founded in 1878 in Baltimore, Maryland, Johns Hopkins is the oldest university press in continuous operation in North America. It is also one of the largest, publishing upward of 170 new books and 50 journals each year with a staff of over 100. Since its founding, the Press has published more than 3,000 books, of which almost half are still in print. It also runs a large programme of scholarly periodicals, including the publishing of these journals online in a program known as Project Muse. Examples of its online projects are *Walker's Mammals of the World* and *The Johns Hopkins Guide to Literary Theory & Criticism*. The site offers links to related sites of scholarly interest.

Houghton Mifflin Company
http://www.hmco.com/
Established in the USA for over a century and a half, Houghton Mifflin is a well-known publisher of textbooks, instructional technology, assessments, and supplementary materials for the elementary and secondary school markets and college markets. It also publishes reference titles, fiction, and non-fiction for adults and young readers, and multimedia entertainment products. Houghton Mifflin Interactive publishes children's and family reference multimedia titles on CD-rom and on the web.

Human Kinetics
http://www.humankinetics.com/
Human Kinetics began in 1974 when Rainer Martens, a professor at the

University of Illinois, decided to publish the proceedings of a sport psychology conference he had organised. Since then the company has become the world's largest producer of information in the physical activity field, with offices in Canada, Europe, Australia, and New Zealand. Its list spans sport and exercise science, physical education, fitness, sports and coaching. Today the company publishes over 90 books and over 20 journals annually.

Humana Press
http://humanapress.com/
Humana is an American publisher of books and journals in molecular biology, neuroscience, cancer research, and medicine. Its most popular titles include *Methods in Molecular Biology*, the *Neuromethods* series, and a new series, *Methods in Molecular Medicine*. It publishes research in *The Journal of Molecular Neuroscience.* Registration gives you full access to articles online. Note: you will need a copy of Adobe Acrobat to view the PDF files.

Hyperion Books
http://www.hyperionbooks.com/
Hyperion, which was founded in 1991, publishes general interest fiction and nonfiction books for adults. It includes Talk Miramax, ESPN Books, ABC Daytime Press, and Hyperion East imprints. The site includes trade information for booksellers as well the general public.

Independent Publishers Group
http://www.ipgbook.com
Founded in 1971, IPG is a book distributor for a large number of independent publishers and small presses throughout the USA and worldwide. On the IPG site you can find an online catalogue of books IPG distributes, information about the services provided to publishers, how to make contact, how to order books, and more. The site includes an A-Z list of publishers distributed by IPG, with links. The Group is a division of the Chicago Review Press.

Johns Hopkins University Press
http://www.press.jhu.edu/home.html
Based in Baltimore, Maryland, Johns Hopkins is the oldest university press in North America in continuous operation, and one of the largest, producing more than 170 books each year and 52 scholarly periodicals. Part of its mission is to publish for a wider general readership. Its list is strong in literary studies, classics, history, economics, political science, and the history of science and medicine, public health, psychology, human development, environmental studies, natural history, the history of technology, and Caribbean studies. It also provides order processing, computer services, warehousing, and shipping for a dozen other publishers.

Jossey-Bass Publishers
http://www.josseybass.com/
Jossey-Bass is based in San Francisco, California. It publishes in the fields of business and management, family and community, education, child development, health, social change, psychology, addictions, sports, public administration and management, religion, counselling, spirituality, and social issues. Its rather functional web site includes links to 100 or more web sites of related interest. It publishes journals, newsletters, and magazines as well as books. The company is a division of Simon & Schuster.

Kensington Publishing
http://www.pinnaclebooks.com/
Founded in 1974 by Walter Zacharius, Kensington Publishing Corporation of New York City claims to be the last remaining independent, full-range book publisher in the United States. During the two decades since its founding, it has developed a mass market and trade program embracing romance, true crime, western, non-fiction and fiction titles, published under the imprints of Kensington Books, Pinnacle Books and Zebra Books. The company has a staff of over 70 editorial, marketing and production people.

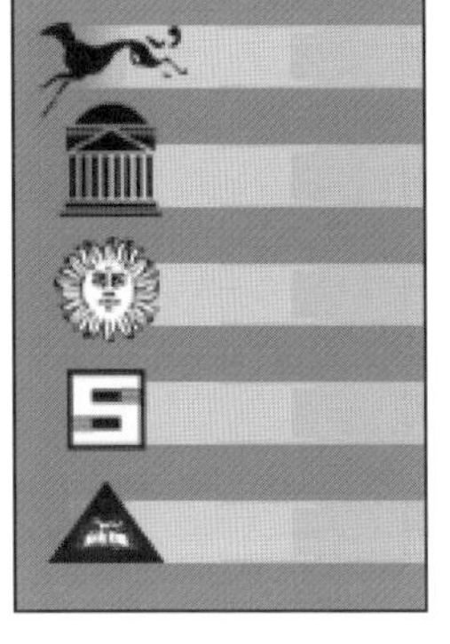

Knopf Publishing Group
http://www.randomhouse.com/knopf/
Founded in 1915 by Alfred A. Knopf, the imprint has long enjoyed a high reputation as a publisher of hardcover trade fiction and nonfiction. It published five of the eleven titles selected by the editors of *The New York Times Book Review* as the Best Books of 1998. Recent titles have included *The American Century*, by Harold Evans, *Glamorama* by Bret Easton Ellis (author of *American Psycho*), and *The New Yorker Book of True Love Cartoons.* Knopf is a division of Random House.

Let's Go
http://www.letsgo.com/
Let's Go is a student-run travel and map guide publishing enterprise, run from Cambridge, Massachusetts. About 200 students each year take part in travelling, researching and writing its thirty or so popular titles, which are distributed around the world, and cover destinations from Alaska and Australia to Turkey and Washington. In addition to travel content of universal interest, the guides include information specially geared to women, disabled, gay and lesbian travellers. The colour pictures of the book covers are quick to load on the site.

Lexis Law Publishing
http://www.lexislawpublishing.com/
Lexis Law Publishing has been a leader in US legal publishing since the early 1800s. Originally known as the Michie Company, it offers more than 700 practice titles, 400 legal publications, and the annotated codes in 35 states and territories. It publishes in a wide range of topics including litigation, torts, business and international law. It is also the

official publisher of the *US Code Service* and *Supreme Court Reports (Lawyers' Edition)*. More than 1,000 people work in its headquarters in Charlottesville, Virginia, and regional offices in Rochester, New York, San Francisco, California and Puerto Rico. Lexis is a division of Reed Elsevier. Its sister companies include Lexis-Nexis, Matthew Bender, Butterworths, Martindale-Hubbell, Shephard's and Capsoft.

Lexis-Nexis
http://www.lexis-nexis.com/
Lexis-Nexis probably leads the world's information industry with the largest one-stop, dial-up information service in existence for legal, business, and government professionals. Its service contains more than one trillion characters and 1.4 billion documents in more than 8,000 databases. It adds over 4 million documents each week. Today, 1.5 million professionals worldwide – lawyers, accountants, financial analysts, journalists, law enforcement officials and information specialists – subscribe to the Lexis-Nexis services, performing more than 300,000 searches a day. The company, a division of Reed Elsevier, is based in Dayton, Ohio, USA, and employs more than 6,000 people around the world.

Library of America
http://www.libraryofamerica.org
The Library of America was founded in 1979 as a non-profit publisher to help preserve the nation's cultural heritage by publishing America's best and most significant writing in durable and authoritative editions. The first volumes were published in 1982. Each one is unabridged and includes a chronology of the author's life and work, notes prepared by a distinguished scholar, and a brief essay on the text selected for each work. The authors run from Henry Adams and James Baldwin to Edith Wharton and Walt Whitman. You can search the web site by category, title and author, and view the lengthy drop-down menu for each. You can also email them for a catalogue by post.

Lippincott Williams & Wilkins
http://www.lrpub.com/
LWW is a global publisher of medical, nursing and allied health information resources in book, journal, newsletter, loose-leaf, and electronic media. Through its newly-formed electronic production department, it aims to become the world leader for electronic delivery of health-science information. It continues to develop new distribution methods for its material including the internet, CD-ROMs, and intranets of hospitals and healthcare organisations. Its impressive web site offers a large online store featuring 4,000-plus titles in over 100 disciplines, content-based sites and online corporate and customer services. Based in Philadelphia, the recently formed company is a subsidiary of the Dutch publishing conglomerate Wolters Kluwer.

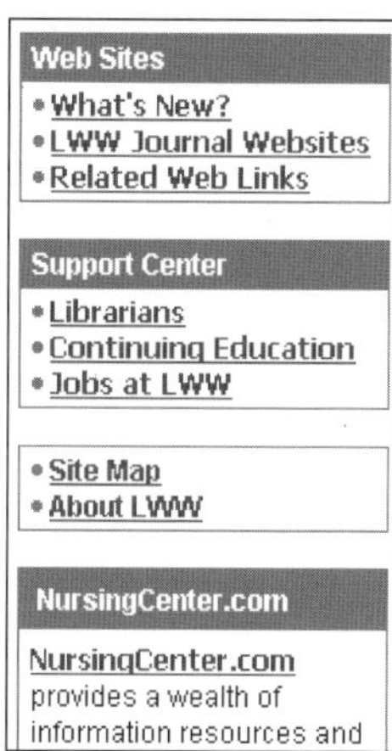

Little Brown
http://www.littlebrown.com
The link for this old-established American publisher now leads you to the

Time Warner Bookmark site, which includes Warner titles as well. The magazine-style site offers a broad range of general interest titles for adults and children.

Llewellyn
http://www.llewellyn.com/
Featuring a waxing moon on its opening page, this is the web site of an old-established new age publishing company, located in St Paul, Minnesota, USA. Llewellyn began as the Portland School of Astrology in 1901 under the leadership of Llewellyn George. Today, its consumer catalogue, *New Worlds* has a circulation of some 200,000. While the imprint has long been known as the Americas' oldest publisher of new age sciences, it is focussing more on tools for self-transformation. The site includes guidelines for writers and artists.

Longman Publishers USA
http://longman.awl.com/
Longman was originally an old British family publishing business. Two centuries later it is an imprint of Addison Wesley Longman, a premiere educational publisher of books, multimedia and learning programs in all major academic disciplines to the primary, secondary, higher education and professional markets throughout the world. Longman itself continues to serve the learning and teaching needs of students and professors in the humanities and social sciences. The company has a distinguished history in these disciplines, dating back to its publication of Samuel Johnson in the 18th century. In more recent years it has focused on textbooks, supplements, and new media for the higher education market.

Macmillan USA
http://www.mcp.com/
Macmillan USA is part of Pearson PLC, an international media company. Its imprints include Que, Sams, BradyGames, the Complete Idiots Guides, and Macmillan Software. Together, they sell around 14 million books worldwide each year. Que produces titles on all major computer and internet topics, for the novice setting up his first PC to the programmer developing leading edge computer software. Sams is another top computing imprint, with around 450 titles in print. The site includes a job opportunities area, where typical vacancies on offer include acquisitions editors, HTML and page layout technicians, and account managers.

Magellan Press
http://www.magellanpress.com
Magellan is a small specialist publisher of American restaurant and travel guides, based in Nashville, Tennessee. Its web site includes links to food, travel, and other related web sites.

Marketing Directions
http://www.marketingdirections.com
Marketing Directions Inc is an American publisher of books and videos on media promotion, employment, interviewing, self-publishing, and

marketing. In 1996 it formed a subsidiary, Book Marketing Works, to help authors self-publish and market their books. Its director, Brian Jud, is founder and president of the Connecticut Authors Association.

Marquis Who's Who
http://www.marquiswhoswho.com/
For nearly a century, *Who's Who in America* has provided concise biographies of notable Americans. Marquis now publishes several such specialised directories, compiled by a variety of criteria, that provide subsets to contemporary biography. Their publications now present biographies of more than 750,000 leaders and achievers from around the world, and from all professions. You can use the web site to nominate a colleague or submit your own personal information. If your name is accepted, be prepared to pay about $370 to obtain a copy of *Who's Who in the World.*

McGraw-Hill
http://www.mcgraw-hill.com
Founded in the nineteenth century, McGraw-Hill has become one of the world's largest technical and educational publishing companies. Building on its original strengths in engineering and science, it has seen an enormous expansion on its publishing on business, management and the social sciences. This impressive web site will tell you all you want to know about the company's history, development, network of subsidiary companies, current publishing programmes, forthcoming titles, news, career opportunities within the group, and more.

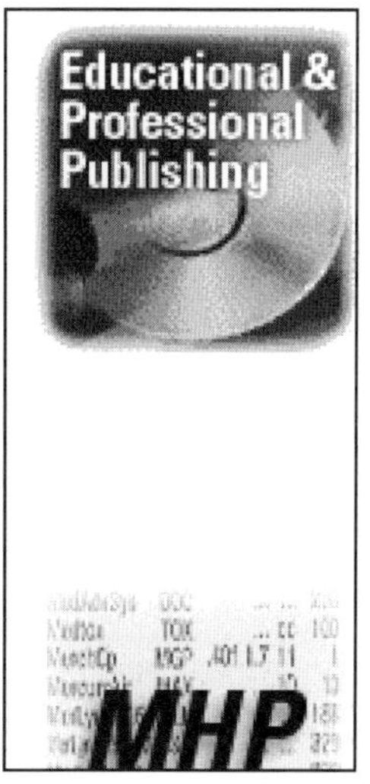

McGraw-Hill Higher Education
http://www.mhhe.com/
The company publishes instructional materials targeted at the higher education market. These include not only texts, lab manuals, study guides and testing materials, but software and multimedia products. Its web site is for both instructors and students. It includes product information, multimedia demos, downloadable ancillaries, interactive features, and more. McGraw-Hill invites you to browse over 5,000 books and digital products in its online catalogue. You can search by author, title, course area, key words or ISBN number.

McPherson & Company
http://www.mcphersonco.com
Founded in 1974, McPherson is an independent literary and arts publishing company operating out of Kingston, New York. The press specialises in four areas: contemporary fiction (mostly American), 'lost' literary works from earlier in the century (the Recovered Classics series), non-fiction books dealing with contemporary art, film, aesthetics, and related cultural issues presented under the Documentext imprint, and translations of 20th century Italian fiction.

Merriam-Webster
http://www.m-w.com/
Merriam-Webster is a prominent American publisher of language reference works. It publishes an array of print and electronic products, including *Merriam-Webster's Collegiate Dictionary* and *Webster's Third New International Dictionary.* Founded in the 1820s by Noah Webster, this publisher has moved strongly into the electronic age, and has everything you want to know about words – American style. This brightly-presented web site offers dictionaries, thesauruses, word games and reference books for all categories of readership and age groups. You can take a brief look at the history of English, and find out how a word gets into a dictionary.

Metropolitan Museum of Art
http://www.metmuseum.org/
The Metropolitan Museum of Art in New York is one of the largest and finest art museums in the world. Its collections include more than two million works of art – several hundred thousand of which are on view at any given time – spanning more than 5,000 years of world culture, from prehistory to the present. This site gives visitors an overview of the collections on display in the Museum's galleries. Also available are a floor plan, which includes information on services for visitors, and the calendar, which offers a detailed current listing of special exhibitions, concerts, lectures, films, and other museum activities. You can also explore the Metropolitan Museum of Art Store, with over 500 popular items available. If you are interested in art this site is a must.

Fig. 51. The Metropolitan Museum of Art web site allows you to view more than 3,500 works of art in its online collection.

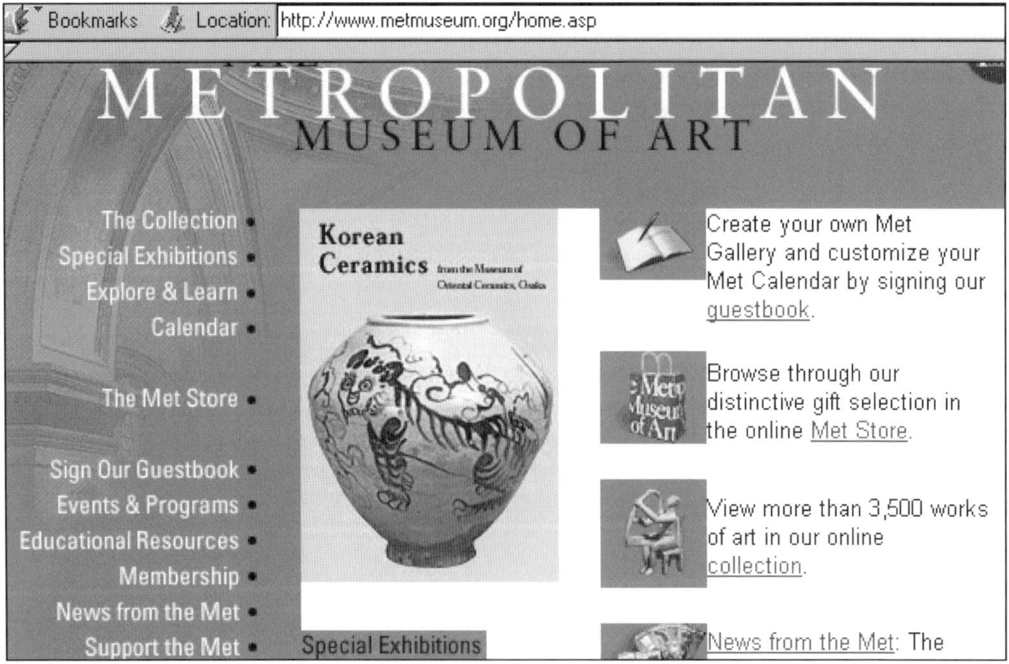

Microsoft Press
http://mspress.microsoft.com/
Microsoft Press offers comprehensive learning and training resources to help new and established users and professionals get the most from Microsoft technology. On this impressive site it offers books, CDs, self-paced training kits, and videos to accommodate different learning styles and preferences. You will also find news, help with certification, chats with technical experts, and more. The search facility and site map are essential for a site of this size. Microsoft Press is also looking for authors with hot ideas for new books on Microsoft products. If you think you fit the bill, or just want more information, take a look at its book proposal guidelines.

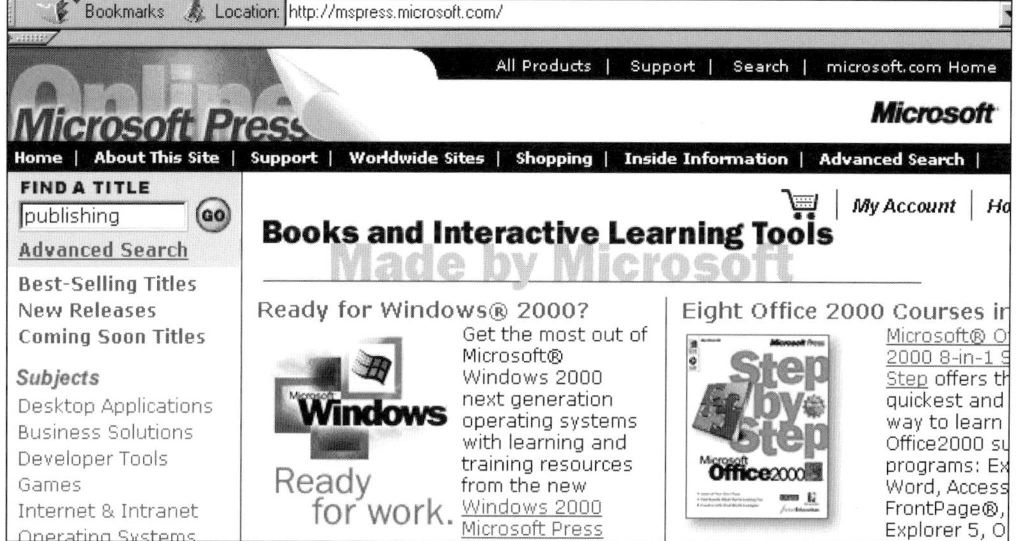

Fig. 52. Microsoft Press offers a large selection of books, courses and software to support the use of Microsoft products in personal and business computing and the internet.

Miller Freeman
http://www.mfi.com/
Miller Freeman is one of the world's largest, oldest and most diversified publishers of business publications. Based in San Francisco, it publishes over seventy business and special interest consumer magazines, a wide variety of newsletters, directories, books and research reports, newsletters, postcard decks, web sites as well as running more than eighty trade shows and conferences around the world. In Europe, London-based Miller Freeman plc publishes over a hundred magazines and forty directories, with particular strength in building, agriculture, medicine, electronics, engineering, pharmacy and the travel trade. Miller Freeman is a United News & Media company.

Modern Age Books
http://www.mabooks.com/
The American publisher Modern Age Books provides digital publishing services, including electronic documentation and online manuals, to companies who publish reference materials. The company has produced

over 800 electronic manuals and CD-roms for major publishing companies such as Microsoft Press, Macmillan, Osborne/McGraw-Hill, and Sybex.

Mojo Press
http://www.mojo.com
Based in Austin, Texas, Mojo is a small independent new publisher of graphic and prose novels. Its main genres are horror, westerns, and science fiction. The word Mojo refers to magic that wards off evil. Other definitions including a term for drugs or when something is cool. This slang word most probably derives from an African tribal language

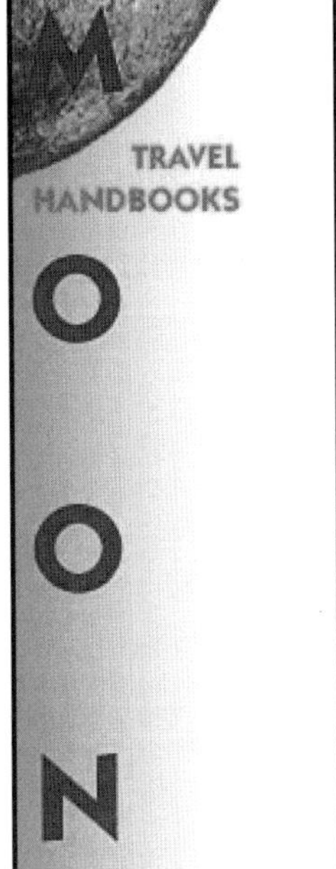

Moon Travel Handbooks
http://www.moon.com/
Moon is an established US-based publisher of travel handbooks. The attractively presented site offers excerpts from new and upcoming Moon titles, visits to exotic worldwide destinations, book and multimedia reviews. You can read *Travel Matters*, Moon's online travel magazine, complete with news, articles, features, and a back-issue archive. The company was founded by Bill Dalton, who chronicles his own latest journeys on the site.

Morgan Kaufmann Publishers
http://www.mkp.com
Morgan Kaufmann was founded in 1984 in Silicon Valley. The founders were Michael Morgan, Nils Nilsson, Professor of Computer Science at Stanford University, and a publishing veteran William Kaufmann. The company has published a range of technical information for computer and engineering professionals. It publishes in book and digital form in such areas as databases, computer networking, computer systems, human computer interaction, computer graphics, multimedia information and systems, artificial intelligence, and software engineering. Located in San Francisco, the company is now a division of Harcourt.

Mosby
http://www.mosby.com/
Based in St Louis, Missouri, and established in 1906, Mosby is an international publisher of nursing, dental and veterinary materials. The site includes expanded descriptions, sample content and information on its latest products. These include books, periodicals and media products, newsletters, videos, posters, brochures, slides, laser discs, CD-roms, seminars, conferences and association management. There is also an author's centre. You can do both quick and advanced catalogue searches. Mosby is a Harcourt Health Sciences Company.

Naval Institute Press
http://www.nip.org
This is the online bookstore of US-based Naval Institute Press, where you can buy naval history and literature books available via a secure, encrypted connection. Currently celebrating 100 years of book publish-

ing, the Press produces more than 70 titles a year, ranging from how-to books on boating and navigation to battle histories, biographies, ship and aircraft guides, and novels. Institute members receive discounts on the Press's nearly 800 books in print. The company is based in Annapolis, Maryland.

Nelson Publishing Company
http://www.nelsonpub.com/
NPC publishes engineering and technical journals including *Evaluation Engineering, Communications News, Modern Applications News,* and *Health Management Technology.*

Netscape Press
http://merchant.netscape.com/netstore/
This is the publishing and bookstore area of Netscape Communications, the company that brought you the Netscape Navigator browser. It offers a range of books and software to help you get the most out of the internet. Netscape is now part of AOL Time Warner.

Norton
http://www.wwnorton.com/
WW Norton & Company Inc is the oldest and largest publishing house owned wholly by its employees. The roots of the company date back to 1923, when William Warder Norton and his wife began publishing lectures delivered at the People's Institute, the adult education division of New York City's Cooper Union. Early on, Norton entered the fields of philosophy, music, and psychology publishing, and has long been known for its distinguished publishing programs in both the trade and the college textbook areas. Since the 1980s, the company has emerged as a prominent international player and now publishes about 300 books a year in hardcover and paperback.

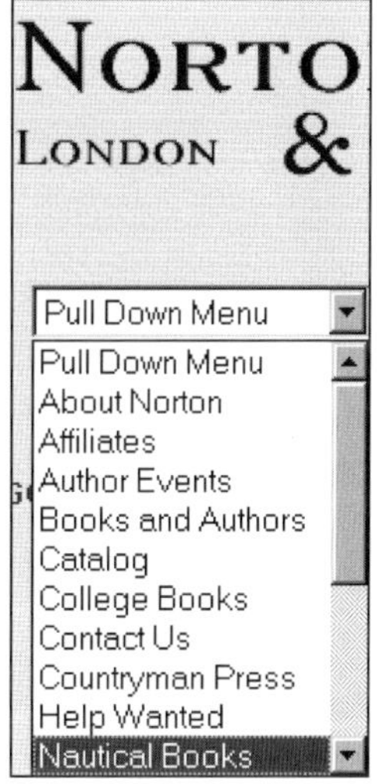

Octavo Corporation
http://www.octavo.com/
Based in Palo Alto, California, Octavo publishes digital editions of rare books and manuscripts. The company forms a partnership with a library, institution, or individual, and works with the librarian or curator to choose books for producing in electronic formats. Its Editions contain facilities to browse, read, and examine files for viewing onscreen. Additionally, there are thumbnails and print files for creating printed references. This is a well-designed and in-depth site which does justice to the range and quality of Octavo's innovative electronic publications, typically priced at $30 to $50.

Oxford University Press (USA)
http://www.oup-usa.org/
This is the American division of the OUP. The impressive and detailed site contains links to academic matters, bibles, business, children and young adults, college/textbooks, dictionaries and reference, electronic publishing, ESL, Oxford paperbacks, journals, music, catalogues, contact an

editor, customer service, employment opportunities, OUP International, the Oxford Reference Book Society, the Oxford University website, permissions, privacy statement, publicity, subsidiary rights, and Y2K information.

Paladin Press
http://www.paladin-press.com/
Based in Boulder, Colorado, Paladin has been called 'the most dangerous press in America. It offers outrageous and controversial books and videotapes on subjects such as weaponry and combat shooting, silencers, sniping, explosives, knives and knife fighting, revenge and humour, lock-smithing, martial arts and self-defence, military and police science, new ID, personal and financial freedom, survival, espionage and investigation, and more.

Paragon Book Gallery
http://www.paragonbook.com/
This Chicago-based company offers a searchable database of titles relating to the arts and antiquities of Asia. You can read book reviews from academics and experts, explore Asian arts on the internet, and join its mailing list to receive email updates.

Parthenon Publishing Group
http://www.parthpub.com
From its offices in New York and London, Parthenon produces a range of books, journals, videos, slide sets and multimedia software for healthcare professionals and environmental scientists around the world. The first link on its web site takes you to news of its latest projects and publications. The second takes you to a selection of books, slide sets, videos and CD-roms from its printed catalogue; and the third link takes you to its journals section, with further links to the contents of recent issues. Examples of recent titles include The *Interactive Atlas of Human Anatomy, Breast Disease for Primary Care Physicians,* and *An Atlas of Multiple Sclerosis*.

Pegasus Press
http://pegasuspress.org
Based at the University of North Carolina, USA, Pegasus offers books for teaching and research in the medieval and Renaissance periods. Its products include a series of Anglo-Saxon manuscripts in microfiche facsimile. It is also developing a CD-rom database of books owned in Renaissance/Restoration England. Its journals include *The John Gower Newsletter, Exemplaria, General Linguistics,* and the *Yearbook of Langland Studies*.

Pelican Publishing Company
http://pelicanpub.com
Louisiana-based Pelican is a growing medium-sized family owned company with a backlist of nearly 500 titles and 50 to 60 new titles produced annually. As a general trade publisher, it produces a wide variety of

travel guides, art and architecture books, Christmas stories, local and international cookbooks, motivational and inspirational works, and children's books, as well as a growing number of social commentary, history, and fiction titles. The site includes author guidelines, a guest book, and details of employment opportunities within the company.

Penguin Putnam
http://www.penguinputnam.com/
This is an American division of the Penguin Group whose imprints and trademarks include Viking, Putnam's Sons, Berkeley Books, Penguin, Dutton, Plume and Signet.

Phoenix Publishing
http://www.phoenixpublishing.com/
This American company publishes books on Wicca, paganism, occult, magic and related topics.

Plenum Publishing Corporation
http://www.plenum.com/
Since 1946, Plenum has provided the international scientific community with leading edge professional books, journals, and databases. Its online catalogue contains over 4,500 titles to choose from, spanning all the physical, life, and social sciences. Its electronic publications include scientific, technical, and medical journals and databases available online or on CD-ROM. An electronic order form is attached to each title. The clearly presented site includes email contacts to its various acquisitions editors. Headquartered in New York, the firm is part of Kluwer Academic.

Plexus
http://www.cyberplexus.com
Publishes a small number of radically practical spiritual wisdom handbooks for the modern age.

Praeger – see Greenwood.

Prentice Hall
http://www.prenhall.com/
Based in the USA, Prentice Hall is one of the leading publishers of college course materials in the world. Its enormous list covers introductory levels to advanced, professional, reference publications, and monographs. There are online search tools to guide you through its extensive academic and reference catalogues. You can order by phone, fax or phone, and there are contact details for ordering in many different parts of the world. The company is a division of Pearson Education.

Prima Publishing
http://www.primapublishing.com/
Established in the USA in 1984, Prima publishes general non-fiction

books, computer user and administrator guides, and strategy guides for computer and video games. It employs more than 200 people in four divisions: Prima Lifestyles, Prima-Tech, Prima Games, and Prima Health, which together publish more than 300 titles a year. There is a site map to guide you around.

Primedia
http://www.primediainc.com/
The quoted US company Primedia provides specialised information for target audiences in the education, business and special interest consumer markets. Its products include *Seventeen, Soap Opera Digest,* and *Ward's*. The Primedia Reference Group includes Funk & Wagnalls, World Almanac Books, World Almanac Education and Facts on File News Services.

Search
New in Print
Browse by Subject
Browse by Series
Catalogs
Join E-mail list
Sample Chapters
Class Use/Exam Copies
Permissions
Recent Prizes
How to Contact Us
Frequent Questions
About the Press
For Book Reviewers
Useful links
Online Ordering

Princeton University Press
http://pup.princeton.edu
Unlike most university presses owned or financially supported by universities, Princeton has always been privately owned and controlled, though it has always maintained a close relationship with the University. Manuscripts are solicited by its staff editors, and referred to outside peer review. The Press sells foreign rights around the world, employs sales representatives in the US and abroad, and warehouses books in New Jersey and England. It publishes about 200 new books in hardcover each year and another 90 paperback reprints. Its titles span more than 40 disciplines from art history to ornithology, population studies to philosophy. There is a secure online order form for the United States, Canada, Latin America, Asia, and Australia (but traditional ordering from the UK).

Prometheus Books
http://www.prometheusbooks.com/
Based in New York State, Prometheus has been publishing books and journals for the educational, scientific, professional, library, popular and consumer markets since 1969. A leading publisher in philosophy, science and critical thinking, Prometheus has more than 1,000 books and journals in print, with an average output of 100 new titles a year. For online ordering, the site is secured by ATT 'secure buy' services.

Prufrock Press
http://www.prufrock.com/
Prufrock is dedicated to supporting the education of gifted and talented children. On its fast-loading site you can find the latest gifted education magazines, research journals, identification instruments, books and more. The company operates out of Waco, Texas,

Public Record Research Library
http://www.brbpub.com
PRRL publishes a series of books and disks dedicated to the understanding of US public records for professional screening or search firms, law

libraries, paralegals, public libraries, human resource professionals, government agencies, private investigators, and investigative reporters.

Putney Press
http://www.sover.net/-ppress/index.html
Based in Vermont, Putney is a specialist publisher in the USA environmental regulatory field.

Quorum – see Greenwood.

Random House
http://www.randomhouse.com/
Founded in 1925, Random House has grown into the world's largest English-language general trade book publisher. It includes an array of famous imprints that publish some of the foremost writers of the age – in hardcover, trade paperback, mass market paperback, audio, multimedia, and other formats. Its many brands include Ballantine, Bantam Books, Broadway Books, the Crown Publishing Group, Dell Publishing, Doubleday and Knopf. The site includes not only catalogues and author details, but also information about permissions and copyrights, and even job opportunities within the group. The site offers online ordering and email updates about forthcoming titles.

Fig. 53. The Random House international web site is packed with news and features about its top selling books and authors.

Reader's Digest
http://www.readersdigest.com/
This is the home page of possibly the world's best-known popular consumer magazine. The site contains a big archive of articles and features, well designed and presented with additional features and links. There are

the famous features of word power, and laugh lines. You can even trace your genealogy here.

Reed Reference Publishing
http://www.reedref.com/
Based in New Providence, New Jersey, Reed Reference comprises Martindale-Hubbell, R.R. Bowker, National Register Publishing, Marquis Who's Who, and Lexis-Nexis Business Information Services.

Rodale Press
http://www.rodalepress.com/
Rodale publishes magazines and books in the areas of sports, health, cooking, woodworking, gardening, quilting and sewing. There are site links to meet Rodale, customer service, company store, career opportunities, news and events, index, retailers, healthy ideas, runner's world online, bookstore, backpacker's base camp, scuba diving, bicycling online, organic gardening and mountain bike daily.

Rutgers University Press
http://rutgerspress.rutgers.edu/
Rutgers is the State University of New Jersey. The site was under construction when reviewed, though there was information on how to submit a manuscript.

Howard W. Sams
http://www.hwsams.com/
Howard W. Sams, located in Indianapolis, Indiana, is a leading publisher of technical documentation and computing materials..

WB Saunders & Baillière Tindall
http://www.hbuk.co.uk/wbs/
Founded in Philadelphia in 1888, WB Saunders Company is a leading international publisher of health science books and periodicals. Baillière Tindall's long publishing history began over 150 years ago as the English branch of a French publishing house that specialised in medicine. Today their combined list of over 2,500 titles contains major textbooks, reference works and periodicals in all medical specialities, from undergraduate textbooks to major reference works; nursing; health-related professions; veterinary medicine and dentistry. The company is a division of Harcourt.

Scribner
http://www.mlr.com/scribner/
Charles Scribner's Sons was founded in 1846, at the Brick Church Chapel on New York's Park Row. Among its many innovative scholarly works over the years were the first *Dictionary of American Biography* volumes published in the 1920s and the first edition of the *Dictionary of American History* published in 1940. In addition to new reference sets and supplements to classic works, its catalogues also offer CD-roms. The firm is now a division of Macmillan Library Reference USA.

Severn House
http://www.severnhouse.com
Severn House publishes editions of contemporary fiction, contemporary and historical romance, crime thrillers, historical sagas, suspense, science fiction, horror, and books on war and military subjects.

Shaw Guides
http://www.shawguides.com/
Established in 1988, New York-based Shaw publishes a series of world-wide guides to activity holidays. These include educational travel, art and craft workshops, cooking schools, recreational golf schools and camps, photography schools and workshops, language vacations, writers' conferences, tennis schools and camps, and water sports schools and camps.

Shelter Publications
http://www.shelterpub.com/
Based in Bolinas, California, Shelter has been issuing trade paperback books for about 28 years. Most of its books are aimed at helping people do things for themselves. They are distributed to the bookstores by Random House. 'We operate out of a production studio built of recycled lumber, set in the midst of a vegetable garden in a small northern California coastal town. Yet we are hooked into the world electronically.' Sample titles include *The Office Fitness Clinic*, and *The Septic System Owner's Manual*.

Signet – see Penguin Putnam.

Fig. 54. The Simon & Schuster web site offers email updates in the subject areas that appeal to you.

Silver Burdett Ginn
http://www.sbgschool.com/
This is the north American publisher's online centre for elementary school teachers and students. It is strong in language, social studies, mathematics and music. Silver Burdett Ginn (together with Scott Foreman) is a division of Pearson Education.

Simon & Schuster
http://www.Simonandschuster.com/
Simon & Schuster is one of the world's top publishing groups. Its imprints include Charles Scribner and Company, and its many notable authors include Ernest Hemingway, Jackie Collins, and Stephen King. Its list spans academic and professional resources, business, cooking and wine, fiction, health and fitness, history, biography, mystery, romance, S&S Classic Editions, The Free Press and eBooks. You can search its database for titles, authors, excerpts and book covers.

Sky Publishing Corporation
http://www.skypub.com/
This company publishes the *Sky & Telescope* magazine, founded in 1941. Using secure ordering technology, its online store offers 'the galaxy's best selection of astronomy books, software, star atlases, observing guides, and related products.' Sky is based in Cambridge, Massachusetts.

Slavica Publishers
http://slavica.com/
Founded by a Professor of Slavic Linguistics at the Ohio State University, Slavica publishes a scholarly books on the languages, peoples, literatures, cultures and history of the former USSR and Eastern Europe. Slavica has been owned by Indiana University since 1997.

Somerville House Books Limited
http://www.sombooks.com/
Somerville is a Canadian book packager and publisher. The firm began life in 1983 as a packager, developing and publishing projects for other companies. It has now developed its own publishing program characterised by fully illustrated children's books combined with a kit or toy. Its products include *The Bug Book and Bug Bottle*, *The Bones Book & Skeleton* and *The Tiny Perfect Dinosaur Series*. It also publishes adult literary fiction and non-fiction books.

Southam
http://www.southam.com/
Southam is a Canadian owned international publishing corporation which produces newspapers, multimedia CD-roms, trade periodicals, trade shows and online databases.

Springer Publishing Company
http://www.springer.co.uk/
This is the US web site of Springer Verlag, offering authoritative books

and journals in the fields of computing, engineering, mathematics, medicine and astronomy. The site includes catalogues, electronic publications, support materials, and information for authors.

St James Press
http://www.stjames.com/
Established in 1968, US publisher St James aims to publish 'exemplary titles with scholarly appeal and contemporary flair in a wide range of disciplines.' Its chosen fields are performing arts, art and architecture, contemporary arts, gay and lesbian studies, contemporary writers, a literary reference guide series and business and general reference titles.

St Martin's Press
http://www.stmartins.com/
New York-based St Martin's Press both publishes and distributes a broad spectrum of books ranging from college texts and scholarly monographs to fiction, biography, mysteries and cookbooks. Its web site (undergoing refurbishment when reviewed) includes links to a number of author sites.

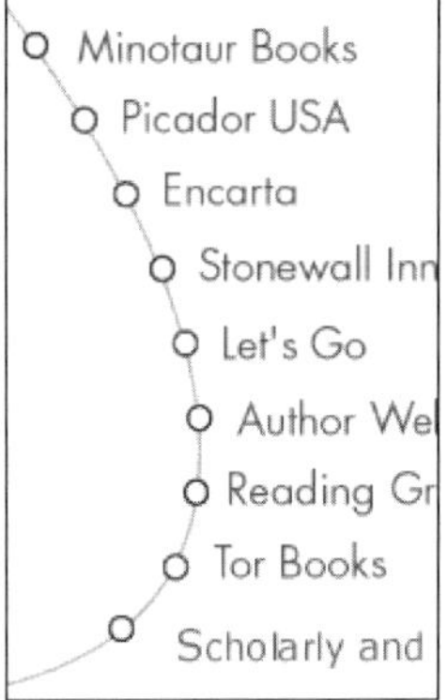

Stanford University Press
http://www.sup.org/
SUP is the academic imprint of Stanford University in California. It furthers the university's research and teaching mission through the publication of works based on significant scholarship. All of its books are approved in advance of publication on the basis of formal, external evaluations. The Press publishes around 110 new books per year, plus new paperback editions. The emphasis is upon the humanities. It is exclusively a book publisher, and does not publish journals, proceedings, symposia, working papers, or unrevised dissertations.

Stemmer House Publishers
http://www.stemmer.com
Founded in 1975, Stemmer is an independent Baltimore-based general trade publisher. Its diversified list encompasses the humanities, art and design, crafts, cooking, children's literature and audiocassettes.

Step by Step Publications
http://www.sbspub.com
SBS runs a self-publishing service from Cloverdale, Indiana.

Sterling Publications
http://www.sterpub.com
Sterling is a privately owned New York publisher formed in 1949. It publishes self-help and how-to books, with more than 3,000 titles in print. Its titles cover art, business, crafts, equestrianism, food, gardening, gifts, health, history, hobbies, home decorating, humour, juvenile, kits, music, natural history, new age, parenting, pets, photography, pre-school, puzzles and games, reference, science, sports and woodworking.

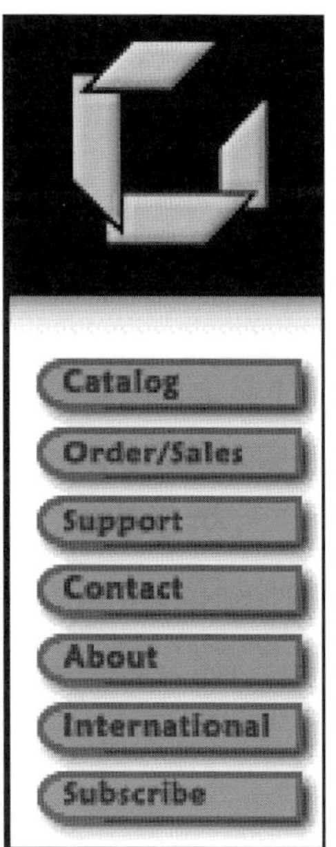

Sybex Computer Books
http://www.sybex.com/
Sybex is well known for its large range of books for graphics and web professionals. The Californian company was founded in 1976 by Rodnay Zaks around the same time as software giants like Apple and Microsoft. Like fellow pioneers Steve Jobs and Bill Gates, Zaks recognised the extraordinary potential of microcomputers. The first Sybex offices were opened in order to train and educate early users and designers worldwide. Today, Sybex is the world's largest independent publisher of computer books, and one of the few independents remaining. Recent titles include *Mastering Adobe InDesign* and *ABC of Windows 98.*

Taunton Press
http://www.taunton.com
Based in Newtown, Connecticut, Taunton is a family-owned publisher of how-to magazines, books and videos for gardening, woodworking, homebuilding, cooking, sewing, and remodelling. You can use its site to explore its magazines: *Fine Woodworking, Fine Homebuilding, Threads, Fine Gardening, Fine Cooking, and Kitchen Gardener.* You can also search through its online book and video catalogues of some 200 titles, join a discussion group at any of its magazine sites, preview videos in its video room, and even apply for a job.

Taurus Publishing
http://www.tauruspub.net
Canadian publisher Taurus was formed in 1994, primarily to self-publish and market the *Maxim Gunn* series of action adventure and espionage novels written by Nicholas Boving.

Templegate Publishers
http://www.templegate.com
Template is a publisher of mainly religious titles, which encompass spiritual handbooks, biographies and anthologies.

Thomson
http://www.thomson.com/
Thomson is one of the world's pre-eminent information publishers, with interests in specialised information worldwide, and newspaper publishing especially in north America. It operates mainly in the US, Canada, and the United Kingdom and has annual revenues of some $6 billion. Its businesses are mainly focused on delivering information-based services and tools to support professionals in private practice, industry, government and academia. Its traditional and electronic products cover legal, financial, health care and scientific disciplines. This main page leads you to the individual web sites of scores of operating subsidiaries from American Banker Online to Winnipeg Free Press Online.

Thomson Learning
http://www.thomsonlearning.com/
'Whether it is in the traditional education setting, the corporate training room, the career school or the virtual classroom: if you are a student, an instructor or trainer, an administrator, a concerned parent, or a bookstore, this site will send you to a rapidly growing list of services, products and information.' In over 100 countries around the world, Thomson provides learning materials in a wide variety of subjects and disciplines. Formerly known as ITP, it publishes for schools, higher education, career and vocational/technical institutions. It is also a growing presence in the world of business, industry and government training.

Time-Life Education
http://www.timelifeedu.com/
'Inspiring young minds' is the slogan of this publisher of colourful educational and reference materials for children and young people. The home page leads you to areas for educators, librarians and students, and to books covering everything from science and nature to history and culture. It also offers general interest publications in such fields as cookery, travel and sports.

Time Warner
http://www.twbookmark.com/
Time Warner has recently merged with America OnLine (AOL) to form the world's biggest entertainment and media group. This magazine-style publishing site offers a broad range of general interest titles for adults and children, published under the separate imprints of Time, Warner and Little Brown. In addition to a large searchable catalogue, its many online features include latest book news, 'the Buzz' (current bestsellers), an author

Fig. 55. Time Warner was recently acquired by America OnLine in the biggest corporate merger in history. The merger was described as a union of 'clicks and mortar' in the way it combined online and traditional products and services.

lounge, live chat with its authors, free chapters of selected titles, details of bookseller services and current job opportunities.

Tradewind Books
http://www.tradewindbooks.com/
Based in Vancouver, Canada, Tradewind is a publisher of illustrated books for young children.

Trafford Publishing
http://www.trafford.com/
Trafford offers a web bookstore and on-demand publishing facilities for authors. Operating from Victoria, British Columbia, it has assisted authors from twelve countries to publish more than 300 titles, 'allowing today's authors to publicise and retail their books on a global scale without leaving their own homes'.

Transaction Publishers
http://www.transactionpub.com
Based in Somerset, New Jersey, Transaction has published topics in international social science since 1962. The home page takes you straight into a secure online bookstore, which also offers large print books. Sample titles include *Anthropology and Ethics* and *Environmental Protection in European Community Law.*

Transworld – see Bantam.

Truman Publishing
http://www.trumanpublishing.com
Located in Kansas City, Missouri, Truman are recently established publishers of books on civic betterment, career and money-making opportunities, mental health, self help, and American history. The site includes submission guidelines for authors.

United Nations
http://www.un.org/
The UN is a major publisher of international materials comprising periodicals available on a subscription basis, documents on demand, microfiche products, mimeograph documents, and an academic textbook programme. The online catalogue lists all titles currently available up to June 1999. Recent titles include *The United Nations and Global Commerce* and *The Age of Space Commercialisation.* You can browse through the alphabetical list or use the subject index to find publications covering specific topics. You can email them to obtain a free copy of the complete *UN Publications 2000* catalogue.

University of Chicago Press
http://www.press.uchicago.edu
UCP offers a broadly based academic and general list including: anthropology, architecture, art history, biological sciences, classics, economics, education, gay and lesbian studies, gender studies, geography and carto-

graphy, history, philosophy, and sociology of science, law, literary studies, musicology, philosophy, political science, reference, religious studies, rhetoric and communication and sociology. You can order books online using their secure shopping cart system.

Vermilion – see Random House.

Viking -see Penguin Putnam.

Wadsworth Publishing
http://www.wadsworth.com/
Wadsworth is a broadly based educational and academic imprint. Its titles include works on anthropology, college help books, communications, counselling, criminal justice, English language, education, history, health, human services, integrated media, music, nutrition, philosophy, political science, psychology, religion, social work and sociology. The company is a division of International Thomson.

John Wiley & Sons
http://www.wiley.com
Said to be the oldest surviving independent publisher in North America, John Wiley develops, publishes, and sells products in print and electronic media for the educational, professional, scientific, technical, medical, and consumer markets worldwide. It offers more than 200 products and services on disk, CD-rom, or by network, and more than 11,000 active book titles and 400 journals. It publishes 1,500 new titles in a variety of formats each year, and has more than 2,100 employees worldwide. The site also gives details of career opportunities at Wiley.

William Morrow & Co
http://www.williammorrow.com
William Morrow are publishers of general trade books for both children and adults, including best-selling fiction, non-fiction, and cookbooks. The site includes pages for authors, and news on job opportunities within the company, which is part of the HarperCollins group. The company does not accept online ordering but includes hyperlinks to the major US bookstore chains.

AUTHOR SITES
Adrain, Lorne A. www.
Altea, Rosemary www
Bach, Richard www.ri
Becker, Walt www.wal
Biker Billy www.bikerb
Chideya, Farai www.p
Chiles, Nick www.cele
Davis, Kenneth C. ww
Dreher, Diane www-a
Dunnigan, Jim www.ji
Fairweather, Lori ww
Flander, Scott http://w
Gutcheon, Beth http://

Williams & Wilkins – see Lippincott Williams & Wilkins.

Williamson Publishing
http://www.williamsonbooks.com/
Williamson publishes a range of illustrated books for young children. Recent sample titles include *Rainy Day Play!* and *The Kids' Science Book.* You can browse their catalogue and order online.

World Book
http://www.worldbook.com/
The multi-volume *World Book Encyclopedia* has been published in America for over 80 years. A World Book Online service is now available

for schools and libraries, and the site gives details of a free 30-day trial. The company is headquartered in Chicago, Illinois.

Ziff-Davis
http://www.ziffdavis.com/
As one of the world's top technology media companies, ZD develops content, community and commerce across the technology marketplace and the internet economy. For thousands of marketers, and millions of consumers, IT professionals and business people, ZD has established itself as a leading source for information, education and market access to the opportunities of the internet age. ZD publishes many of the world's leading technology magazines such as *Computer Shopper* and *PC Magazine*.

Zondervan Publishing House
http://www.zondervan.com/
Founded in 1931 during the Great Depression, Zondervan describes itself as a 'Christian communications company'. Recent sample titles from its large list include *Boundaries in Marriage* and *The Bible Jesus Read*. Its home page allows you to search the bible (various versions) for key words and phrases. The company is based in Grand Rapids, Michigan, USA, and is now a division of HarperCollins Publishers.

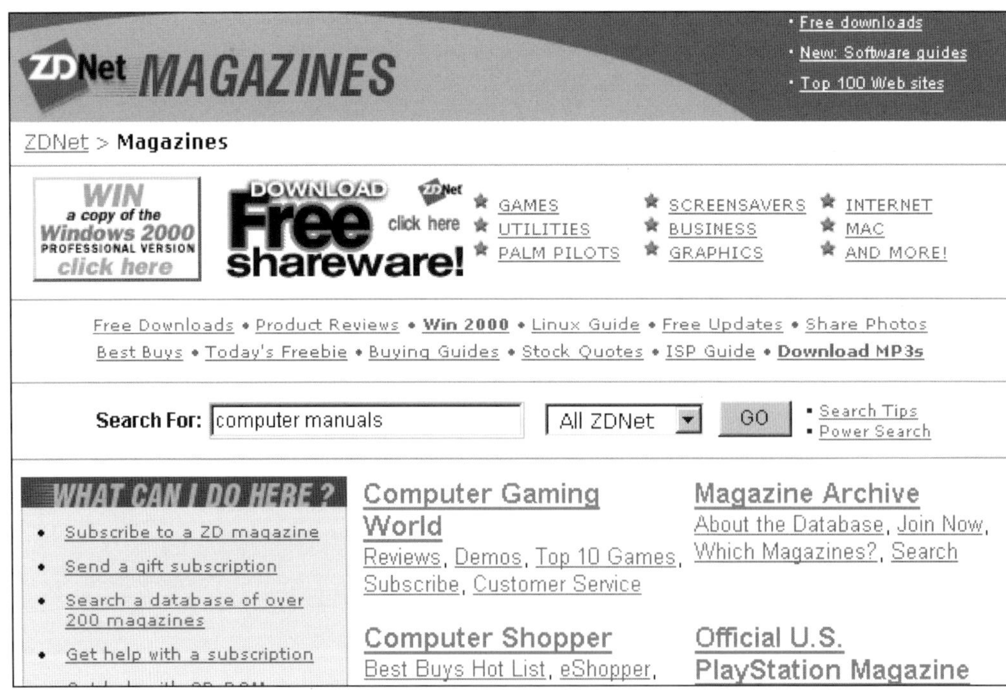

9 Asia and Australasia

In this chapter we will explore:

- *trade associations*
- *book fairs*
- *publishers A-Z*

The development of web sites by publishing firms across Asia/Australasia is still at a fairly early stage. Online contact with publishing organisations in the Republic of China and several other countries remains a hit and miss affair, with servers frequently down or unobtainable. Government censorship and control of internet service providers is the norm in several Asian countries. This section focuses in providing online contacts for the better-known media groups with a physical presence in the region's free world, and the ability to view their web pages in English.

Trade associations

Australian Publishers Association
http://publishers.asn.au/index.htm
Formed in 1948, the APA is main representative organisation for about 150 Australian publishers. Its web site includes a handy membership directory. About half of these have email contacts and hyperlinked web addresses.

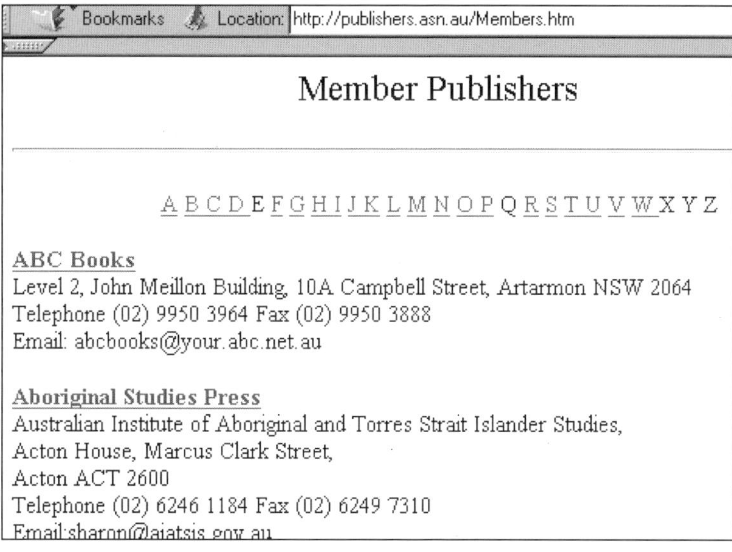

Fig. 56. The Australian Publishers Association offers quick and functional links to its member firms.

Japan Book Publishers Association
http://www.jbpa.or.jp/
The JBPA represents more than 500 publishers. The site can be viewed in both Japanese and English. The membership database is searchable by name (with erratic results), but there does not appear to be a complete visible A-Z list of member firms.

Book fairs

Asia International Book Fair
http://www.aibf.com.sg
Held in Singapore, this event is held primarily to encourage Asian publishers to do more business among themselves as well as those in developed countries, and to support the efforts of publishers from the West to sell more books in Asia.

About the JIBF
Exhibitor Information
Visitor Information
Events Calendar
Editorial Fellowship
Jerusalem Prize
Aspen-JIBF Forum
Reading Symposium
Travel/Tourism
Catalogue
Contact Us

Jerusalem Book Fair
http://www.jerusalembookfair.com/
Held in June each year, the 20-year old JIBF is considered one of the leading book fairs in the world, combining a lively business environment with literary and cultural encounters of an international standard. The focal point of business activity at the fair is its Editors, Agents and Foreign Rights Centre, which serves the needs of attending literary agents and rights representatives from around the world.

Tokyo Book Fair
http://www.reedexpo.co.jp/tibf/english/index.html
Open to both the book trade and general public, this major book fair takes place each April. The organisers are Reed Exhibitions.

Publishers

Addison Wesley Longman
http://www.awl.com.au/
This is the Australian web site of the global educational publishing group.

Allen & Unwin Australia
http://www.allen-unwin.com.au/
Allen & Unwin began publishing in Australia in 1976 as a division of Allen & Unwin UK. In 1990, following the purchase of the UK parent company by HarperCollins, the directors organised a management buy-out and the company became fully independent, owning the Allen & Unwin imprint throughout the world. It publishes about 250 titles a year, ranging from fiction and general non-fiction through an academic list specialising in the social sciences and health, to the Little Ark children's list. The company has distribution arrangements in the US, UK, Singapore, Hong Kong, Japan, Canada, New Zealand and South Africa and its books can also be ordered on this web site.

Butterworths Australia
http://www.butterworths.com.au/
The site contains full details of Butterworths' wide range of legal, business and professional publications in print, CD and online formats. It also offers a 'net search' facilty to help you track down all kinds of Australian web sites from those dealing with professional and reference topics to those dealing with entertainment and media, travel, hobbies and sports, business and other subject categories. You can browse an online catalogue for more information about its titles. Butterworths is a division of Reed International.

Butterworths New Zealand
http://www.butterworths.co.nz/
This is the home page of the New Zealand branch of the world's foremost legal publisher, and division of Reed International. The site features a useful collection of links to law firms and law resources around the world.

Federal Publications see Times Publishing Group (below).

HarperCollins Publishers Australia
http://www.harpercollins.com.au/
HarperCollins Publishers Australia is a general publishing house that incorporates the great literary heritage of Australia's oldest publisher Angus & Robertson. It offers a wide variety of tittles in the following categories: health, lifestyle, homes and gardens, history, cookery and wine, general and literary fiction, science fiction and fantasy, biography, business, religion and spirituality, plus an extensive range of children's books.

India Bookhouse & Journals
http://indiabookhouse.com/
Established on the internet for three years, the company handles general trade books, magazines, newspapers, dictionaries, cook books, religious books, books on sports, yoga, audio cassettes, film star posters, novels in Hindi, Urdu, Punjabi, and Gujarati, different language learning books, greeting cards and handicraft items. In total there are some 4,500 items in its online catalogue.

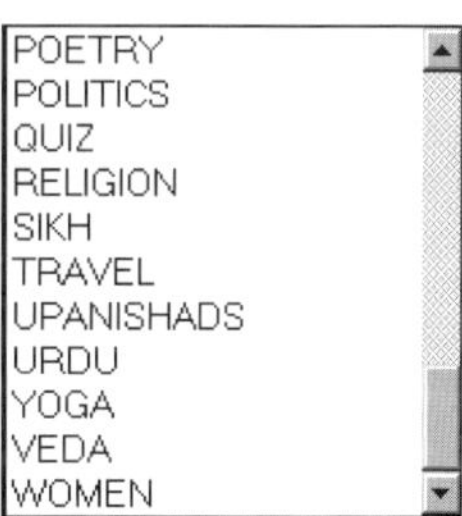

Kodansha
http://www.kodansha.co.jp/index.e.html
Kodansha is one of Japan's largest publishers, both of books and magazines. Founded in 1909 with a magazine for public speakers, it now publishes 56 weekly and monthly magazines, ranging from comics to consumer magazines. Kodansha sells over 50 million books a year, and publishes over 2,000 new titles. This URL takes you to the English version of the web site.

Lothian Australia
http://www.lothian.com.au/
The site of this old-established Australia educational and trade publisher and book distributor was under development when reviewed.

Marshall Cavendish
http://www.mcmedia.com/
For more than 25 years, Marshall Cavendish has been the market leader in 'part work' publishing. The company pioneered the idea of collectible magazines in the UK, and now has over 100 successful series to its credit, with new ones being added every year. The subjects range from fine arts to domestic skills, science to sex, from the natural to the supernatural world. Marshall Cavendish is now owned by the Times Publishing Group of Singapore.

Maruzen
http://www.maruzen.co.jp/index-j.html
Maruzen is one of Japan's best known general publishing, bookselling and book distribution groups. The web site, which can be viewed in English as well as Japanese, incorporates an internet bookshop, news, company information and other features, plus a lengthy and useful A to Z list of hyperlinks to western publishers. It is developing an ambitious online network called MaruNet, linking together all those individuals and organisations with whom the company has a relationship.

Fig. 57. Maruzen of Japan. This well-produced site features MaruNet, a network designed to link together the company, its customers and suppliers online.

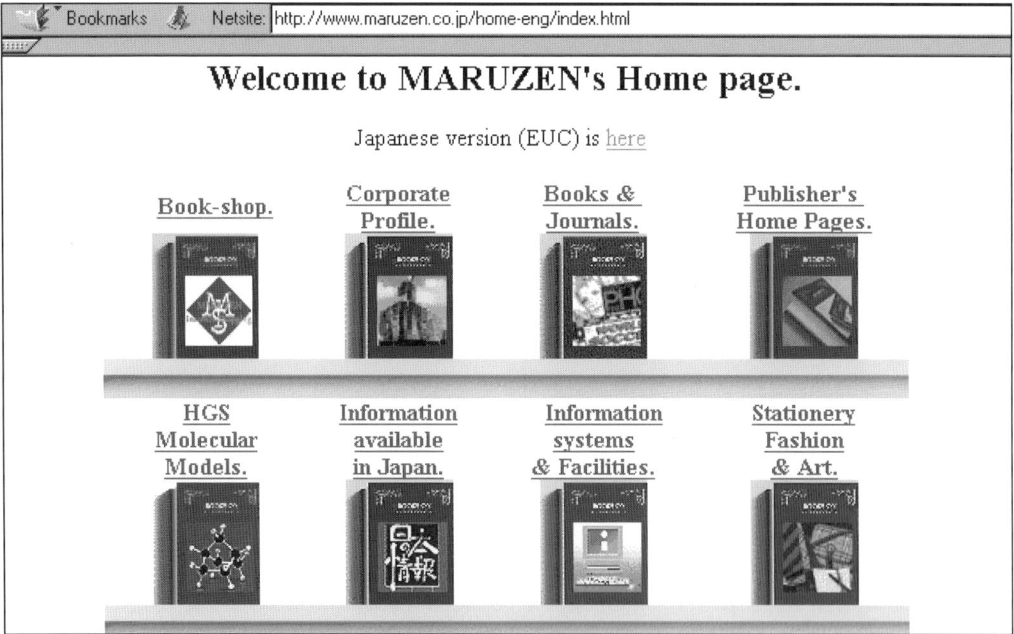

McGraw-Hill Book Company Australia
http://www.mcgraw-hill.com.au/
McGraw-Hill Australia is one of the country's leading educational publishers. Incorporated in 1964, it is a wholly owned subsidiary of the McGraw-Hill Group, distributing to customers throughout Australia, New Zealand, and South Africa. Its three main divisions cover higher education, school, and professional reference. It has recently purchased Science Research Associates.

Penguin Books Australia
http://www.penguin.com.au/
This is the orange and black home page of Penguin Australia, one of the country's leading publishers and distributors of new Australian and international books, and 1999 Australian Publisher of the Year. The site features author profiles, competitions, reading groups, help and FAQs, and you can even send electronic postcards to your friends, using a selection of cover images from the latest books. Penguin is a Pearson company.

Post Books of Thailand
http://www.bangkokpost.net/postbooks/
Owned by the *Bangkok Post*, Post Books is a publisher of general interest non-fiction paperbacks and illustrated hardcover books on Thailand and south-east Asia. Its catalogue includes books on expatriate life, arts, culture, travel, language, and food. Prices are quoted in US dollars. You can order online (not secured), by fax or telephone or post the order form.

Reed Books Australia - see Butterworths (above).

Tata McGraw-Hill
http://www.tatamcgrawhill.com/
Established in 1961, the Indian company of Tata McGraw-Hill is a market leader in educational books covering all subjects and areas of interest.

DW Thorpe
http://www.thorpe.com.au/
Part of the Reed Elsevier group of companies, Thorpe is a foremost bibliographic and reference publisher based in Melbourne, Australia, with a regional office in Auckland, New Zealand. Operating since 1921, it publishes information about the ANZ book industries in journal, volume, microfiche and CD rom formats. It also represents many of the world's other leading bibliographic publishers.

Times Publishing Group (Singapore)
http://www.tpl.com.sg
Headquartered in Singapore, Times Publishing has been in the communication business for more than two decades. It is an international Asian group involved in print and multimedia publishing, commercial printing, distribution, direct sales, retailing of books, partworks, directories and magazines, the distribution of recorded music, audio and video tapes and hi-fi accessories, the provision of educational facilities, and the organisation of conferences and exhibitions. Its many operating divisions include Far East Trade Press, Federal Publications, Marshall Cavendish, and United Publishers Services.

Toppan
http://www.toppan.com/
Toppan is a substantial Japanese manufacturing company, with sub-

stantial interests in printing and publishing. The site can be viewed in English.

UBS Publishers Distributors Ltd
http://www.ubspd.com/
UBS began operations in 1963 in New Delhi, India. It has branches in seven major cities of India and a head office in Delhi. There are resident representatives in major Indian cities, and eight export managers. It represents over two million titles and about 300 Indian publishers.

Fig. 58. The web site of UBS Publishers Distributors, the leading exporter of books from India.

Newsgroups

Accessing newsgroups

There are normally two ways of accessing newsgroups using your web browser, or using a newsreader.

- *Using your web browser* - Just type in the name of the newsgroup into the address panel in your browser window, prefixed with 'news:' (omitting the punctuation marks). For example:

  news:alt.books

- *Using your newsreader* - If your browser is Microsoft Internet Explorer, your newsreader will probably be Microsoft Outlook (Click Tools, then Newsgroups). If your browser is Netscape 4, your newsreader will probably be Netscape Messenger (click Communicator, then Collabra Discussion Groups).

The newsgroups

These are some of those dealing with books and writers, though such a list can never be exhaustive. The ones in bold type are of wide general interest.

alt.books
alt.books.anne-rice
alt.books.arthur-clarke
alt.books.beatgeneration
alt.books.brian-lumley
alt.books.bukowski
alt.books.cait-r-kiernan
alt.books.carl-sagan
alt.books.chesterton
alt.books.clive-barker
alt.books.crichton
alt.books.cs-lewis
alt.books.cs.lewis
alt.books.dan-simmons
alt.books.david-weber
alt.books.dean-koontz
alt.books.dennis-brumm
alt.books.deryni
alt.books.destroyer
alt.books.dylan-thomas
alt.books.george-fraser
alt.books.george-orwell
alt.books.ghost-fiction
alt.books.gor
alt.books.h-g-wells
alt.books.iain-banks
alt.books.inklings
alt.books.isaac-asimov
alt.books.jack-chalker
alt.books.james-joyce
alt.books.jean-auel
alt.books.jerry-chavez
alt.books.john-grisham
alt.books.julian-may
alt.books.karin-lynne.intermill
alt.books.kurt-vonnegut
alt.books.larry-niven
alt.books.lars-eighner
alt.books.louis-lamour
alt.books.lynn-luxner
alt.books.m-lackey
alt.books.moorcock
alt.books.mysteries
alt.books.raymond-feist

Newsgroups

alt.books.reviews
alt.books.robert-rankin
alt.books.roger-zelazny
alt.books.sebar
alt.books.sf.melanie-rawn
alt.books.thomas-pynchon
alt.books.toffler
alt.books.tom-clancy
alt.books.stephen-king
alt.books.suelette-dreyfus
alt.books.technical
alt.books.terry-brooks
alt.books.the-waste-land.jug.jug.-jug
alt.books.thomas-ligotti
alt.books.nabokov
alt.books.nancy-drew
alt.books.orson-s-card
alt.books.outlander
alt.books.pat-conroy
alt.books.peter-straub
alt.books.phil-k-dick
alt.books.poppy-z-brite
alt.books.pratchett
alt.books.purefiction
alt.books.pynchon
alt.books.ray-bradbury
alt.books.valdemar.fanfic
alt.books.zogoiby
alt.boomerang
alt.marketplace.books
alt.marketplace.books-on-tape
alt.marketplace.books.sf
rec.arts.books
rec.arts.books.childrens
rec.arts.books.hist-fiction
rec.arts.books.marketplace
rec.arts.books.reviews
rec.arts.books.tolkien
rec.arts.comics.alternative
rec.arts.comics.creative
rec.arts.comics.dc.lsh
rec.arts.comics.dc.universe
rec.arts.comics.dc.vertigo
rec.arts.comics.elfquest
rec.arts.comics.european
rec.arts.comics.info
rec.arts.comics.marketplace
rec.arts.comics.marvel.universe
rec.arts.comics.marvel.xbooks
rec.arts.comics.misc
rec.arts.comics.other-media
rec.arts.comics.reviews
rec.arts.comics.strips
rec.collecting.books
uk.adverts.books
uk.media.books.sf

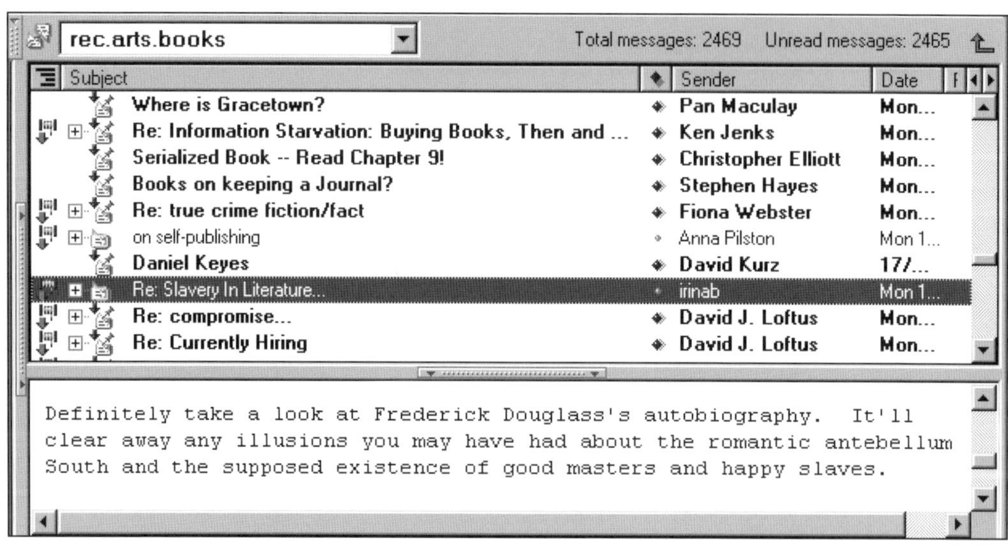

Publishing Qualifications

A publishing qualification can be obtained from several UK higher education institutions. Check their web sites for details of current courses and entry requirements.

Course providers

London College of Printing (BA, Postgraduate Certificate & Postgraduate Diploma in Publishing)
http://www.lcp.linst.ac.uk

Middlesex University (BA Writing and Publishing)
http://www.mdx.ac.uk

Napier University in Edinburgh (BA Publishing)
http://www.napier.ac.uk

Oxford Brookes University (BA Publishing)
http://www.brookes.ac.uk

University of Plymouth (Postgraduate Diploma & MA Publishing)
http://www.fae.plym.ac.uk

University of Stirling (MPhil Publishing)
http://www.stir.ac.uk

West Herts College in Watford (BA/BSc Publishing)
http://www.westherts.ac.uk

Other useful contacts

The Paul Hamlyn Foundation
http://www.phf.org.uk

The Publishing Training Centre
http://www.train4publishing.co.uk

Glossary of Internet Terms

Access provider – The company that provides you with access to the internet. This may be an independent provider or a large international organisation such as AOL or CompuServe. See also **internet service provider**.

Adobe Acrobat – A type of software required for reading PDF files ('portable document format'). You may need to have Adobe Acrobat Reader when downloading large text files from the internet, such as lengthy reports or chapters from books. If your computer lacks it, the web page will prompt you, and usually offer you an immediate download of the free version.

Address book – A directory in a web browser where you can store people's email addresses. This saves having to type them out each time you want to email someone. You just click on an address whenever you want it.

AltaVista – One of the half dozen most popular internet search engines. Just type in a few key words to find what you want on the internet.

AOL – America On Line, the world's biggest internet service provider, with more than 20 million subscribers, and now merged with Time Warner. Because it has masses of content of its own - quite aside from the wider internet - it is sometimes referred to as an 'online' service provider rather than internet service provider. It has given away vast numbers of free CDs with the popular computer magazines to build its customer base.

Ask Jeeves – A popular internet search engine. Rather than just typing in a few key words for your search, you can type in a whole question or instruction, such as 'Find me everything about online investment.' It draws on a database of millions of questions and answers, and works best with fairly general questions.

ASP – Active Server Pages, a filename extension for a type of web page.

Attachment – A file sent with an email message. The attached file can be anything from a word-processed document to a database, spreadsheet, graphic, or even a sound or video file. For example you could email someone birthday greetings, and attach a sound track or video clip.

Bandwidth – The width of the electronic highway that gives you access to the internet. The higher the bandwidth, the wider this highway, and the faster the traffic can flow.

Banner ad – This is a band of text and graphics, usually situated at the top of a web page. It acts like a title, telling the user what the content of the page is about. It invites the visitor to click on it to visit that site. Banner advertising has become big business.

Baud rate – The data transmission speed in a modem, measured in bps (bits per second).

BBS – Bulletin board service. A facility to read and to post public messages on a particular web site.

Blue Ribbon Campaign – A widely supported campaign supporting free speech and opposing moves to censor the internet by all kinds of elected and unelected bodies.

Bookmark – A file of URLs of your favourite internet sites. Bookmarks are very easily created by bookmarking (mouse-clicking) any internet page you like the look of. If you are an avid user, you could soon end up with hundreds of them! In the Internet Explorer browser and AOL they are called 'favourites'.

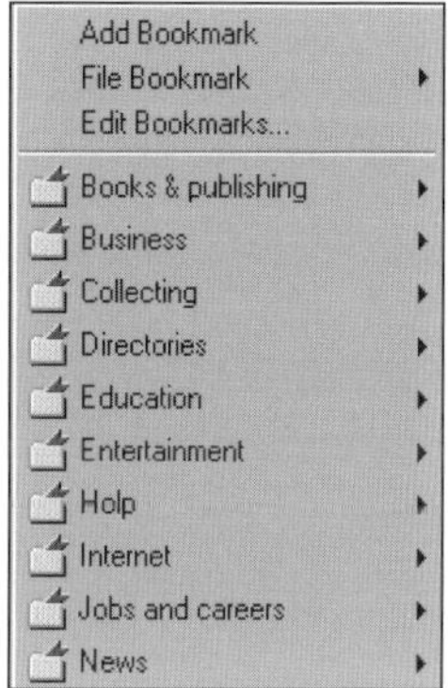

Boolean search – A search in which you type in words such as AND and OR to refine your search. Such words are called 'Boolean operators'. The concept is named after George Boole, a nineteenth-century English mathematician.

Bot – Short for robot. It is used to refer to a program that will perform a task on the internet, such as carrying out a search.

Browser – Your browser is your window to the internet, and will normally be supplied by your internet service provider when you first sign up. It is the program that you use to access the world wide web, and manage your personal communications and privacy when online. By far the two most popular browsers are Netscape Communicator and its dominant rival Microsoft Internet Explorer. You can easily swap. Both can be downloaded free from their web sites and are found on the CD roms stuck to the computer magazines. It won't make much difference which one you use - they both do much the same thing. Other browsers include Opera and NetCaptor.

Bulletin board – A type of computer-based news service that provides an email service and a file archive.

Cache – A file storage area on a computer. Your web browser will normally cache (copy to your hard drive) each web page you visit. When you revisit that page on the web, you may in fact be looking at the page originally cached on your computer. To be sure you are viewing the current page, press **reload** – or **refresh** – on your browser toolbar. You can empty your cache from time to time, and the computer will do so automatically whenever the cache is full. In Internet Explorer, pages are saved in the Windows folder, Temporary Internet Files. In Netscape they are saved in a folder called 'cache'.

Certificate – A computer file that securely identifies a person or organisation on the internet.

Client – This is the term given to the program that you use to access the internet. For example your web browser is a web client, and your email program is an email client.

Closed areas – Those areas of a web site that only registered users can enter.

Community – The internet is often described as a net community. This refers to the fact that many people like the feeling of belonging to a group of like-minded individuals. Many big web sites have been developed along these lines, such as GeoCities which is divided into special-interest 'neighbourhoods', or America OnLine which is strong on member services.

Compression – Computer files can be electronically compressed, so that they can be uploaded or downloaded more quickly across the internet, saving time and money. If an image file is compressed too much, there may be a loss of quality. To read them, you uncompress or 'unzip' them.

Crash – What happens when a computer program malfunctions. The operating system of your PC may perform incorrectly or come to a complete stop ('freeze'), forcing you to shut down and restart.

Cybercash – This is a trademark, but is also often used as a broad term to describe the use of small payments made over the internet using a new form of electronic account that is loaded up with cash. You can send this money to the companies offering such cash facilities by cheque, or by credit card. Some Internet companies offering travel-related items can accept electronic cash of this kind.

Cyberspace – Popular term for the intangible 'place' where you go to surf - the ethereal and borderless world of computers and telecommunications on the internet.

Dial up account – This allows you to connect your computer to your internet provider's computer remotely.

Digital – Based on the two binary digits, 1 and 0. The operation of all computers is based on this amazingly simple concept. All forms of information are capable of being digitalised – numbers, words, and even sounds and images – and then transmitted over the internet.

Domain – A domain is a specific area on the internet and identifies to the computers on the rest of the internet where to access particular information. Each domain has a name. The domain for Internet Handbooks for instance is: www.internet-handbooks.co.uk

Download – 'Downloading' means copying a file from one computer on the internet to your own computer. You do this by clicking on a button that links you to the appropriate file. Downloading is an automatic process, except you have to click 'yes' to accept the download and give it a file name. You can download any type of file - text, graphics, sound, spreadsheet, computer programs, and so on.

E-cash – Short for electronic cash. See cybercash.

Email – Electronic mail, any message or file you send from your computer to another computer using your 'email client' program (such as Netscape Messenger or Microsoft Outlook).

Encryption – Encoding for security purposes. Email and any other data can now be encrypted using PGP and other freely available programs. Modern encryption has become so amazingly powerful as to be to all intents and purposes uncrackable. Law enforcers world wide are pressing their governments for access to people's and organisation's passwords and security keys. Would you be willing to hand over yours?

Excite – A popular internet directory and search engine used to find pages relating to specific keywords which you enter. See also Yahoo!.

E-zines – The term for magazines and newsletters published on the internet.

FAQ – Frequently Asked Questions. You will see 'FAQ' everywhere you go on the internet. If you are ever doubtful about anything check the FAQ page, if the site has one, and you should find the answers to your queries.

Favorites – The rather coy term for **bookmarks** used by Internet Explorer, and by America Online.

File – A file is any body of data such as a word processed document, a spreadsheet, a database file, a graphics or video file, sound file, or computer program.

Filtering software – Software loaded onto a computer to prevent access by someone to unwelcome content on the internet, notably porn. The well-known 'parental controls' include CyberSitter, CyberPatrol, SurfWatch and NetNanny. They can be blunt instruments. For example, if they are programmed to reject all web pages containing the word 'virgin', you would not be able to access any web page hosted at Richard Branson's Virgin Net! Of course, there are also web sites that tell you step-by-step how to disable or bypass these filtering tools.

Firewall – A firewall is special security software designed to stop the flow of certain files into and out of a computer network, e.g. viruses or attacks by hackers. A firewall would be an important feature of any fully commercial web site.

Form – A means of collecting data on web pages, using text boxes and buttons. For example quite a few commercial sites will ask you to register by completing an online form.

Forums – Places for discussion on the internet. They are rather like usenet newsgroups and allow you to read, post and reply to messages. See also **bulletin board services.**

Frames – A web design feature in which web pages are divided into several areas or panels, each containing separate information. A typical set of frames in a page includes an index frame (with navigation links), a banner frame (for a heading), and a body frame (for text matter).

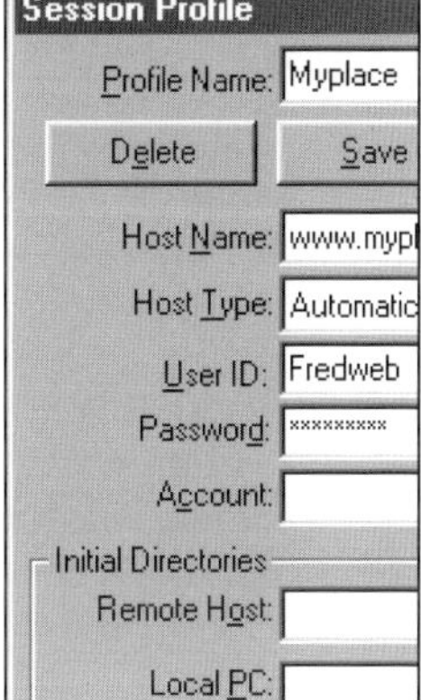

FTP – File transfer protocol, the method the internet uses to speed files back and forth between computers. Your browser will automatically select this method, for instance, when you want to download your bank statements to reconcile your accounts. In practice you don't need to worry about FTP unless you are thinking about creating and publishing your own web pages: then you would need some of the freely available FTP software. Despite the name, it's easy to use.

Hacker – Someone who makes or seeks to make an unauthorised entry into someone else's computer system or network.

History list – A record of visited web pages. Your browser probably includes a history list. It is handy way of revisiting sites whose addresses you have forgotten to bookmark - just click on the item you want in the history list. You can normally delete all or part of the history list in your browser. However, your ISP may well be keeping a copy of this information (see **internet service providers**, above).

Hits – The number of times a web page has been viewed.

Host – A host is the computer where a particular file or domain is located, and from where people can retrieve it.

HotBot – This is a popular internet search engine used to find pages relating to any keywords you decide to enter. 'Bot' is short for robot. In internet terms it means a piece of software that performs a task on the internet, such as searching.

HTML – Hyper text markup language, the universal computer language used to create pages on the world wide web. It is much like word processing, but uses special 'tags' for formatting the text and creating hyperlinks to other web pages.

Hyperlink – See **link**.

Infoseek – One of the ten most popular internet search engines.

Internet – The broad term for the fast-expanding network of global computers that can access each other in seconds by phone and satellite links. If you are using a modem on your computer, you too are part of the internet. The general term 'internet' encompasses email, web pages, internet chat, newsgroups, and video conferencing. It is rather like the way we speak of 'the printed word' when we mean books, magazines, newspapers, newsletters, catalogues, leaflets, tickets and posters. The 'internet' does not exist in one place any more than 'the printed word' does.

Internet Explorer – The world's most popular browser software, a product of MicroSoft and rival to Netscape (recently taken over by America On-Line).

Internet service providers – ISPs are commercial, educational or official organisations which offer people ('users') access to the internet. The well known commercial ones in the UK include AOL, CompuServe, BT Internet, Freeserve, Demon and Virgin Net. Commercial ISPs may levy a fixed monthly charge, though the worldwide trend is now towards free services. Services typically include access to the world wide web, email and newsgroups, as well as others such as news, chat, and entertainment. Your internet service provider will know everything you do on the internet - emails sent and received, web sites visited, information downloaded, key words typed into search engines, newsgroups visited and messages read and posted. This is why many of them are willing to offer their services free. What do they do with all this data? How long do they store it? Do they make it discreetly available to enforcement agencies? Do they allow the police private access? There are some major issues of personal privacy and data protection in all this, at both a national and European level, and state surveillance is expanding fast. At the very least, check out your service provider's privacy statement – but it may have very little value.

ISDN – Integrated Services Digital Network. This is a high-speed telephone network that can send computer data from the internet to your PC faster than a normal telephone line.

JavaScript – A simple programming language that can be put onto a web page to create interactive effects such as buttons that change appearance when you position the mouse over them.

Link – A hypertext phrase or image that calls up another web page when you click on it. Most web sites have lots of hyperlinks, or 'links' for short. These appear on the screen as buttons, images or bits of text (often underlined) that you can click on with your mouse to jump to another site on the world wide web.

Linux – A new widely and freely available operating system for personal computers, and a potentially serious challenger to Microsoft. It has developed a considerable following.

Listserver – A listserver is an automated email system whereby subscribers are able to receive and send email from other subscribers to the list.

Log on/log off – To access/leave a network. In the early days of computing this literally involved writing a record in a log book. You may be asked to 'log on' to certain sites and particular pages. This normally means entering your user ID in the form of a name and a password.

Lurk – The slang term used to describe reading a newsgroup's messages without actually taking part in that newsgroup. Despite the connotations of the word, it is a perfectly respectable activity on the internet.

Mail server – A remote computer that enables you to send and receive emails. Your internet access provider will usually act as your mail server.

Mailing list – A forum where messages are distributed by email to the members of the forum. The two types of lists are discussion and announcement. Discussion lists allow exchange between list members. Announcement lists are one-way only and used to distribute information such as news or humour. A good place to find mailing lists is Liszt (http://www.liszt.com). You can normally quit a mailing list by sending an email message to request removal.

Marquee – A moving ('scrolling') line of text on a web site, often used for eye-catching advertising purposes.

Media player – Software on a personal computer that will play sounds and images including video clips and animations.

Metasearch engine – A site that sends a keyword search to many different search engines and directories so you can use many search engines from one place.

Modem – An internal or external piece of hardware, one end of which is plugged into your PC. The other end is plugged into a standard phone socket, thereby linking you to the internet. The word is short for MOdulator/DEModulator.

MP3 – An immensely popular audio format that allows you to download and play music on your computer. See http://mpeg.org for further technical information, or the consumer web site www.mp3.com.

Navigate – To click on the hyperlinks on a web site in order to move to other web pages or internet sites.

Net – A slang term for the internet. In the same way, the world wide web is often just called the web.

Netiquette – Popular term for the unofficial rules and language people follow to keep electronic communication in an acceptably polite form.

Netscape – After Internet Explorer, Netscape is the most popular browser software available for surfing the internet. An excellent browser, Netscape has suffered in the wake of the rise of Microsoft's Internet Explorer, mainly because of the success of Microsoft in getting it pre-loaded on most new PCs. Netscape Communicator comes complete with email, newsgroups, address book and bookmarks, plus a web page composer, and you can adjust its settings in all sorts of useful ways. Netscape was taken over by America Online for $4 billion.

Newsgroup – A Usenet discussion group. Each newsgroup is a collection of messages, usually unedited and not checked by anyone ('unmoderated'). Messages can be placed within the newsgroup by anyone including you. It is rather like reading and sending pubic emails. The ever-growing newsgroups have been around for much longer than the world wide web, and are an endless source of information, gossip, news, entertainment, sex, politics, resources and ideas. The 50,000-plus newsgroups are collectively referred to as Usenet, and millions of people use it every day.

News reader – A type of software that enables you to search, read, post and manage messages in a newsgroup. It will normally be supplied by your internet service provider when you first sign up, or preloaded on your new computer. The best known are Microsoft Outlook, and Netscape Messenger.

News server – A remote computer (eg your internet service provider) that enables you to access newsgroups. If you cannot get some or any newsgroups from your existing news server, use your favourite search engine to search for 'open news servers' - there are lots of them freely available. When you have found one you like, add it to your news reader by clicking on its name. The first time you do this, it may take 10 to 20 minutes to load the names of all the newsgroups onto your computer, but after that they open up in seconds whenever you want them.

Online – Being connected to the internet.

Pentium – The name of a very popular microprocessor chip in personal computers. The first Pentium IIIs were supplied with secret and unique personal identifiers, which ordinary people surfing the net were unwittingly sending out, enabling persons unknown to construct detailed user profiles. After a storm of protest, Pentium changed the technology so that this identifier could be disabled. If you buy or use a Pentium III computer you should be aware of this risk to your privacy when online.

PGP – Pretty Good Privacy. A method of encoding a message before transmitting it over the internet. With PGP, a message is first compressed then encoded with the help of keys. Just like the valuables in a locked safe, your message is safe unless a person has access to the right keys. Many governments (as in France today) would like complete access to people's private keys. New Labour wanted access to everyone's keys in the UK, but dropped the initial legislation after widespread protests. Unlike in many countries, there is no general right to personal privacy in the UK.

PoP – Point of presence. This refers to the dial up phone numbers available from your ISP. If your ISP does not have a local point of presence (i.e. local access phone number), then don't sign up - your telephone bill will rocket because you will be charged national phone rates. All the major ISPs have local numbers covering the whole of the country.

Portal site – Portal means gateway. A portal site includes the one that loads into your browser each time you connect to the internet. It could for example be the front page of your internet service provider. Or you can set your browser to make it some other front page, for example a search engine such as Yahoo!, or even your own home page if you have one.

Post, to – The common term used for sending ('posting') messages to a newsgroup. Posting messages is very like sending emails, except of course that they are public and everyone can read them. Also, newsgroup postings are archived, and can be read by anyone in the world years later. Because of this, many people feel more comfortable using an 'alias' (made-up name) when posting messages.

Privacy – You have practically no personal privacy online. Almost every mouse click and key stroke you make while online is being electronically logged, analysed and possibly archived by internet organisations, government agencies, police or other surveillance services. You are also leaving a permanent trail of data on whichever computer you are using. But then, if you have nothing to hide you have nothing to fear... To explore privacy issues worldwide visit the authoritative Electronic Frontier Foundation web site at www.eff.org, and for the UK, www.netfreedom.org.

Protocol – Rules. It is the technical term for the method by which computers communicate, for example http (hyper text transfer protocol) or ftp (file transfer protocol). It's not something to worry about in ordinary life.

Quicktime – A popular free software program from Apple Computers that will play sounds and images including video clips and animations on both Apple Macs and personal computers.

Register – You may have to give your name, personal details and financial information to some sites before you can continue to use the pages. Site owners may want to produce a mailing list to offer you products and services. Registration is also used to discourage casual traffic.

Registered user – Someone who has filled out an online form and then been granted permission to access a restricted area of a web site. Access is usually obtained by logging on, in other words entering a password and user name.

Search engine – A search engine is a web site you can use for finding things on the internet. Popular search engines are big web sites and information directories in their own right. There are hundreds of them; the best known include AltaVista, Excite, Infoseek, Lycos and Yahoo!.

Secure servers – The hardware and software provided so that people can use their credit cards and leave other details without the risk of others seeing them online. Your browser will tell you when you are entering a secure site.

Shareware – Software that you can try before you buy. Usually there is some kind of limitation to the game such as a time limit, or limited features. To get the registered version, you must pay for the software, typically \$20 to \$40. A vast amount of shareware is now available on the internet.

Shockwave – A popular piece of software produced by Macromedia, which enables you to view animations and other special effects on web sites. You can download it free and in a few minutes from Macromedia's web site. The effects can be fun, but they slow down the speed at which the pages load into your browser window.

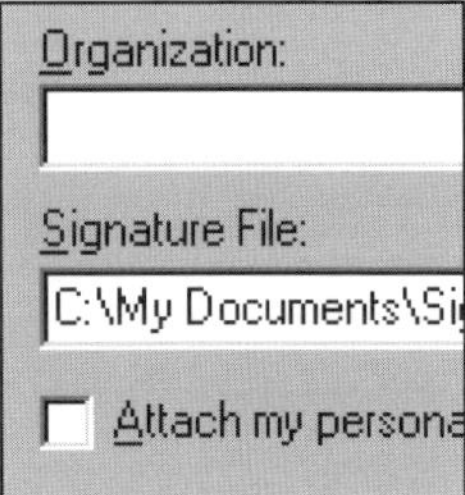

Signature file – This is a computer file in which you can place your address details, for adding to email and newsgroup messages. Once you have created a signature file you can append it to your emails as often as you like.

Spam – The popular term for electronic junk mail – unsolicited and unwelcome email messages sent across the internet. The term comes from Monty Python. There are various forms of spam-busting software which you can now obtain to filter out unwanted email messages.

Subscribe – The term for accessing a newsgroup in order to read and post messages in the newsgroup. There is no charge, and you can subscribe, unsubscribe and resubscribe at will with a click of your mouse. Unless you post a message, no-one in the newsgroup will know that you have subscribed or unsubscribed.

Surfing – Slang term for browsing the internet, especially following trails of links on pages across the world wide web.

TCP/IP – Transmission Control Protocol/Internet Protocol, the essential technology of the internet. It's not normally something you need worry about.

Thread – An ongoing topic in a usenet newsgroup or mailing list discussion. The term refers to the original message on a particular topic, and all the replies and other messages which spin off from it. With news reading software, you can easily 'view thread' and thus read the related messages in a convenient batch.

UNIX –This is a computer operating system that has been in use for many years, and still is used in many larger systems. Most ISPs use this operating system.

URL – Uniform resource locator – the address of each internet page. For instance the URL of Internet Handbooks is:

http://www.internet-handbooks.co.uk

Usenet – The collection of well over 50,000 active newsgroups that make up a substantial part of the internet.

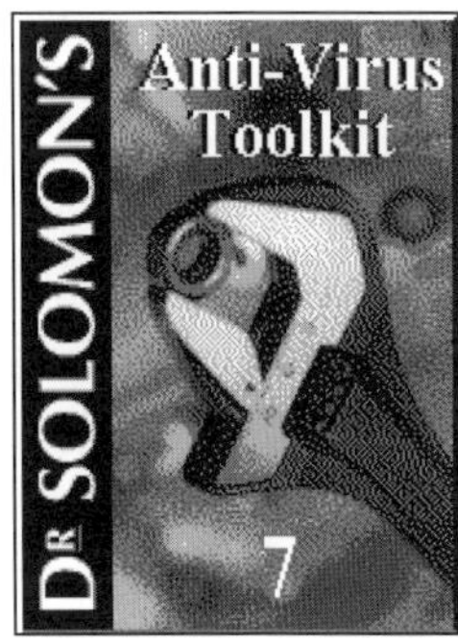

Virus – A computer program maliciously designed to cause havoc to people's computer files. Viruses can typically be received when downloading program files from the internet, or from copying material from infected disks. Even Word files can now be infected. You can protect yourself from the vast majority of them by installing some inexpensive anti-virus software, such as Norton, McAfee or Dr Solomon.

Webcrawler – A popular internet search engine used to find pages relating to specific keywords entered.

Webmaster – Any person who manages a web site.

Windows – The ubiquitous operating system for personal computers developed by Bill Gates and the Microsoft Corporation. The Windows 3.1 version was followed by Windows 95, further enhanced by Windows 98 and Windows 2000 is next.

WWW – The world wide web. Since it began in 1994 this has become the most popular part of the internet. The web is now made up of more than one billion web pages of every description, typically linking to other pages. Developed by a British computer scientist, Tim Berners-Lee, its growth has been exponential and is set to continue so.

Yahoo! – Probably the world's most popular internet directory and search engine, and now valued on Wall Street at billions of dollars.

Zip/unzip – Many files that you download from the internet will be in compressed format, especially if they are large files. This is to make them quicker to download. These files are said to be zipped or compressed. Unzipping these compressed files generally refers to the process of returning them to their original size. Zip files have the extension '.zip' and are created (and unzipped) using WinZip or a similar popular software package.

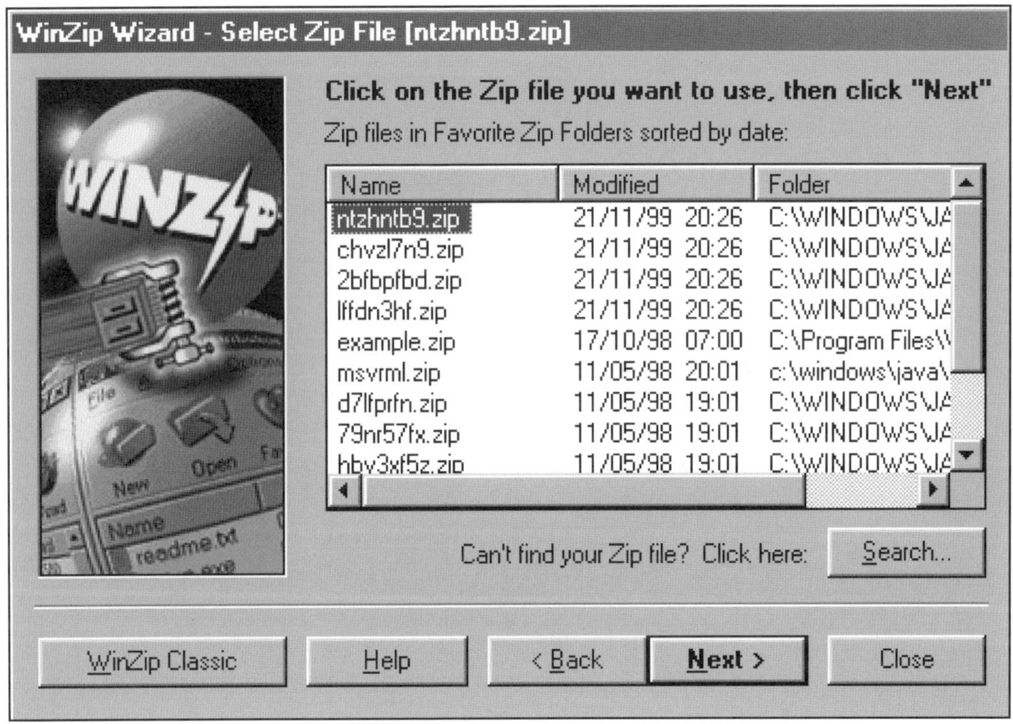

Index

Index

Index

Index